D0205645

# AMERICAN FILM
# IN THE DIGITAL AGE

**New Directions in Media**
*Robin Andersen, Series Editor*

# AMERICAN FILM
# IN THE DIGITAL AGE

Robert C. Sickels

**New Directions in Media**
Robin Andersen, Series Editor

 PRAEGER

AN IMPRINT OF ABC-CLIO, LLC
Santa Barbara, California • Denver, Colorado • Oxford, England

**Library of Congress Cataloging-in-Publication Data**

Sickels, Robert C.
  American film in the digital age / Robert C. Sickels.
    p. cm. — (New directions in media)
  Includes bibliographical references and index.
  ISBN 978-0-275-99862-2 (hard copy : alk. paper) — ISBN 978-0-275-99863-9 (ebook)
1. Motion pictures.   2. Motion picture industry.   I. Title.
  PN1994.S532   2011
  791.43—dc22        2010034690

ISBN: 978-0-275-99862-2
EISBN: 978-0-275-99863-9

15  14  13  12  11    1  2  3  4  5

This book is also available on the World Wide Web as an eBook.
Visit www.abc-clio.com for details.

Praeger
An Imprint of ABC-CLIO, LLC

ABC-CLIO, LLC
130 Cremona Drive, P.O. Box 1911
Santa Barbara, California 93116-1911

This book is printed on acid-free paper  (∞)

Manufactured in the United States of America

The sun shines every day in Hollywood.
—Ernst Lubitsch

# Contents

# ACKNOWLEDGMENTS

First and foremost, special thanks are due to my editor Daniel Harmon, who was infinitely patient and supportive in his shepherding of this project. I'd also like to thank Yannis Tzioumakis and Annie Petersen for their willingness to write pieces for this book, which is much better as a result of their contributions. Thanks to my home institution, Whitman College, for helping to support this project via their generous sabbatical policy. Thanks to the Fulbright Scholar Program, which afforded me the life-changing opportunity to live and work in Hong Kong. Thanks to Tim Meade for helping to ease my culture shock while I was doing so. Thanks to Professors Tom Reck, Robert Merrill, Michael Branch, and Robert Withycombe for what has now been many years of guidance, mentoring, inspiration, and friendship. Thanks to Ben Kegan for turning me on to the young Next Wave filmmakers whose work found its way into this book. Thanks to the men of The Green Lantern and old Mr. Overholt for their staunch companionship during the very necessary fun breaks I took from the writing of this book. Thanks to Bishop Allen, Drive by Truckers, and KEXP Seattle's Song of the Day podcast for providing the primary background soundtrack to which this book was written. Thanks to my children, Dutch and Tallulah, for allowing me to see the magic of the movies through their eyes. Lastly, thanks to my Mom and Dad for everything. This one is for Ginny.

# Chapter 1

## INTRODUCTION: AMERICAN FILM IN THE DIGITAL AGE

Creations of the spirit are not just commodities; the elements of culture are not pure business. Defending the pluralism of works of art and the freedom of the public to choose is a duty. What is at stake is the cultural identity of all our nations. It is the right of all peoples to their own culture. It is the freedom to create and choose our own images. A society which abandons to others the way of showing itself . . . is a society enslaved.

—François Mitterand, 1993, quoted in Jeancolas (57–58)

Not long ago I was a part of a global studies seminar in which college professors from across the academic disciplines met to exchange ideas about possible ways we can work together to make our departmental curricula more global in nature. As part of the endeavor, we had nightly homework for which we read various articles about a variety of subjects. For our final assignment we watched James Cameron's *Avatar* (2009) and read a number of pieces on it. In our discussion the next day, my colleagues were almost exclusively interested in discussing whether or not the film was racist and sexist. They all thought it was and were quite concerned with what they saw as the reinforcement of negative stereotypes that the film propagates. As a college professor, I've certainly spent my fair share of time analytically interpreting and discussing texts in ways that revolve around race and gender (and class, for that matter). More often than not, whether with colleagues or students, these have been fruitful, illuminating, and rewarding conversations. While there may be truths in some of my colleagues' points of view, this was nevertheless not one of those instances. *Avatar* provides a unique lens through which to think about the context of globalism as it applies to the film industry; the movie is, after all, the most financially lucrative film in the history of the world. As such, while I value specific interpretations of the film, in this case I believe thinking about and understanding the production, distribution, and exhibition of *Avatar* tells us much more about the landscape of global media than a more strictly singular, close textual analysis ever could. I mentioned this to my colleagues, and they vociferously disagreed; in fact, when prodded to consider what kind of thinking might have been behind the decisions that ultimately led to the green-lighting of the film, one colleague went so far as to say, "Who cares about what a bunch of guys in a room are talking about? That's just boring."

And my colleague may have a point. Having never been privy to the rarified high-level, insiders-only conversations that result in movies being produced, I concede he may well be right. Those types of conversations may well be boring as all get out. But where I respectfully disagree is that even if the conversations are boring, the decisions that result from them are anything but, as the choices studio execs make dictate what the whole world will be watching and that's no small thing, especially given that global or world cinema doesn't mean the same thing it once did. Indeed, I would go so far as to say that world cinema as we once knew it is dead. I know the rebuttals: "What about the DIY Nollywood phenomenon in Nigeria?" "What about Bollywood?" "What about Iranian cinema?" "What about this great French film I saw?" "What about this amazing Brazilian movie I saw in South America last summer?" These are all valid points, but they also serve to underscore my argument. In the not too distant past there was a global cinematic exchange. You may have had to look a bit for foreign films, as they were not often widely distributed nationwide, but if you wanted to see one in America, you could. Indeed, the entire generation of young American filmmakers that so electrified Hollywood and the world in the late 1960s and throughout the 1970s was inspired in no small part by the innovations of the great European filmmakers of the late 1950s and early 1960s, whose films that generation of American filmmakers saw in movie theaters. And that has become increasingly difficult to do. So my answer to the rebuttals is simple: "When is the last time you saw a Nollywood/Bollywood/Iranian/name-the-country, etc., film in an American movie theater or on American television?" It's not a question people typically have an answer for, unless they're both hardcore cinephiles and lucky enough to live in one of the handful of U.S. cities that may intermittently play these kinds of films. As A. O. Scott plaintively asks, "The whole world is watching, why aren't Americans?"

But the opposite isn't even remotely true. Go to any country in the world and you can see just about any mainstream American movie, à la *Avatar,* playing on the big screen. The primary exceptions are in countries whose governments prohibit or limit American media. And even then, there's almost always a fecund market for pirated American movies. Take Iran, for example, in which, as Brain T. Edwards observes, their most internationally celebrated filmmaker, Abbas Kiarostami, isn't much cared for by many Iranians. Conversely, among the most popular images in Iran's capital is that of DreamWorks Animation's *Shrek,* which "appears everywhere throughout Tehran: painted on the walls of DVD and electronics shops, featured in an elaborate mural in the children's play area at the Jaam-e Jam mall," and so on (6). Where are the equivalent familiar icons from foreign films in American culture? They just don't exist and they're not going to anytime soon, if ever. There is precious little market for foreign films in the United States, whereas in many countries around the world, the thriving legitimate and black markets for cinema and television are fueled by an insatiable desire for American products. John Powers observes that "really all over Asia people are making movies, all over Europe people are making movies, and a lot of those movies are good. . . . [But in other] countries, their stars don't get much attention because the American stars sort of suck up all of the oxygen or a movie like *Avatar* is just everywhere" (Gross).

The piracy problem is one that has Hollywood perhaps justifiably up in arms. According to a study conducted in 2005 by the Motion Picture Association–International, "the major U.S. motion picture studios lost $6.1 billion to piracy worldwide in 2005," 80 percent of which was a result of overseas' piracy (MPA-I, "Global Losses"). But it's no secret that the U.S. government has long believed American popular culture to be key in winning over foreign nations to the beauty of democracy. Edwards thinks differently, arguing that, "When American State Department officials imagine that the export of Hollywood film . . . can be [a] simple weapon . . . in the battle for 'hearts and minds' of other cultures (as so many of the champions of so-called 'cultural diplomacy' do these days), they are suffering from a Cold War hangover" (10). Perhaps. But some folks think otherwise, specifically that foreign governments, while publicly limiting or banning altogether American cinema, are all too happy to turn a blind eye to the piracy that occurs as a result of their strictures. I recently had a chance to interview a high-ranking official of the Asia Pacific branch of the Motion Picture Association–International and he told me that he believes the problems with piracy in China and its territories—in which the 90 percent piracy rate is the highest in the world (MPA-I, "Cost")—are in large part because the government has no will to intercede. They'd rather have their populace caught up in American entertainment than worrying about what their government is doing, an opinion that gives whole new meaning to Marx's maxim about the "opiate of the masses."

I was fortunate enough to spend the first 6 months of 2010 in Hong Kong as a Fulbright Senior Scholar, and one of my favorite things to do while speaking to groups in Asia was to ask how many of them had seen a movie featuring their native language on a movie screen in the previous month. More often than not, just 2 or 3 people in an audience of 30 or more would raise their hands. But when I asked how many had seen an American movie in a theater over the same time frame, typically 10 or more people would raise their hands. The numbers became even more skewed if I took the theater out of the equation and asked how many of them had watched a native-language movie anywhere—TV, laptop, iPod, and so on—in the previous month. The number stayed about the same, 2 or 3. But asked the same question about American movies, it was almost always 100 percent. This is certainly an unscientific exercise, and there's no doubt that there are many places I didn't visit in which the locals would have seen many more of their own movies, but I think it's pretty revealing nonetheless. So when I say that world cinema as we once knew it is dead, I'm not claiming that there aren't vibrant filmmaking cultures the world over; there absolutely are and their filmmakers' work should be seen and celebrated. What I am claiming is that with very little exception, world cinema doesn't mean what it once did. Films from most national cinemas rarely transcend borders and get worldwide distribution, which means foreign cinema stays that way, local or regional instead of international. But this doesn't at all apply to American cinema, which, for better or worse, is the dominant national cinema to play in wide release theatrically and via satellite, DVDs (legitimate or not), and so forth the world over. In other words, American cinema is global cinema.

What does transcend borders is money, and that's an important thing to realize. In some ways it's kind of silly to even be talking anymore about movies in terms of country of origin, in no small part because financing for productions of all sizes is increasingly international and multifaceted, so that several entities from a variety of world locales can and often do play a part in producing a film ostensibly originating from a given country. Additionally, people of all nationalities work side by side in filmmaking the world over, coming together in a smorgasbord of global talent. Even though we cling to the idea of national cinemas, many films are made from an amalgam of international financing and, often, talent as well. But still, the cinema Americans traditionally view as foreign, especially non-English-language movies, is increasingly never coming to the States, whereas American cinema is becoming increasingly international in terms of who sees it and where. Why is this? And what does it mean for cinema in America and abroad? Again, part of this has to do with money, and as of this moment, six companies—the Comcast Corporation (which as of this writing is awaiting FCC approval of its purchase of NBC Universal from General Electric), The Walt Disney Company, Fox News Corporation, Time Warner, Viacom, and the Sony Corporation, the so-called Big Six—control the lion's share of the world's major filmed entertainment companies, as well as the infrastructure needed to distribute and exhibit their product. (Although they don't own movie studios, there is definitely a case to be made for also including CBS in this group.) These are huge multinational corporations that aren't in business for the public good; they exist to make money. And, as such, having the movie business as a part of their vertically and horizontally integrated monopolies is a legitimate business strategy. Conversely, radio and television, at least initially, were thought of as public entities that had the potential to educate and enlighten. They are under the purview of the Federal Communications Commission (FCC), which tries to ensure that at least a portion of the respective mediums' programming is in the interest of the public good. But the American movie industry never had such a mandate, nor has it ever been federally controlled. The business of the movies has always been to make money. This is the great conflict of the industry, as artists are eternally trying to reconcile their visions with the financial realities of the system, a conflict that has become even more exacerbated as industry control has become concentrated in the hands of so few companies.

Again, this doesn't mean that there aren't people who passionately believe in the power of the cinema as an art form. But if you pay to see a movie on a big screen or buy or rent it through a legitimate outlet after its theatrical run, it also means that someone, somewhere, believed that the film you are paying to watch, regardless of its artistic intent or social importance, could also make money and invested in it accordingly. It's called "the business of entertainment" for a reason. Movies of all shapes and sizes can make money, but this is where it gets complicated and especially pertinent to the text you now hold in your hands. To make the kind of return on investment required to be deemed worthwhile by a subsidiary of a Big Six company, a film has to transcend national borders; it has to play widely the world over. And in that case, the language of origin, though normally English, hardly matters a lick. What matters most is that it be simplistic and broad enough that the events on-screen can be followed regardless of the native language of the audience. This applies to films that the studios make, but also to those made outside of the system, or at least to those that aspire to studio distribution. For example, film festivals are also markets where people pitch their products in the hopes of making "presales" (cash up front in exchange for domestic and/or international distribution rights) that will net them the capital required to go into production. Not surprisingly, as the American Film Market's Jonathan Wolf observes about film festival marketplaces, "Those that have projects tend to stay more into genres that translate easily—horror, erotic thrillers, action-adventures, comedies that are based on the visual and not on the words—because those are easy to understand and easy to convey to the buyer and are less sensitive to a successful execution by the director" and therefore not tied to a particular language (Masters, "Cannes"). Accordingly, when making a film that you hope will play worldwide, the visual language of cinema becomes much more important than the film's spoken language. Cultural specificity and nuance go by the wayside, as they aren't globally marketable; in their place are beautiful people engaged in spectacle and bombast. As it turns out, everyone likes a visually spectacular sequence, or at least enough people do to make spectacle the lingua franca of Hollywood cinema. Certainly over the years many have lamented this state of affairs, including David Foster Wallace, who blames James Cameron's (not coincidentally *Avatar*'s writer/director as well) *Terminator 2: Judgment Day* (1991) for inaugurating the rise of what he calls Hollywood's "special new genre of big-budget film: Special Effects Porn. 'Porn' because, if you substitute F/X for intercourse, the parallels between the two genres become so obvious they're eerie." Similarly, in his review of the remake of *Clash of the Titans* (Leterrier 2010), released almost 20 years after the original, David Edelstein says, "There's no shame in loving spectacle. In the *Poetics,* Aristotle recognized it as an important component of drama although much further down the list than plot, characters, and dialogue. But Aristotle never saw *Avatar.* Spectacle in movies goes a long way. We crave amazement. . . . [But the] dirty secret of the gods who call the shots in Hollywood is that they are boring."

While I do sometimes get tired of seeing what appear to be the same kind of things recur on-screen over and over again, I don't necessarily agree with Wallace or Edelstein, and for the purposes of this book, it doesn't matter whether I do or not. Their criticisms are value judgments about individual films, which are useful and important but beside the point for what I'm interested in exploring here. Rather than lament the kinds of films that now predominate Hollywood's output, I think it's more useful at this moment to accept them for what they are and instead focus on broader questions: How did we get here? What does it mean for the industry and consumers now that we've arrived? And where do we go from here? I am talking about nothing less than the future of the movies, about which David Thomson, at the turn of the 20th century, posited, "We're on the edge . . . of an explosive end to cinema, as a way of remaking society" (476). To believe that statement, you have to believe that cinema—or at least mainstream cinema—was ever a way "of remaking society" to begin with, and I'm far from convinced that it was. Regardless though, because of the kind of money an individual film can now bring in—in extreme cases $1 billion or more in its theatrical release alone, which is just the tip of the total financial iceberg (the Motion Picture Association–International says only 16% of a movie's profits come from its theatrical run, while "the remaining whopping 84% stems from the home environment—via DVD and VCD, pay-TV and free-to-air TV" [MPA-I, Asia Pacific])—I think the evolution of the movies has to this point been nothing if not predictable. In a capitalist system, the function of a business is to maximize its profits, and that's exactly what the Big Six companies have done. They shouldn't be made villains for doing that which they are supposed to do, whether you like their product or not.

But there's no question that the movies have changed. Although maybe "changed" isn't the right word, as blatantly commercial movies have always been made; but because of the present financial imperatives of the industry, certain kinds of films have been given primacy over others. Whether finances have degraded the overall quality of cinema is in the eye of the beholder, although I think you can argue, as Edward Jay Epstein does,

> that movies have been juvenilized if not degraded. Brought down in their age level and intelligence by the requisites and realities of what a studio needs to do to keep money flowing in. I think that everyone in Hollywood would like to make socially relevant . . . movies . . . really good movies. The problem is that they know that they need an audience to come to the theaters that they can find and that audience tends to be teenaged and high school students and people that basically want action in movies. So more and more they produce the movies that will produce the money they need and somehow they hope that a little money will be available to make the *Hurt Lockers* or the other movies that they would really prefer to make if they had their way about it—if they had the ability to do what they wanted to do.

Perhaps nothing provides better evidence of the infantilization of movies than the trend to adapt children's games into feature films, which has led us to the present moment in which movies based on games and toys such as Battleship, Ouija Board, Candy Land, Risk, Stretch Armstrong, View-Master, and the Magic 8 Ball are now in Hollywood's development and production pipeline (Masters, "Sexual Banter"). Can this be a good thing for those of us who believe in the power of movies to do more than simply entertain? As the Magic 8 Ball might say, "Outlook not so good." And this brings us back to James Cameron's *Avatar*, which as of this writing, at $2.7 billion and counting in noninflation-adjusted dollars, is the most financially successful theatrical release in the history of the planet (boxofficemojo. com).[1] It's a film that's perfectly reflective of the contemporary industry: narratively simplistic and visually stupendous, thus its near-universal appeal. To be sure, different cultures respond to the film in varying ways so that what people think about it in America isn't necessarily akin to the way it is viewed in China, Iran, or Brazil. But while the responses are multitudinous, the fact remains that its narrative broadness and visual enticements are so appealing that it plays well across all cultures. Just as *Gone with the Wind* (Fleming 1939) was the pinnacle of the classical-era Hollywood studio system, so too is *Avatar* the pièce de résistance of the nascent digital age of Hollywood filmmaking. But that doesn't mean that all is rosy at the present moment.

As digital technology becomes ever more ubiquitous, it's having a profound effect on the way audiences consume their media, which has resulted in the crumbling of the nearly century-old production, distribution, and exhibition model of the American film industry. This doesn't mean that the industry is going away—or that the importance of controlling production, distribution, and exhibition will become any less essential. But it does mean that the industry has to reinvent itself in the wake of the onslaught of new technologies, as the tried and true process of giving a film a grand opening to garner the reviews that will bolster its subsequent wide distribution seems positively antique in this day and age of instantaneous communication and social networking. The film industry has been given permission by the FCC to disable home DVRs so as to prevent the recording of their films (Poirier). This is a huge deal, as it will ultimately lead to the bursting of the dam as concerns the simultaneous day and date multiplatform release of movies. No longer will you have to go to the theater to watch a movie, nor will you have to wait months to rent it on DVD or via pay-per-view online or on your TV. It will all be available simultaneously the same day the film is released in theaters. And for a lucky few, the industry's ride towards reinventing how it operates will be amazing and result in great riches. But just as digital technology will create tons of new opportunities, so too will it leave others behind. Take, for example, digital 3D, which

is on the one hand the great mantra for Hollywood. On the other hand it's like the Freddy Krueger for people around the rest of the world . . . because we already live in a time when 5% of the movies made occupy 95% of the screens and with the growth of 3D it seems likely to shift so that an even smaller percentage of films will get even more screen space. Part of the problem for the 3D technology as it now exists is, one, it costs a lot of money to make [at least for those sans studio affiliation], and, two, it limits the kinds of stories you can tell. You know, what really is the point of having a small-scale but beautiful film about monks if you're just shooting it in 3D and there's no real action sequence in it? So that 3D in its very technological nature seems to provoke a certain kind of storytelling, which is anti-thetical to much of what the storytelling is around the world. . . . [As a result], the excited side . . . is the money people, and the artistic people are all freaking out, thinking that 3D is just going to gobble up all the screens and art movies are going to be even more endangered. (Masters, "Cannes")

There's no doubt that the industry is undergoing nigh-unprecedented seismic shifts, and no one is certain where it will go and how it will get there and what it will look like once it reaches the mature phase of the digital age it's now entering. Who will get left behind and who will get to come along for the ride and why? How will the industry go about monetizing new technologies and what will that mean for consumers? What does the digital future hold not only for blockbuster studio filmmaking but for independent and foreign filmmakers as well? What will the new paradigm mean for audiences and their relationship to the cinema? Will the industry even be able to reinvent itself so as to survive relatively intact? The only thing that seems certain to remain unchanged is the fact that the tense rela-tionship between art and commerce that has always been at the root of the business of entertainment will remain firmly in place. And so the industry moves forward in fits and starts to meet the digital future that is arriving at breakneck speed. As Margo Channing (Bette Davis) says in the classic film *All About Eve* (Mankiewicz 1950), "Fasten your seatbelts, it's going to be a bumpy night."

## NOTE

1. As concerns the dollar figures for production budgets and box office returns used in this book, keep in mind that these numbers are notoriously inaccurate. While they all come from the *Internet Movie Database* (*imdb.com*), the affiliate site *Box Office Mojo.com*, or some other reputable source, these sources are merely noting the figures made public by the companies involved. For a variety of reasons—publicity, taxes, self-preservation, and so on—these companies, when they can, tend to make public the figures that present their endeavors in the most flattering light; therefore you shouldn't take any of these numbers as gospel truth. That said, they are nevertheless typically somewhere in the ballpark of plausibility, which allows us to use them in such a way as to arrive at certain assumptions about the industry and that's what I've tried to do throughout this book, even if the num-bers don't always line up with what might be the literal truth.

## WORKS CITED

*Box Office Mojo.com.* "Avatar." 2009.
Edelstein, David. "A *Titans* Remake: Clashing with Everything in Sight." *NPR's Fresh Air Podcast.* April 2, 2010.
Edwards, Brian T. "Watching *Shrek* in Tehran: The Seen and the Unseen in Iranian Cin-ema." *The Believer,* March/April 2010: 5–11.
Epstein, Edward Jay. (Interviewed by Dave Davies). "Crunching Numbers in the Holly-wood Economy." *NPR's Fresh Air Podcast.* April 1, 2010.

Gross, Terry. "John Powers' Reflections on Cannes." *NPR's Fresh Air Podcast.* May 27, 2010.

Jeancolas, Jean-Pierre. "From the Blum-Byrnes Agreement to the GATT Affair." In *Hollywood and Europe: Economics, Culture, National Identity: 1945–95*, ed. Geoffrey Nowell-Smith and Steven Ricci, 47–62. London: British Film Institute, 1998.

Masters, Kim. "Sexual Banter, Tantrums, Abuse: Hollywood's Work Environment." *KCRW's The Business Podcast.* May 3, 2010.

Masters, Kim. "Cannes Market Report." *KCRW's The Business Podcast.* May 24, 2010.

Motion Picture Association–International (MPA-I). "Global Losses to Piracy Top US $6.1 Billion." *MPA-I.org.*

Motion Picture Association–International (MPA-I). "The Cost of Movie Piracy." *MPA-I.org.*

Motion Picture Association–International (MPA-I). "Asia Pacific Technology Initiatives." *MPA-I.org.*

Poirier, John. "U.S. Approval Allows First-Run Movies to TV Sets." *Reuters.com.* May 7, 2010.

Powers, John. "A *Titans* Remake: Clashing with Everything in Sight." *NPR Fresh Air Podcast.* April 2, 2010.

Scott, A. O. "The Whole World Is Watching, Why Aren't Americans?" *The New York Times.com.* Jan. 21, 2007.

Thomson, David. *The New Biographical Dictionary of Film.* New York: Alfred A. Knopf, 2002.

Wallace, David Foster. "F/X Porn." *Waterstone's* magazine. Winter/Spring 1998. http://www.badgerinternet.com/~bobkat/waterstone.html.

# Chapter 2

# FROM THE BUSINESS OF FILM TO THE BUSINESS OF ENTERTAINMENT: HOLLYWOOD IN THE AGE OF DIGITAL TECHNOLOGY

*By Yannis Tzioumakis*[1]

In his influential 2002 article "Digital Cinema: A False Revolution," film historian John Belton has no equivocations about the nature and the objectives of what has been labeled "the digital revolution" when it comes to the field of cinema. Although the introduction of this technology has been taking place in a number of phases since the late 1980s and has involved such distinct elements of filmmaking as the digitization of special effects, the digitization of sound, and in more recent years the gradual adoption of digital film production and projection systems, it nonetheless has not been driven by "any desire to revolutionise the *theatrical* moviegoing experience." Rather, Belton suggests, "the digital revolution is part of a new corporate synergy within Hollywood, driven by the lucrative home entertainment market" (100).

This synergy has been based on new and improved corporate partnerships between the Hollywood majors and manufacturers of home theater appliances (who are often are under the same corporate umbrella), while later owners of new entertainment digital delivery systems (digital cable, satellite, and the Internet) also joined in to provide consumers with an increasing number of media-based entertainment options for consumption in the comfort of their own home. To facilitate this provision, major corporate players from the consumer electronics industry, the telecommunications industry, the information technology industry, and the media industry invested heavily in digital technology, which in the past two decades has made such giant strides that the term "digital revolution" is now an integral part of the everyday lexicon.

Thus this view necessarily suggests that digital technology has been utilized as a means to an end, as the best available vehicle for the domination of the global entertainment market by a small number of giant corporations. In this respect, one could argue, and Belton implicitly does, the real revolution has not been the technological wonders of digital technology when applied to the creation and delivery of media-based entertainment. Instead, the real revolution has been the manner in which this handful of corporations whose economies are larger than the economies of many nations used digital technology to create a global entertainment market that revolved around media consumption in the domestic space and to install a "transnational media corporate economy" that has swiftly crushed any oppositional or alternative economic models (Zimmermann 247).

Although corporate players from industries such as Sony, Toshiba, and Matsushita (consumer electronics); IBM and Microsoft (information technology); and AT&T, TCI, and Comcast (telecommunications) have certainly been influential in shaping the landscape of the entertainment and leisure industry, it was the Hollywood majors that were at the epicenter of these synergistic trends. With their unquestioned oligopolistic control of the global film market since the late 1910s, their stronghold on television through the provision of programming since the 1950s, and their domination of the home video market since the 1980s, the old studios had amassed vast libraries of film and television titles. These titles, especially the film ones, had been utilized as software for the introduction and widespread market penetration of home entertainment hardware, such as the VCR (from the mid-1970s), and of entertainment delivery systems, especially cable (from the late 1960s).

However, as the global video market started showing signs of sluggish growth in the 1990s, some of the Hollywood majors started becoming more proactive in seeking new ways to exploit their library of titles and establishing novel platforms and interfaces to repurpose their existing and increasingly expanding software (McDonald 92). With consumer electronics companies desperate to upgrade home entertainment hardware as VCRs had reached extremely high levels of penetration of television households in most major international markets,[2] and the telecommunications and information technology companies vying to enter the home and bring further entertainment options through cable, satellite, and the Internet, it was clear that the Hollywood majors were holding the key for any future developments. As an executive of European consumer electronics giant Philips put it with regard to the potential success of DVD technology almost a year before its introduction in the U.S. market, "without the support of software, it's a nonstarter," highlighting clearly the centrality of the Hollywood ex-studios in the introduction and adoption of home entertainment technology in general and DVD more specifically (Hettrick, "Panel").

In this respect, both the nature of the corporate synergies and, especially, the direction of the digital revolution were shaped to a large extent by an agenda set by the Hollywood majors. This agenda saw the majors siding initially with the consumer electronics companies to reignite the sluggish home video market through the introduction of videodisc technologies (DVD and Divx), and therefore competing against telecommunications and information technology companies who at the same time had started to introduce video on demand and pay-per-view services targeting the same home entertainment market (Brinkley B1). In the late 1990s and early 2000s, however, this agenda was modified and Hollywood embraced equally telecommunications companies, especially when the majors realized that video entertainment consumption had stopped being purely home based and was becoming increasingly mobile. By that time, all Hollywood majors had become divisions of corporations alongside other gigantic companies representing the other relevant industries.

This essay charts the evolution of Hollywood from a film business into an entertainment business by reviewing the synergistic trends and corporate strategies of the major Hollywood players in order to reveal the factors that have influenced the setting of the majors' agenda in the digital era, factors that often made those same companies adopt disparate, even conflicting, attitudes regarding the future direction of the film/entertainment business. To illustrate this, the focus will be primarily on the corporate marriages between the ex-studios and the consumer electronics companies that facilitated the introduction of DVD technology. Besides highlighting once again the centrality of the Hollywood majors as producers and publishers of software in the shaping of the digital era, the ensuing discussion argues that the evolution of Hollywood into an entertainment business had been well under way before the benefits of digital technology for the consumption of entertainment in the home had become obvious. In this respect, digital technology in general and the Digital Video Disc in particular became vehicles for the execution of a corporate restructuring plan in Hollywood, the origins of which are located back in the analog era.

The corporate restructuring transformed Hollywood in fundamental ways as it created a market that was infinitely larger in size and scale than the film market could ever be and companies infinitely larger and more powerful than the ex-studios. It also necessarily affected the types of films made by or for the Hollywood majors, while it initially also created a sizable niche for smaller, indie productions. It is the actual execution of this restructuring process that came to depend heavily on the benefits of digital technology.

## HOLLYWOOD IN THE AGE OF ANALOG ENTERTAINMENT

To make sense of the corporate plans and synergistic tendencies in Hollywood in the 1990s and 2000s, one needs to go back almost half a century, to the early years of analog television. From the very beginning, the eight Hollywood studios (MGM, Warner Bros., 20th Century Fox, Paramount, RKO, Universal, Columbia, and United Artists) that dominated the film industry from the second decade of the twentieth century objected to the idea of television, as they believed that free home entertainment would ultimately devalue their films and their stars. As a result, the television industry was shaped without the involvement of the studios, which allowed new corporate players, the three broadcasting networks (ABC,

NBC, and CBS), to emerge. The studios, however, maintained a strong foothold in the television business by providing programming for the networks, as they were the best-resourced outfits to deliver programming in high volume.

In 1955, however, RKO became the first film studio to collapse financially. In the ensuing liquidation, the management of the studio agreed to sell its pre-1948 library of titles for $15 million to General Telesales (Balio, *UA* 105), a television sales company servicing several major metropolitan areas, including Los Angeles and New York. In the same year, Warner Bros. sold its own pre-1948 catalogue of titles to Associated Artists Production, while by 1958 almost 3,700 pre-1948 films had been sold or leased for television consumption by the studios for an estimated $220 million (Ibid.). Although all this product was sold for use in the syndicated television and not the network television market, it nevertheless made Hollywood studios realize that the then new medium of television was actually providing a significant afterlife for product the studios until then thought had little or no future economic potential. As Jim Hillier suggests, during the golden years of Hollywood, films were considered products that made only "immediate profits," with the studios collecting 80 percent of the film's value within a year after its release and 100 percent within two years (12). Only on rare occasions did major successes such as *Gone with the Wind* (Fleming 1939) or Disney films like *Snow White and the Seven Dwarfs* (Hand et al. 1937) bring additional income through one or more theatrical re-releases in later years. In this sense, television became the first significant ancillary market for the film industry, and this at a time when the studios had been experiencing significant economic difficulties following the effects of the Paramount Decree of 1948 (especially the loss of income from the theater divestiture) and of the continual audience decline after the peak of 1946.

More important, however, the studios' provision of programming for the networks and their film sales to syndicated television, alongside the expansion of small independent company Walt Disney Pictures to television with the incredibly successful *Disneyland* (shortly thereafter renamed *The Wonderful of Disney*), which advertised both Disney films and the company's amusement park in California, signaled the incipient phase of Hollywood's diversification (Schatz 460). Although revenue from television would remain at relatively low levels until the 1960s, when deals like the one between NBC and United Artists for a package of 70 post-1960 pictures released theatrically by the latter would bring to the major $125 million, the 1950s did provide the studios with a blueprint for creating a new market by means of exploiting their library of titles through a new technology (Balio, *UA* 112). In the words of Peter Lev, "television provided the film industry with new opportunities that laid the groundwork for diversification and concentration that characterised the entertainment industry at the end of the century" (146).

Although diversification and expansion towards other media markets continued in the 1960s, with Universal's takeover by talent agency Music Corporation of America (MCA) in 1962 providing the key example of the formation of an early entertainment conglomerate, near the end of the decade varying factors that

TABLE 2.1: THE CONGLOMERATION OF HOLLYWOOD

| YEAR | STUDIO | CONGLOMERATE/BUYER |
|---|---|---|
| 1966 | Paramount | Gulf+Western |
| 1967 | United Artists | Transamerica |
| 1969 | Warner Bros | Kinney National Service |
| 1969 | MGM | Tracy Investment Company |
| 1962 | Universal | Music Corporation of America (MCA) |
| 1970s | 20th Century-Fox | Self-conglomerated |
| 1970s | Columbia | Self-conglomerated |

included the dismal box office failure of a number of films produced and/or distributed by the majors[3] and the continuing audience decline, which reached an ultimate low of 15.8 million people per week in early 1971 from almost 100 million in 1946, put the major studios in a precarious financial position (Cook 22). It was at this point that the film industry ceased to exist as a single, autonomous entity as the diversification process entered a second, very different phase. This phase involved the corporate takeover of four major studios by conglomerates, "diversified company[ies] with major interests in several unrelated fields," within the space of three years (Balio, *UA* 303). With Universal already conglomerated after its takeover by MCA, the remaining two studios also became conglomerates themselves, through a program of aggressive diversification. Table 2.1 summarizes the corporate takeover of the American film industry in the late 1960s and early 1970s.

## THE CONGLOMERATION OF HOLLYWOOD

Conglomerates like Gulf+Western, which among its holdings included companies specializing in automobile parts, considered film studios like Paramount fine targets for corporate takeovers in the economic climate of the late 1960s (Monaco 31). This was because the studios' stock was significantly undervalued as a result of the poor box office of recent films, but also because of their significant real estate holdings in and around the city of Los Angeles. Equally important, however, the conglomerates were aware of the increasing value of the studios' film libraries and wanted to exploit them on cable and pay-TV, two additional exhibition windows that had started emerging in the United States in the 1960s (Balio, *UA* 303).

The conglomeration of the American film industry had far-reaching implications for the structuring and organization of the film business. As I have discussed elsewhere, the conglomerates allowed their newly acquired subsidiaries to take increasingly expensive gambles with films that had the potential for huge payoffs at the box office (Tzioumakis, *American* 196). This was mainly because the financial basis on which conglomerates operated was big enough to easily absorb box office losses. In this respect, the conglomerates can be credited for cultivating the blockbuster mentality that took the industry by storm, especially from the mid-1970s onwards. Furthermore, they imposed modern business techniques and methods in their attempt to rationalize film production and distribution and therefore reduce the sizable financial risks for which the film business has been notorious. These methods included the installation of university-trained management regimes; the adoption of various scientific audience research mechanisms to measure tastes, preferences, and viewing habits; and the implementation of decision-making structures that depended on research reports, charts, and data.

More important, the conglomerates, as experts in matters of corporate diversification, recognized immediately the significance of opening up to new markets and creating more outlets for the commercial exploitation of the product their subsidiaries produced and distributed. For that reason, they actively encouraged the expansion of the majors to media- and leisure-related fields with an eye to create new profit centers for a commodity that was already produced and therefore in need of only additional marketing and advertising costs.

The significance and value of the ex-studios in the new conglomerate structure became so evident to the management of the parent companies that from the early 1980s onwards, all the ex-studios found themselves amidst a new, this time internal, restructuring process. With cable television having become another very significant ancillary market, accounting for 17 percent of all film revenues in 1982 (Hillier 15), and with VCR households in the United States increasing from 1,850,000 in 1980 to 8,300,000 in 1983 (*Velvet Light Trap* Editors 86), it became clear that the potential for further revenue from the exploitation of an ex-studio's library of films was enormous. The internal restructuring, then, aimed to "deconglomerise" Hollywood, that is, to divest off "unrelated market segments in order to concentrate on related areas of operation and to facilitate ongoing merger-and-acquisition activities" (Prince 60).

Gulf+Western, parent company of Paramount, arguably became the model for such deconglomeration. By 1980 the company consisted of a large number of subsidiaries operating under the umbrella of seven unrelated divisions, including apparel and home furnishings, consumer and agricultural products and auto parts. Nine years later and after implementing a program with which it "began to redeploy its resources by trimming its corporate structure, strengthening its financial position, and divesting operations that did not fit its evolving corporate profile," the company emerged consisting of only two divisions, entertainment (centered on Paramount) and publishing (centered on giant publishing house Simon & Schuster) (Prince 63). The new structure allowed the company to become much more focused and to specialize in a variety of related areas and products, while also exploiting the considerably enhanced potential for synergies and cross-promotion (Ibid.). For instance, Paramount films and television programs could promote books and other services offered by the other division, while the huge number of titles published by Simon & Schuster (which includes such major publishing imprints as Pocket Books) could promote Paramount films, their stars, etc.

To complete the restructuring process, the new company changed its name from Gulf+Western to Paramount Communications, highlighting once again the significance of the ex-studios, this time not only as copyright holders of invaluable filmed entertainment but also as globally recognizable brand names whose brand identity was essential in the reshaping of the company and of the sector. This was also reflected in Transamerica's decision not to change the name of United Artists to Transamerica Films in 1980 (Bach 22). Likewise, for the short time that MGM continued its operations under Las Vegas financer and hotelier Kirk Kerkorian's Tracy Investment Company, before its partial liquidation and severe downsize in 1973, it also maintained its name. And so did Columbia, which as early as 1968 had merged with its subsidiary Screen Gems, thereby creating an "integrated entertainment complex" under the name Columbia Pictures Industries (Cook 315).

The road to deconglomeration, however, had been paved in the early 1970s with the development of Warner Bros. as part of Kinney National Service. Under the management of Steven J. Ross, an early advocate of television technologies, Warner and all other media-related holdings of Kinney (including companies that published the Batman and Superman comic magazines) were pooled together under the name Warner Communications, Inc. (WCI), while the rest of the parent company's assets that included companies in such unrelated areas as funeral parlors and parking lots were regrouped under the Kinney National brand (Cook 307). Following this reshuffle, Ross started adding to his WCI holding companies that specialized in exhibition technologies with the explicit intention of expanding the available distribution windows for Warner titles. Warner Communications became the company that took Hollywood "into the business of directly operating cable TV systems," as it established Home Box Office (HBO) in 1975, a cable television system that has dominated the landscape of cable television in the United States ever since and has recently emerged as the producer of incredibly popular series like *The Sopranos* (1999–2007) and *Sex and the City* (1999–2004) (Gomery 52).

This trend was not only symptomatic of the policies in the top echelon of the film business, as new independent companies and mini-major studios of the early 1980s also followed similar business tactics. Arguably the most important independent company of the period, Orion Pictures, tried to compete with the Hollywood majors by adhering to a strong program of diversification, moving to areas that could generate synergies with its films and divesting itself of subsidiaries with little or no overlapping potential with its core film business. In this respect, almost immediately after establishing Orion as a distribution company by taking over Filmways, Orion's management sold subsidiaries that were originally part of Filmways' portfolio in the areas of publishing, slide mounting, and radio hardware, while later in the decade the company branched out to television with Orion Television and

**TABLE 2.2: THE DECONGLOMERATION OF THE FILM INDUSTRY**

| ORIGINAL STUDIO | DECONGLOMERATED MAJOR |
| --- | --- |
| Paramount | Paramount Communications (name change in 1989) |
| United Artists | MGM/United Artists Entertainment Company |
| Warner Bros | Warner Communications |
| MGM | MGM/ United Artists Entertainment Company |
| Universal | MCA/Universal |
| 20th Century-Fox | Self-conglomerated (kept its name after takeover by oilman Barry Davis in 1981) |
| Columbia | Columbia Pictures Industries |

Orion Pictures Television (Tzioumakis, "Major" 98, 123). Table 2.2 summarizes the evolution of the film industry and its move "from movies to communications" by the early 1980s (Hillier 15).

It is clear then that corporate synergies, which expanded the business of film to a more loosely defined but one with much greater economic potential entertainment, media, and leisure business, were well under way before the 1980s' merger mania. In this respect, digital technology became the lynching pin for the undertaking of more audacious, elaborate multibillion dollar synergies that came to characterize the industry from the late 1980s to date.

## HOLLYWOOD IN THE AGE OF DIGITAL ENTERTAINMENT

In 1982, soft drink giant Coca-Cola broke the wave of deconglomeration by buying Columbia Pictures Industries. Although its ownership of the ex-studio would last only seven years, as the years of conglomerates with subsidiaries in unrelated fields had passed, it nevertheless understood precisely why a subsidiary like Columbia could prove to be a real gold mine with the corporate support of a parent company like Coca-Cola behind it. As a Coca-Cola statement read:

> The entertainment business in general and the motion picture business in particular are undergoing significant changes, primarily due to technological developments which have resulted in the availability of alternative forms of leisure time entertainment, including expanding pay and cable television, video cassettes, video discs, and video games. (quoted in Prince 40)

Besides underscoring the increasing importance of various other forms of distribution and exhibition technologies, Coca-Cola correctly identified the evolution of the business in which companies like Columbia and the rest of the other ex-studios were leading the way. As the above statement suggests, the business was "leisure time entertainment," though at that time such entertainment had increasingly started targeting the home as opposed to the theater or the video arcade. And while the diversification and deconglomeration processes had placed the ex-studios in pole position for achieving this objective, the increasing significance of digital technology to bring (more) entertainment into the home upped the financial stakes, created more "urges to merge" (Balio, "Adjusting" 27), and shaped an entertainment business landscape where the ex-studios have been increasingly defined by their status as entertainment software authors and copyright holders of invaluable content.

## LEADER OF THE PACK

The Hollywood major that initiated this new phase in the evolution of the film business was 20th Century Fox, after its takeover by Rupert Murdoch's News Corporation in 1985. By acquiring a diversified Hollywood ex-studio, the holdings of which included companies with interests in film, broadcasting, resorts and recreation, theaters outside the United States, and soft drinks bottling, News Corporation built on its own global holdings in the areas of media entertainment, which centered mainly on newspapers and magazines (Prince 5). With the potential for synergies and cross-promotions on a global scale significantly enhanced, News Corporation immediately proceeded to branch out to television in order to include this lucrative market/business segment alongside film and publishing under the same corporate umbrella. Not surprisingly, Murdoch chose the brand name Fox for his television operations in the U.S. market and invested billions of dollars in launching and supporting Fox Television, which became the first outfit to break the oligopoly of the three established television networks that had held since the 1940s.

Although Fox's integration into Murdoch's media and entertainment empire was seemingly a case of more aggressive diversification with the objective of exploiting more synergies on a truly global level, it nevertheless departed significantly from the diversification that occurred in the earlier years. First, there was the field of operations in which the new parent company specialized. While the conglomeration of the film industry in the 1960s saw a number of huge companies moving into the film industry from the outside, News Corporation was the first company (barring MCA in 1962) with interests in the media market to acquire an ex-studio (especially as the most recent major takeovers before that were again from companies from outside the sector—Fox's by oilman Barry Davis, and Columbia's by Coca-Cola). Second, the new parent company operated on a global level, with major interests in the United States; Australia; Eastern markets, especially India and China; South America; and Britain. Although conglomerates like Gulf+Western and Transamerica also operated on a global level, they nevertheless lacked the coherence of News Corporation, the interests of which were in media-related areas across the board. Third, the owner of the ex-studio was not American. Although Gulf+Western was also owned by a non-U.S. citizen, this was never perceived as a problem given the conglomerate's lack of market specialization and therefore lack of interest in controlling a nation's media. News Corporation, however, owned influential newspapers and magazines, a film studio, and, by the end of the 1980s, a U.S. television network, which meant that a large section of the nation's media and their channels of distribution were increasingly concentrated under the control of one agency.

Finally, and more important, Fox's takeover by News Corporation was only one (but arguably the most significant) corporate move towards the development of a new super-company, a transnational entertainment corporation that would continue to expand horizontally in order to own all available entertainment distribution and exhibition windows, while also controlling the huge volume of programming that is required for all those windows to operate efficiently. This means that companies like News Corporation, after the takeover of 20th Century Fox and the establishment of the Fox Network in the United States, the launch of BSkyB in 1990 in the United Kingdom, and various other media services the world over, have not only been able to grow horizontally and play the synergy game at an unprecedented level, they have also managed to expand vertically and control a sector from production to distribution to exhibition. With the ex-studios having amassed years of expertise in all three aspects of the business during the cinema years, it is clear that their role in the new companies would be of utmost significance, given also their ownership of vast libraries of titles of filmed entertainment.

## THE RISE OF THE TRANSNATIONAL ENTERTAINMENT ECONOMY

With Fox changing hands and becoming part of a vast and constantly expanding horizontally and vertically entertainment empire, the rest of the majors followed suit. The year 1989 proved to be a key year for Hollywood as both Warner and Columbia changed hands and ended up parts of vast integrated entertainment complexes, while Disney started an aggressive program of diversification and joined the established superpowers. Warner merged with publishing and cable television giant Time Inc., creating Time Warner, then the "world's pre-eminent media conglomerate valued at $14 billion" (Balio, "Adjusting" 29). Columbia, which by 1987 had been spun off from Coca-Cola and had stand-alone status, accepted a takeover by Japanese consumer electronics manufacturer Sony.

While the Time Warner merger seemed to be following the example set by News Corporation, that is, bringing together interests in the publishing business (Time) and filmed entertainment business (Warner), and therefore enriching the potential for synergies in both companies, it is arguably more important that the merger was about Warner Communications acquiring a foothold in Time's vast cable television business (Gomery 52). Already controlling a considerable part of cable television in the United States through HBO and its Cinemax entertainment package, Warner further strengthened its position in that market, which by 1989 boasted 21 million addressable cable households (up from 1.5 million in 1982) and 27.07 million pay cable subscribers (up from 13.4 million in 1982) (*Velvet Light Trap* Editors 87). As Douglas Gomery puts it, "The Time Warner merger was simply another step in logically expanding the 'ancillary markets' for Warner's television programmes and films, furthering vertical integration, making even more money and in the process remaking Hollywood" (53).

Columbia's takeover by Sony, however, was again driven by the possibilities of cross-promotion (Sony's home entertainment electronics being promoted by and promoting Columbia's filmed entertainment), though the emphasis was clearly on the Japanese giant's effort to secure software support for its many electronics products. To this end, Sony had already spent $2 billion in 1987 to buy CBS Records, therefore securing content for its audio systems, while the takeover of Columbia could offer Sony important leverage in future video technology innovations (Hillier 25). This was desired in part because Sony had experienced a number of defeats in video and audio format wars in the 1970s and 1980s, respectively (with Sony's Betamax losing the VCR battle to JVC's VHS format, while Sony's digital audio tape and minidisc were also defeated as audio technologies by competitors like Philips). With a major ex-studio and record label under its corporate umbrella, Sony would be in a position to compete more effectively against other global entertainment conglomerates in the next stage of the home entertainment revolution (Philips would try to introduce CD-interactive, or CD-i, as the first example of digital video as early as 1991) or to lead the way through DVD in 1996 (McDonald 53).

Sony's takeover of a Hollywood major certainly did not remain unnoticed in the Japanese consumer electronics industry. A little more than a year later, Matsushita, arguably Sony's main competitor and bitter rival in the video wars of the 1970s and 1980s, proceeded to take over first MCA and through this deal Universal, the first media-centered Hollywood corporation. Paying double the amount of money to purchase its own Hollywood major—$6.6 billion against Sony's $3.3 billion—Matsushita's entrance to the entertainment market underscored further the scale of the stakes and the significance of content as produced and administered by the Hollywood majors (McDonald 137). This was highlighted even further by Toshiba's decision to also enter the emerging entertainment market through buying a significant stake at Time Warner, making it the third Japanese consumer electronics company with a piece in the Hollywood pie.

Disney also emerged as a global entertainment player through the establishment of two additional production labels (Touchstone Pictures in 1983 and Hollywood Pictures in 1988) that would provide the company with an increased number of titles, through creating its own cable channel, the Disney Channel (in 1983), and through starting to finally release its extremely popular animation titles on video. As a result, Disney started gaining ground in the entertainment market at a time during which the industry was moving in giant strides and managed to become "a film producer and distributor on a par with the other majors" (Prince 74).

With the rest of the majors having changed hands and restructured anew in order to locate themselves at the strongest possible position at the dawn of the transnational entertainment economy, Paramount became the major to close this phase of corporate restructuring and consolidation. Five years after its deconglomeration and emergence as Paramount Communications, the company was taken over by Viacom, a then leading television syndication and cable network company, for $8.2 billion (Balio, "Major" 67). Although film historians, like Balio, writing closer to the time of this particular takeover, have argued that rather than being the last move in a cycle of mergers, Paramount's takeover by Viacom was the first in a wave of mergers that involved cable and network television (Ibid.), in hindsight, it is more constructive to see this move as part of the earlier restructuring phase. Like the takeover of Fox, Paramount also changed ownership after a media-related buyer took over the major's parent company. Furthermore and again like in the case of Fox, the new owner used the company to branch out to network television through the creation of United Paramount Network (1995), while a year earlier and almost immediately after taking over Paramount, Viacom had moved to add Blockbuster Entertainment, the biggest chain of video stores in the United States for $7.6 billion (Ibid.), under its corporate umbrella, thereby creating a giant entertainment empire on a par with the competition.

Alternatively, it could be argued that it was the next major corporate transaction in the entertainment industry that signified a new cycle, and that was Disney's 1996 takeover of Capital Cities, a communications company that owned ABC, one of the three established U.S. television networks. This was because until that point the three key corporate players in network television, ABC, CBS, and NBC, had stayed away from the emerging transnational entertainment empires and therefore it was their time to realign themselves corporately or else miss the train to the new media order. One should also add the fact that the three networks had already started experiencing intensified competition from the new networks like Fox Television and United Paramount Network, which of course could benefit from the many media sister companies under News Corporation and Viacom, respectively, in ways that the established networks could not. Following ABC's lead, the other two remaining networks also found new corporate parents, with CBS adding yet more diversity and strength to the already vast corporate edifice created by Viacom in 1999, and in 2004 NBC merging with Universal, which by that time had been part of the European-based Vivendi group, thus creating yet another giant transnational corporation under the corporate leadership of General Electric. In this respect, it is more constructive to see the takeover of Paramount by Viacom in 1993 as the last move in a cycle. Table 2.3 summarizes the entertainment landscape by the mid-1990s,

**TABLE 2.3: THE ENTERTAINMENT LANDSCAPE IN THE UNITED STATES IN THE MID-1990S**

| ORIGINAL STUDIO | MEDIA ENTERTAINMENT CONGLOMERATE |
| --- | --- |
| Paramount | Viacom |
| Columbia | Sony |
| Warner Bros | Time Warner |
| 20th Century-Fox | News Corporation |
| Universal | Matsushita |
| Disney | Walt Disney Pictures |
| MGM/UA | Remained as relatively small stand alone corporations |

## THE ROLE OF DIGITAL TECHNOLOGY

It was during the particular restructuring phase of the 1980s to mid-1990s that digital technology started becoming a major factor. On the one hand, by 1989, the home entertainment market had become a significant ancillary market for the ex-studios and the companies that controlled or were about to control them. On the other hand, though, VCR technology had already reached very high levels of penetration, especially in the United States and western Europe, which in effect meant that the days of the exponentially expanding market of the 1980s had slowed down considerably. Thus while, as we saw earlier, in 1983 there were 8.3 million VCR households in the United States, by 1989 the number had reached an incredible 69.26 million, or 67.6 percent of the television households (*Velvet Light Trap* 86).

While the ex-studios remained indifferent to the slowing down of VCR technology penetration as it affected little their status as software providers when the retail market for videocassettes had been more buoyant than ever, with sales of prerecorded videocassettes jumping from 135 million in 1988 to 200 million in 1989, the home entertainment hardware manufacturers had started feeling the pressures of a gradually saturating global VCR market (*Velvet Light Trap* 87). Interim innovations such as the laserdisc had not taken off as mass entertainment technologies, and under the best of circumstances had created only niche markets. More important, however, there was no evident demand by consumers to replace or upgrade the existing technology, as video's two main benefits, individually chosen prerecorded entertainment and time shifting, had provided consumers with a flexibility in entertainment that seemed to cover their needs in the late 1980s and early 1990s' consumer media environment. Even later in the 1990s, this demand for replacing video remained low, and it was the consumer electronics industry, which by then was in desperate need to innovate, that had started pushing for the introduction of an upgraded digital video home exhibition technology (Roberts 42).

Around the late 1980s and early 1990s, the wonders of digital technology in the area of special effects had started becoming manifest in U.S. cinema. Such effects-laden films as *The Abyss* (Cameron 1989), and especially *Terminator 2: Judgment Day* (Cameron 1991) and *Jurassic Park* (Spielberg 1993), became block-buster successes (especially the latter two) and made digital technology visible to a wide cinema-going public. At the same time, the introduction of digital sound in 1990—featured in such popular films as *Dick Tracy* (Beatty 1990), *Edward Scissorhands* (Burton 1990), and *The Doors* (Stone 1991)—gave further momentum to the use of digital technology in cinema, and together with the developments in effects promised a bright future for the on-screen realization of images, sounds, and ideas that were hitherto impossible to imagine (Belton 101).

Digital technology (or, to be more precise, one particular application of digital technology), however, was not new, especially for the vast majority of the Western population. As a matter of fact, its benefits had been utilized in the very recent past to introduce and market an audio technology that would replace the long-established record players and vinyl long-playing records (LP) as well as cassette recorders and cassette audio technologies. This technology was the compact disc player and the compact disc (CD). Introduced commercially in 1983, the compact disc digital audio technology (as was its full name) became the first successful mass-marketed home entertainment digital technology. Integral to its commercial success was the aura of unprecedented quality in terms of digital sound reproduction, which made established audio technologies pale in comparison (McDonald 52).

Although this technology did not take off immediately, with only 35,000 CD players sold in its debut year in the United States (Nichols n.p.), it nonetheless proved to be exceptionally successful later in the decade, with almost 1.5 billion units of music sold in the CD format only eight years later (1991) against 291.6 million vinyl LPs and 997.5 million cassettes (McDonald 52). A major factor in the eventual triumph of CD technology was the availability of content that mounted to its support, as one of the main companies behind the Compact Disc technology was Sony, which had partnered with CBS Records with the intention of making popular music titles immediately available in the new format (Ibid.). Besides un-paralleled quality and fidelity of sound, digital technology equipped CD players with random access functionality, enabling consumers to access the content of the recordings in individualistic ways.

One particularly interesting outcome from the success of the CD technology was that consumers did not only use the format to acquire new product, irrespective of the fact that new titles normally drive new media technology markets (Nichols n.p.). Rather, consumers used the technology to replace their existing record and cassette collections with the better quality compact discs. According to Paul McDonald, this proved to be a major lesson for all parties involved in digital video technology and home entertainment a few years later, namely that "digital media provide lucrative platforms for new but also old media content, adding to the value of the music, film or television libraries kept by rights holders" (52).

With digital audio technology having provided both a blueprint and a useful precedent, and with the forces behind that technology, the consumer electronics companies, being considerably more integrated in the structures of the emerging transnational entertainment economy after their corporate marriages with several Hollywood majors, digital home video technology became the logical next development. Indeed, the first efforts to replace VCRs and VHS technology appeared in the market as early as 1993 with the commercial introduction of CD-interactive (CD-i) and of video compact disc (VCD). However, neither technology caught on with media consumers. On the one hand, CD-i was not supported by the necessary availability of titles, which highlights in the most emphatic way the centrality of the Hollywood majors (Lieberfarb, quoted in Weiner and Stalter 52). On the other hand, VCD failed to impress consumers as it was launched with limited data storage capacity that made it difficult to prerecord feature-length films, while on many occasions image quality was not of the standard anticipated by the promises of digital technology (McDonald 54).

Despite these early failures and consumers' initial reluctance to rid themselves of almost $30 billion worth of investment in video hardware in the United States and of a comparable figure in the rest of the world, the introduction of digital home video technology had become an inevitability (Roberts 43). By 1993, the year of the introduction of both CD-i and VCD, VCR penetration had surpassed 75 percent of all television households in the United States, in effect making it a saturated market (Levy 41). This meant that consumer electronics companies had to introduce a new video technology or end up losing a lucrative line of manufacturing, not to mention writing off billions of dollars' worth of investing in research and development. To realize this objective, recent advances in digital technology would provide the technological foundation and the ex-studios' libraries of film entertainment would provide the software, while the horizontal structure of the industry would use its might to create a new market or, to be more precise, to expand the entertainment and leisure market in a new direction.

Arguably the most important development towards establishing what eventually became the DVD market was the "relative consensus" under which the specifications of the digital video format were agreed upon by the involved parties (Keane 23). This does not mean that the technology was adopted without problems, delays, or moves that threatened yet another long video format war, like the one between Sony's Betamax and JVC's VHS formats that had scarred the introduction of the original video technology in the late 1970s and early to mid-1980s. As it happened, the development of digital video was characterized by two mini format wars, which nonetheless were resolved relatively quickly and with minor casualties for the industry as a whole.

Even from the research and development stage and despite the establishment of a pressure group consisting of the major ex-studios, which requested a unified digital disc standard, the consumer electronics industry had been developing two competing formats: the multimedia CD (MMCD), which was backed by Sony and Philips, and the super density (SD) format, developed by Toshiba and Time Warner and supported by Matsushita, Hitachi, Mitsubishi, and a few other home electronics manufacturers (McDonald 55). With the prospect of a new format war that could prove costly for all parties clearly on the horizon, and with each side counting on the presence of major forces in the relevant industries, it came down to the intervention of an outside party, but one that was also bound to be affected by the imminent war format: information technology giant IBM (Roberts 43). Alongside other information technology and computer manufacturers, who were originally attracted to digital discs because of their increased data capacity that could be utilized in personal computing, IBM successfully lobbied the opposing groups to come to an agreement in September 1995. The agreement saw both sides make concessions and eventually support one unified format under the name DVD (McDonald 55–56).

Besides showcasing the power of IBM and the interest in the digital video format by the computer industry, this brief clash in format development demonstrated that despite a common interest in the establishment of a new format for the distribution and exhibition of their product, the Hollywood majors were actually divided in their approach. This was mainly because of the majors' new corporate owners, who were counting on their subsidiaries' support in their continued efforts to innovate the video market. Writing in *Newsweek* in August 1996, half a year before the introduction of the DVD in the U.S. market, and under the telling title "The Disc Wars," Johnnie L. Roberts noted the schism in Hollywood, with Japanese-owned companies "count[ing] as DVD bulls" but with the rest of majors, which, significantly, were owned by non-home entertainment hardware manufacturing parent companies (Paramount, Disney, and Fox), being "far less enthusiastic" and not able to "see compelling reasons for consumers to dump their videotape for digital discs" (43).

Equally important, however, this schism attained further rationale from the actual structure of the entertainment industry, which, increasingly, had started to see sister companies under the same corporate umbrella competing against each other rather than working together and achieving the desired synergies. For instance, Viacom's vast Blockbuster video rental chain, with over 3,500 stores in the United States (Balio, "Major" 67), would seemingly stand to lose ground to Paramount Home Entertainment, as the DVD targeted the sell-through/retail market, which meant that consumers would be tempted to stop renting videocassettes from Blockbuster and start buying DVDs supplied by Paramount Home Entertainment (Roberts 43). Disney, though, whose video releases in the mid-1980s had been instrumental for popularizing video, would now have to also consider its cable operations and its ultra-successful Disney Channel, which often premiered Disney feature films in the home entertainment market before their release on video (Lyons 1). For these reasons, it might not have been coincidental that Disney and Paramount were the only two Hollywood majors that refused to take sides in the early format clash, opting to refrain from supporting MMCD or SD (McDonald 56).

While the standards format clash was resolved quickly, the next stage in the introduction of digital home video technology presented a more serious challenge to Hollywood's delicate balance, to the extent that for a period of a little over two years, from March 1997 to July 1999, the entertainment industry experienced uncertainty about the future and the direction of the technology in question. This was because yet another pair of formats competed against each other for the attention of media consumers, despite the September 1995 agreement. On the one hand, there was the digital video disc (DVD), which had been supported by Sony (Columbia) and Toshiba (Time Warner) and their many subsidiary media companies. On the other hand, there was Digital Video Express (Divx), "a pay per view hybrid" (Brown n.p.) that gave consumers the option to either watch a film once and/or to proceed to buying it.

Although the latter had been developed outside Hollywood, it nevertheless found support from the majors as they liked the possibilities it offered in terms of allowing only one authorized viewing of the content on the disc and of having stronger protection from unauthorized copying. Thus while by late 1997 Disney and Universal had decided to align themselves with DVD, they also endorsed Divx with a view to release films on both formats, while Fox and MGM decided to release their films exclusively on Divx, leaving only Paramount and Dreamworks (a new privately owned film company that had been established in 1994) in the "undecided" camp (McDonald 146–47).

While Divx seemed to gain ground compared to DVD, a number of factors, which included hardware pricing--Divx was more expensive than DVD players (McDonald 148); lack of support from the video rental market, the representatives of which thought that Divx would kill the market in question (Brinkley B4); lack of support from retailers, who thought that Divx was confusing potential customers (Moosebrugger B3); and the backing DVD had been gaining outside the United States as international consortia had been forming to speed up the arrival of DVD in many international markets (Frater and Franklin 1), changed matters by the middle of 1999. Divx lost the battle of the formats and its backers paid the price with an after tax-loss of $114 million (McDonald 149).

Despite the fact that all of the above factors in the defeat of Divx were important, it was arguably the influence and leverage of Toshiba/Time Warner and Sony/Columbia, the main supporters of DVD, that caused the demise of the rival format. As these two companies had the most to lose given their corporate ties with hardware manufacturers, they took the necessary measures to obtain advantages for DVD against Divx. Thus during the launch period of Divx, Warner, by far the biggest provider of titles and the market leader for DVD in the early years with an incredible 44 percent of all DVD sales for the first half of 1998 (Grove n.p.), responded by lowering the prices of its discs for the sell-through market, while also announcing a national rental program that in effect meant it could match the benefits of Divx (McDonald 148). Warner also teamed up with Buena Vista to distribute popular Disney titles in a large number of territories outside the United States, and made concrete plans for an even "more aggressive" push of DVD technology for 1999 (Hettrick, "Study" 1, 6). With the vast resources of the Hollywood majors working overtime to protect its investment in digital video, it is not surprising that Divx could not compete.

With the format issue settled by mid-1999, DVD technology was ready to conquer the global entertainment market. Indeed, DVD player sales in 1999 were three times those of 1998 (Sweeting n.p.), while three years later, DVD penetration had reached 25 percent of television households in the United States (McDonald 149). As it turned out, DVD became "the fastest selling technology in the history of consumer electronics," thus providing the majors with an ancillary market from which the revenues often surpassed the revenues from the theatrical box office (McDonald 93). Furthermore, and due to the phenomenal success of the technology, it was not long before the entertainment giants moved to the next generation of digital video technology, demonstrating that they had learned their lesson well when it came to creating new lucrative exhibition platforms for their new and old product. What they did not learn well, however, was the necessity to standardize format from the beginning, as yet another pair of competing advanced digital video formats were launched at the same time: Sony's Blu-ray and Toshiba's High Definition DVD (HD DVD).

Although this format battle between the former allies during the development and launch of the first generation of DVDs commenced recently (2006), once again it proved to be a relatively short one, with Sony's Blu-ray winning the battle due to its much stronger position in the market. This is because, in this case, Sony's synergies have proven to be stronger than Toshiba's, as the former launched in 2007 the third generation of its extremely popular games console PlayStation 3, which was also equipped to play Blu-ray discs. And while PlayStation 3 has not proved to be as successful as its predecessors, it nonetheless sold enough units worldwide to give Sony a strong consumer base for its Blu-ray format. With 10.5 million consoles sold by February 2008, Blu-ray hardware holders outnumbered those who opted for HD DVD by 10 to 1, which caused Toshiba to cancel its HD DVD production that same month (Elliot). Sony's eventual success proved beyond a doubt that control of the digital video market is dependent on control of other areas in the constantly expanding area of home entertainment, which in recent years has also become characterized by a widespread penetration of game consoles and an increasing pervasiveness of high-definition televisions and home theater sound systems.

## CONCLUSION: EMBRACING THE (MOBILE) FUTURE

With DVD reviving the home video business and ushering it into "a second period of innovation and growth," especially during the end of the 20th century and the first years of the 21st, the entertainment media empires turned their attention to telecommunications in order to capture yet another new development in the leisure and entertainment market, which this time involved the provision of mobile video entertainment (McDonald 42). The staggering level of penetration of mobile telephony, the incredible success of Apple's iPod MP3 players, Sony's successful launch of a portable PlayStation (PSP), and a host of other developments that made media mobile have made the provision of video content to mobile media users an inevitability. It was time for the Hollywood studios to start participating anew in corporate takeovers and elaborate partnerships that facilitated the convergence of the telecommunications, computing, and Hollywood entertainment industries.

The takeover that started this new restructuring phase and set a new standard for the increasingly expanding entertainment industry was that of Time Warner by AOL in 2000, a corporate transaction that was valued at $95 billion (Byron). Although the vast new super-company proved to be cumbersome and dysfunctional to the extent that it downsized significantly in 2004, and the name AOL removed from corporate logos, it nonetheless paved the way for a future where only an even smaller number of incredibly large-sized corporations would dominate the global entertainment market. This was confirmed in 2005 when telecommunications giant Comcast, after failing to take over Disney, partnered with Sony in order to acquire MGM and United Artists, thus bringing together three ex-studios under the same corporate structure (Eller and Bates). During the same year, NBC Universal partnered with computer hardware and software leader Apple to provide television entertainment to Apple's iTunes store (Cohen and Darlymple). Two years later, Viacom and Microsoft signed an agreement to share content, with Microsoft using Viacom-administered content for its Xbox games and with the two giant companies participating in collaboration and synergies (Hayes).

These three deals are the tip of the iceberg that includes a large number of other smaller-scale corporate moves that have brought further consolidation to the vast media entertainment landscape. This is because leading players from the telecommunication and computing industries became further integrated to its structures, creating even larger super-powers that own, control, or have significant stakes in every conceivable distribution outlet possible due to digital technology allowing the compression and transmission of huge volumes of data whether through satellite, cable, or on DVDs. However, it is the actual content that has been and will be produced and administered through Hollywood's ex-studios (and a large number of smaller outfits) that feeds those expanding distribution pipelines, which means that it is the Hollywood majors that have been the most important players in shaping the direction the market has taken since the early television years of the 1950s. In this respect, there might have been a digital revolution driving technological development in the media market, but it is Hollywood's agenda that has actually shaped the direction of this revolution. Having invigorated the home entertainment market through the ultra-successful launch of DVD, Hollywood has then set its sights on mobile entertainment, helping to establish yet another strand to what seems to be a limitless entertainment market. Digital technology then has served the long-established Hollywood objective of creating an increasing number of lucrative ancillary markets for its filmed product.

## NOTES

1. This essay is Tzioumakis's translation of his original Greek version: "Apo ti viomihania tou kinimatografou stin viomihania tis psihagogias: To Hollywood stin epohi tis psifiakis tehnologias" [From the Business of Film to the Business of Entertainment: Hollywood in the Age of Digital Technology]. In *Psifiaka Mesa: O Politismos toy Ixou kai tou Theamatos* [*Digital Media: the Culture of Sound and Spectacle*]. Ed. Mihalis Kokonis, Grigoris Paschalides & Philemon Bantimaroudis, 47–81. Athens: Kritiki, 2010. It is published here by kind permission of Kritiki.

2. For instance, VCR penetration in the United States had reached 75 percent of television households (Grant and Meadows, 2006 35).

3. These films included *Doctor Dolittle* (Fleischer 1967), *Star!* (Wise 1968) and *Hello Dolly* (Kelly 1969), *Camelot* (Logan 1967), *Chitty Chitty Bang Bang* (Hughes 1968), *Sweet Charity* (Fosse 1969), and *Paint Your Wagon* (Logan 1969).

## WORKS CITED

Bach, Steven. *Final Cut: Dreams and Disasters in the Making of Heaven's Gate*. London: Faber and Faber, 1986.

Balio, Tino. *United Artists: The Company That Changed the Film Industry*. Madison: University of Wisconsin Press, 1987.

Balio, Tino. "Adjusting to the New Global Economy: Hollywood in the 1990s." In *Film Policy: International, National and Regional Perspectives,* ed. Albert Moran, 23–38. London: Routledge, 1996.

Balio, Tino. "'A Major Presence in All of the World's Important Markets:' The Globalisation of Hollywood in the 1990s." In *Contemporary Hollywood Cinema,* ed. Stephen Neale and Murray Smith, 58–73. London: Routledge, 1998.

Belton, John. "Digital Cinema: A False Revolution." *October* 100 (Spring 2002): 98–114.

Brinkley, Joel. "DVD Leads Race for TV Disks, but It Is Looking Over Its Shoulder." *The New York Times,* July 6, 1998: B1, B4.

Brown, Colin. "*Titanic* Floats Divx: Studios Back PPV Disc Format: Ready US Launch for Summer." *Screen International,* Feb. 27, 1998: n.p.

Byron, Christopher. "The AOL Time Warner Black Hole." *Fox News.com. New York Post.* April 29, 2002.

Cohen, Peter, and Jim Darlymple. "NBC, Apple Announce iTunes TV Show Deal." *Macworld.com. Playlist Magazine.* Dec. 6, 2005.

Cook, David A. *Lost Illusions: American Cinema in the Shadow of Watergate and Vietnam, 1970–1979*. Berkeley: University of California Press, 2000.

Eller, Claudia, and James Bates. "Sony Deal for MGM Would End a Long Run." *Los Angeles Times.com.* Sept. 14, 2004.

Elliot, Phil. "Playstation 3 Sales Hit 10.5 Million: Console Effect Gave Blu-ray a Massive Lead over HD DVD." *Gamesindustry.biz.* Feb. 19, 2008.

Frater, Patrick, and Anne Franklin. "Studios Give DVD Faster Spin." *Screen International,* July 10, 1998: 1, 6.

Gomery, Douglas. "Hollywood Corporate Business Practices and Periodizing Contemporary Hollywood History." In *Contemporary Hollywood Cinema,* ed. Stephen Neale and Murray Smith, 47–57. London: Routledge, 1998.

Grant, August E., and Jennifer H. Meadows. *Communication Technology Update, 10th edition.* Burlington, MA, and Oxford, England: Focal Press, 2006.

Grove, Christopher. "More Studios Hope on Disc Express." *Daily Variety,* Sept. 1, 1998: n.p.

Hayes, Dade. "Viacom, Microsoft Ink $500 Mil Deal Pair Teams on Ads, Content, Events." *Variety.com.* Dec. 19, 2007.

Hettrick, Scott. "Panel: DVD Is the Future for Sell-through Market." *Hollywood Reporter,* Feb. 22, 1996: n.p.

Hettrick, Scott. "Study: DVD's Future Is Bright." *Hollywood Reporter,* Aug. 13, 1998: 1, 6.

Hillier, Jim. *The New Hollywood.* London: Continuum, 1994.

Keane, Stephen. *Cinetech: Film Convergence and New Media.* Basingstoke: Palgrave Macmillan, 2007.

Lev, Peter. *The Fifties: Transforming the Screen, 1950–1959.* New York: Scribners, 2000.

Levy, Jonathan D. "Evolution and Competition in the American Video Marketplace." In *Film Policy: International, National and Regional Perspectives,* ed. Albert Moran, 39–61. London: Routledge, 1996.

Lyons, Charles. "Disney Animation Leaps into DVD." *Daily Variety,* Aug. 18, 1999: 1, 10.

McDonald, Paul. *Video and DVD Industries.* London: BFI, 2007.

Monaco, Paul. *The Sixties 1960–1969.* Berkeley: University of California Press, 2003.

Moosebrugger, Ed. "Digital Video Discs Get Popular." *The Hollywood Reporter Outlook,* March 4, 1998: B3.

Nichols, Peter M. "Debut of DVD Exceeds 'Rivals,'" *The New York Times,* Jan. 16, 1998: n.p.

Prince, Stephen. *Hollywood under the Electronic Rainbow: 1980–1989.* Berkeley: University of California Press, 2002.

Roberts, Johnnie L. "The Disc Wars." *Newsweek,* Aug. 26, 1996: 42–43.

Schatz, Thomas. *The Genius of the System: Hollywood Filmmaking in the Studio Era.* New York: Metropolitan Books, 1996.

Sweeting, Paul. "DVD Success Viewed with Mixed Emotions." *Weekly Variety,* Dec. 20, 1999: n.p.

Tzioumakis, Yannis. "Major Status, Independent Spirit: The History of Orion Pictures (1978–1992)." *The New Review of Film and Television Studies* 2.1 (2004): 87–135.

Tzioumakis, Yannis. *American Independent Cinema: An Introduction.* Edinburgh: Edinburgh University Press, 2006.

*Velvet Light Trap* Editors. "The 1980s: A Reference Guide to Motion Pictures, Television, VCR, and Cable." *Velvet Light Trap* 27 (Spring 1991): 77–88.

Weiner, Rex, and Katherine Stalter. "DVD Dividing Hollywood." *Weekly Variety,* March 17, 1997: 1, 51, 52.

Zimmermann, Patricia R. "Digital Deployment(s)." In *Contemporary Independent American Film: From the Margins to the Mainstream,* ed. Chris Holmlund and Justin Wyatt, 245–64. London: Routledge, 2005.

# Chapter 3

# THE GUILLOTINE HAS FALLEN AND THE BEACHES OF MALIBU ARE LITTERED WITH CARCASSES: THE DEATH OF AMERICAN INDEPENDENT MOVIES

When people think of independent films, they often think of Miramax, which is a perfectly reasonable association to make with the indie scene of the past 20 years, even though what we now think of as an independent film often isn't in any way, shape, or form independent. Still, the evolution of Miramax certainly played a huge role in influencing the industry and bringing the state of indies to where it currently resides, which, arguably, is either on its deathbed or buried deep underground, already snuggly ensconced in its coffin. This is neither to say that indies don't exist nor to claim that they won't once again rise, like the phoenix, reborn to see another golden era. Rather, it's to claim that just as the industry is now caught in lurching haphazard transition as it makes its way from the old analog era to the nascent digital age, so too is the independent branch of that industry struggling to find a path for success in the newly arrived digitally dominated world of filmic entertainment. Where we go from here is anybody's guess, but in tracing how we got to where we currently are, we can certainly look into the near future and get a good idea of the possibilities and what they might mean for the industry and the business of independent filmmaking.

Miramax was founded in 1979 by the infamously bombastic brother duo of Harvey and Bob Weinstein. In a sweetly personal touch, the company is named after their parents, Miriam and Max. The Weinsteins cannily saw a market for the distribution of films that wouldn't otherwise be seen on American screens. The business model was simple and at times highly profitable: see an independent film that you think has popular potential and buy it for a flat fee, which will allow you to keep all of the profits the film makes beyond the outlay of your acquisition, distribution, and prints and advertising (P & A) costs. Because the Weinsteins were initially focused on small films made outside of the Hollywood system, their investment costs were typically comparatively little, whereas their return on investment could be much larger than it would have been had they paid for production from scratch.

In addition to leveraging the market for the release of foreign films without distribution, the Weinsteins had the good fortune to be working in the right time and place in cinema history for their vision to achieve maximum success. This is not to say that they didn't work as hard or harder than their competition—they did—or that they're not enormously talented at what they do—they are. But in any instance in which a business' success changes the modus operandi of an entire industry, there's usually a bit of historical luck involved, and the Weinsteins were no exception to this rule. In 1978, the year before the Weinsteins hung out their shingle, the US Film Festival made its debut in Utah. This festival would ultimately become known as the Sundance Film Festival and it would also provide the Weinsteins with the opportunity to purchase many of the films that would be among their greatest successes. Sundance was the first major festival to focus on American films made outside of the studio system, which were coincidentally a perfect fit for the Miramax business model. These films were often made on a wing and a prayer and the filmmakers were happy to just make their production budgets back so as to live to film another day. And the Weinsteins, if they thought a film had commercial appeal, were all too delighted to come in and pick up the films for distribution. Miramax was really the first company to see the commercial viability of doing so and they did it with a vengeance. By the time other companies both big and small saw the beauty of their model and tried to copy it, Miramax, with the success of films like *sex, lies, and videotape* (Soderbergh 1989), *Tie Me Up, Tie Me Down* (Almodóvar 1990), *The Crying Game* (Neil Jordan 1992), *Reservoir Dogs* (Tarantino 1992), and *Clerks* (Smith 1994), had already established its reputation as the world's major player in independent and foreign film acquisition and distribution.

Still, that didn't stop other companies from jumping into the independent sector, including THINKFilm, Killer, October, and many others, all of whom became competitors with Miramax. But Miramax ruled the roost, and it was their success not only financially but also in the way of industry accolades that would cause the tremors that would subsequently lead to the quakes that have shaken the indie community to its core. Miramax was financially successful with a number of films—enormously so if you consider money earned to money invested—but was nonetheless relatively small potatoes in the context of Hollywood movie studios. Even so, a relatively small company with a nice return on their investments is an attractive object for a bigger fish, and sure enough, in 1993 The Walt Disney Corporation bought Miramax for a reported $80 million to serve as its new "specialty" division (Holson). This was not without benefits for the Weinsteins, especially as concerns capital; their being acquired significantly upped their ability to pay top dollar for the films they picked up as their yearly operating budget eventually climbed to the $700 million range (Eller and Munoz). Additionally, it allowed them the chance to be not just a distribution company, but a full-blown production company as well. (Although they had produced films previously, these had been primarily foreign art films and documentaries.)

Among their first productions under the auspices of Disney was Quentin Taran-tino's *Pulp Fiction* (1994), an $8 million film that became the first "independent" film to gross over $100 million domestically and cumulatively earned $213 mil-lion worldwide (*Box Office Mojo.com*). And it was also nominated for seven Acad-emy Awards, though it would win only one, Best Original Screenplay. At the time, $100 million was the gold standard for a hit, and Oscar nominations only added to a film's bottom line. With the Disney money in their coffers, the Wein-steins would spend buckets of money on their films' Oscar campaigns, which beginning in 1992 resulted in the studio having an unprecedented run of at least one film in competition for Best Picture for 11 consecutive years (Horn, "Best-Picture"). The Hollywood majors weren't used to getting this competition from a so-called independent studio (although technically Miramax wasn't an inde-pendent anymore—it just played one in the media). Other big studios wanted in on the game. Sony had already created Sony Pictures Classics in 1991, while Fox News Corp. combined some of its extant subsidiaries into Fox Searchlight Pictures in 1994. In 1996 Time Warner purchased New Line Cinema, not only for New Line but also for Fine Line Cinema, which was started in 1992 and would become Warner's specialty division; Viacom's Paramount Vantage (née Classics) was started in 1998; and Universal's Focus Features was founded in 2002, although it began as Gramercy Pictures in 1992 (parent company GE sold NBC/Universal to Comcast in 2010). And so the independent sector was now consolidated and dominated almost entirely lock, stock, and barrel by the majors; this marked the short-lived nadir of American indies, which, unbeknownst to the major players, began the process of dying off not long after their production largely shifted from actually being independent to instead being the output of the specialty arms of the major studios. In hindsight, their death seems inevitable— after all, when you are owned by a major, you are by definition no longer inde-pendent—but no one seemed to know it at the time, or we wouldn't have had the subsequent irrationally exuberant decade plus long flurry of acquisitions and vanity productions that we did.

There's no doubt that in the early years Miramax flourished at Disney. But just as clearly, there's also no doubt that there was conflict between the Weinsteins and their new corporate masters. Prior to selling controlling interest of Miramax to Disney, the Weinsteins had made their reputation on the merits of a successful run of producing and/or distributing films like Errol Morris's *The Thin Blue Line* (1988), Steven Soderbergh's *sex, lies, and videotape* (1989), Jim Sheridan's *My Left Foot* (1992), and Chen Kaige's *Farewell My Concubine* (1993). While Miramax's sale ostensibly took the pressure off them as independent financiers, it clearly in some ways actually increased the pressure in that their parent company was a huge multinational media conglomerate that wasn't interested in the idea of making artistic statements that may or may not make money. As a result, it can be argued that even though their films were often financially successful and some-times critically successful, they lost their edge, moving closer to the mainstream and becoming less risky: *The English Patient* (Minghella 1996), *Shakespeare in Love* (Madden 1998)—both of which won the Oscar for Best Picture—*Emma* (McGrath 1996), *Good Will Hunting* (Van Sant 1997), *Cider House Rules* (Hallström 1999), *Chocolat* (Hallström 2000), *Chicago* (Marshall 2002), and so on. They were not really true independents—much more centrist, more glossy, more predictable, and a lot more expensive to make than we're used to seeing in independents.

Did the Weinsteins consciously lose their desire for edgier fare or were their tastes changing? Likely neither. But they are smart and pragmatic businessmen. They released the films that they could through Disney, but they also had very public spats with the mouse house over a number of films, most notably Larry Clark's *Kids* (1995) and Michael Moore's *Fahrenheit 9/11* (2004), both of which they tried to produce and/or distribute through Disney only to be denied due to the films conflicting with the parent company's desired corporate image. Still, despite some bumps, Disney's acquisition of Miramax was at the time seen in the industry as a win-win situation for both companies. When other companies followed suit and purchased or created their own specialty arms for the acquisition, production, and distribution of smaller more artistic films, the American cinema, fueled by an influx of new voices with deeply personal and often iconoclastic visions, went through an artistic renaissance not unlike that which occurred during the period of industry consolidation and subsequent conglomeration of the late 1960s and early 1970s, to which the era from the early 1990s to the early 2000s is eerily similar. Just as the auteur-driven era of the 1970s would meet its demise in the wake of the rise of the summer blockbuster, so too would the indie auteurs who came to prominence in the late 1980s and throughout the 1990s see their opportunities for making the kinds of films they wanted to make diminish in the wake of the industry's retooling itself towards more exclusively large-scale entertainment.

There are many good things that came from the major studios' entry into the specialty business. More companies in the business meant more opportunities for indie filmmakers to secure distribution deals for their films. For the studios, distribution was the best of all worlds, or at least it was before the prices for acquisitions went off the deep end. The beauty of a festival acquisition is that ostensibly costs can be controlled, whereas in production, things sometimes have a way of spiraling totally out of control. Truly independent filmmakers are normally under immense financial pressure, having had to beg, borrow, and steal from friends, family, and credit card companies for the money to make their movies. Not surprisingly, they are often content to sell their film for a flat fee covering the money they owe, or not much more. The purchasing studio then invests in whatever additional post production a film needs and outlays the P & A and distribution costs. Whatever money the film makes beyond their investment is theirs to keep. It can be a slim profit margin, but with fiscal discipline and a little luck, a company can be quite successful. As Anne Thompson notes, "The advantages are clear for experienced indie execs with enlightened management—from Fox

Searchlight and Sony Pictures Classics to Miramax and Focus Features—who understand the intricacies of the sector" ("Niche"). And while it might seem like a bad deal for the filmmakers, if their film is good and handled well by the studio, they've a lot to gain. In addition to getting out of debt (which is no small thing), a successful theatrical run can become an industry calling card that gets them noticed and allows them to continue making films. The list of current well-known directors who've followed this route is long, including luminaries such as Spike Lee, P. T. Anderson, Wes Anderson, Bryan Singer, Christopher Nolan, Darren Aronofsky, Steven Soderbergh, and countless others.

And there's the chance of striking gold in a way that is harder to do when also producing a film, which requires a much greater initial cash outlay. While it's rare, it does happen, and when it does, much lore comes to surround the film's success, as replicating it is the Holy Grail for indie producers and filmmakers the world over, not to mention the studios that are insatiable for profitable content. So take a film like *My Big Fat Greek Wedding* (Zwick 2002), the $5 million budget of which was financed through a joint effort of Gold Circle Films and a TV presale to HBO (which means you sell the rights for your film to play on TV prior to its being made so as to use the cash to go towards production—these are not easy deals for an indie producer to secure, but they do happen). After being passed on by several studios, in part because the producers wanted to separate distribution rights and marketing costs, IFC Films agreed to distribute the film for a flat $200,000 fee and Gold Circle paid for the marketing and would reap the lion's share of the profits if any were to be had. It's hard to know what Gold Circle saw in the film, which on the surface appears to contain nothing extraordinary. But Gold Circle stuck by the movie, giving it a platform release—a slow rollout in which the film plays in a few key cities for a number of weeks so as to build word of mouth buzz, which is accompanied by putting the film in more and more theaters as time goes on (Fonseca). This is the exact opposite of the saturation release most films, even indies, currently get. But it worked, and the film went on to gross an astounding $241 million in worldwide box office, making it among the most profitable movies ever made (*Box Office Mojo.com*).

Among the first films that really became a touchstone blueprint for 1990s indie filmmakers—even though duplicating its history has proven to be nearly statistically impossible—is Kevin Smith's *Clerks* (1994), which was one of Miramax's first important successes after the Disney buyout. *Clerks* was famously financed by Smith's 10 credit cards for $27,575 (or about what Miramax paid for the music licensing costs for the soundtrack they added after purchasing the film) and shot in grainy 16mm over a 21-day period at the New Jersey Quick Stop and RST Video stores at which Smith actually worked. After being seen by a Sundance Advisory Council member at the Independent Feature Film Market, it played at Sundance in 1994, where it was acquired for distribution by Miramax. Its often profane and sexually frank (and hilarious) dialogue resulted in its initially receiving an NC-17 from the Ratings Board of the Motion Picture Association of America (MPAA), which led Miramax to hire Alan Dershowitz to make its case before the appeals board ("Clerks"). He won, and the film was released sans cuts in 1994 and went on to earn critical acclaim as well as $3.15 million despite never being released on more than 96 screens at its widest point (*Box Office Mojo. com*). It's an irreverent and unusual film, and its visual aesthetic (or lack thereof) and shambling narrative worked in its favor as audiences overlooked its comparative lack of polish and embraced its original narrative and anarchic spirit. And it's rightly seen as a highpoint of independent filmmaking in the 1990s and lives on as a revered cult classic that has inspired countless independent filmmakers intent on duplicating its success.

Another notable indie that's achieved legendary status in the business is Jared Hess's *Napoleon Dynamite* (2004), as bizarre and unlikely a film that has ever struck gold. The film was written by Hess and his wife and cowriter, Jerusha, and starred John Heder. All of them attended Brigham Young University, which is about as far from a hotbed of Hollywood filmmaking as one can imagine. Made for a paltry $400,000, the quirky film, which tells the tale of geeky high school student Napoleon Dynamite's (Heder) attempts to find love and happiness in Preston, Idaho (Hess's real hometown), debuted at Sundance in 2004, where a bidding war for its acquisition broke out, with Fox Searchlight winning the rights over Warner Independent by ponying up $3 million. Fox would go on to partner with Paramount and MTV Films to release the picture, with the latter's partnership being of key importance, as the film was advertised heavily on MTV's networks, which perfectly cater to the film's demographics. (On a personal note, I knew something magical was happening with this film when I saw it at a matinee in the summer of 2004. In my late thirties at the time, I was the only person in the audience over the age of 18. Everyone else there had clearly seen the film several times, as they spoke lines of dialogue verbatim well in advance of the characters, and repeatedly squealed in anticipation for the delight of coming scenes. It was like seeing *The Rocky Horror Picture Show* [Sharman 1975], but the difference was *Napoleon Dynamite* had only been out for about a week and kids were already this enraptured with it.) The film would go on to earn over $42 million domestically, making it one of the more successful films of its era, at least as concerns return on the dollar (*Box Office Mojo.com*). More important, like *Clerks, El Mariachi* (Rodriguez 1992), and *The Blair Witch Project* (Myrick and Sánchez 1999), it became another one of those lo-fi film successes that had the twofold result of inspiring novice filmmakers to believe "if they can do it, we can do it" and also of inspiring investors to believe that with a little luck and the right guidance, money was there for the taking in independent filmmaking, just as it was in the stock market, and outside investors began to flock to the industry in increasing numbers.

More recently, and against seemingly insurmountable odds, Paramount struck gold with Oren Peli's *Paranormal Activity,* which was made in 2007 but not released until 2009. Ironically, the film was ultimately shepherded to the big screen in part by Jason Blum, a producer who had earlier passed on *The Blair Witch Project* back when he worked in acquisitions at Miramax. That he had done so is no cause for shame—so had a ton of other Hollywood folks, and not without reason. They thought it was basically a home video with little chance of success. Who knew it would go on to gross almost $250 million worldwide (*Box Office Mojo.com*)? So when Blum first saw *Paranormal Activity*, the similarities didn't escape him: it was a grainy amateur-looking film that was shot on digital video over the course of a couple of weeks in a nondescript San Diego tract house. But Blum overlooked the surface obstacles facing the film and instead absorbed the events that occurred on-screen, and he immediately decided the movie was original, ingenious, and scary and that if he could get it released, then good things would come. Blum thought there was something special there, and after a tumultuous couple of years that included the support of Steven Spielberg and DreamWorks, the film was finally released in partnership with Paramount in the fall of 2009. The release pattern was in part what made the film's success so unusual, at least in the contemporary market. Rather than releasing the film wide, Paramount instead chose to market the film heavily online while releasing the film in a highly limited number of carefully selected college towns, in which there would be midnight screenings. As word of mouth began to grow, the *Paranormal Activity* Web site added a link that allowed potential viewers who hadn't yet seen the film to vote for it to come to their town, the idea being that once a locale got a big enough number of votes, the film would play there (Masters). The film caught fire online and via word of mouth and went on to earn an international gross of more than $153 million, which, given its $14,000 production budget, made it the most profitable film in Hollywood history (*Box Office Mojo.com*). Whether or not the film's ingenious marketing campaign, unusual distribution approach, and diverse online strategy are a filmic blip or something that will have long-lasting influence within the industry remains to be seen; regardless, the film is now one of the small handful of essentially homemade truly independent films that gives hope to filmmakers everywhere working outside of the industry.

And at this point it's probably best to address the question that hangs over the industry: What, exactly, is it that makes a film independent? The traditional definition is a film that's been produced entirely outside of the Hollywood system, sans stars and budgets, exactly as films such as *Clerks, El Mariachi,* and *Napoleon Dynamite* were. Ultimately, no film that gets picked up for distribution—either theatrically and/or for home video—remains wholly independent. If you've seen it in a way that requires you to pay for it (or, if you're pirating, should be paying for it—movies actually don't want to be free), then somebody, somewhere, believed that film could be profitable and invested the money required to bring it to the market. In the director's commentary on the DVD of *El Mariachi,* when the Columbia Pictures' logo comes on-screen at the film's start, Robert Rodriguez calls it a $1 million shot, a half-joking reference to the money Columbia poured into the $7,000 film after picking it up for distribution. But having a company, major or otherwise, pick your film up for distribution doesn't hurt your film's indie cred; indeed, selling your film is the ultimate goal and everyone understands that doing so requires participating in the part of the industry from which you've to date been independent. After all, that's the point isn't it? Few filmmakers want to toil away in obscurity. You make your films in the hopes of getting them seen by the widest possible audience, and doing so ultimately requires the financial participation of industry players and, in some cases, a devil's bargain as well, in which you might have to cut your precious baby in particular ways the distributor believes might make your film more marketable.

Beginning in the late 1980s, this formula proved a boon to independent film-makers, who tried to make the best films they could and get them into high-profile film festivals in the hopes of selling them to the highest bidder and gaining entrée into the mainstream industry. But by necessity they typically made films that were different from their studio brethren; they didn't have the money to make high-concept films laden with special effects, and so instead they intention-ally focused on what they could do, and that was make small, character-driven films that would, whether intentionally or not, result in their becoming fod-der for counterprogramming, which proved to have the capacity to be lucrative. There was an audience that wanted what for lack of a better word we can call "smarter" films. And they turned out to see them in sufficient enough numbers to result in a golden age of independent production that led to the festival circuit becoming a marketplace dominated by Miramax and other comparatively small, early-adapting acquisition and distribution companies who realized the beauty of a system in which they didn't have to pay for the production costs of their prod-uct. Not surprisingly, as previously mentioned, many directors of note rode the wave of their earlier, more independent success to mainstream dominance, in-cluding such industry stalwarts as Christopher Nolan, who first made *Following* (1998) and *Memento* (2000) and then went on to helm *Batman Begins* (2005), which rebooted the flagging franchise; Doug Liman, who started with *Swingers* (1996) before graduating to the *Bourne Identity* (2002); Bryan Singer, whose suc-cess with *The Usual Suspects* (1995) eventually led to his directing the first two *X-Men* (2000, 2003) movies; and Sam Raimi, who began his career with the leg-endary ultra-low budget horror film *The Evil Dead* (1981) and would go on to direct the first three *Spider Man* (2002, 2004, 2007) movies.

But almost as soon as the boom began, the seeds of the death of a flourishing American independent cinema were sown. And just as Miramax's success helped to start the independent boom, so too did it also help to kill it, at least indirectly. Miramax was a smart company that made good purchases and got lucky (again, this is not a criticism—some bit of luck, even if it's the result of sound strategy, is a vital part of success in the film industry) and their successes not only led to their purchase by Disney, they also led to many other small companies joining the fray and, perhaps most consequentially, to other majors getting involved in the indie business as well. To whit, as Ian Mohr notes, "In 1996 there were only four major specialty arms, Miramax, Sony Pictures Classics, Fine Line, and Fox Searchlight. By 2006 there were many more companies, Focus Features, Magnolia, Picturehouse, Screengems/Tristar Pictures, Warner Independent et. al., both studio and otherwise, competing for the same piece of the pie, making it increasingly difficult to get market share." And this doesn't even take into account the increase in the accessibility of other digital media that were also in direct competition with the theatrical and home video ends of the movie industry. The resultant increase in competition meant that there were a lot more companies competing for product, which drove up the costs of acquisition, which, in turn, drove up the costs of P & A as a film now had to earn back a higher gross to net a profit. And while the indie sector did make a number of people rich, the key to its success was always in part due to the willingness of its investors to operate with fiscal discipline. But when all these companies became competitors, the result was a lot of stupid decisions, some of the most famous of which were made by Miramax itself, which spent a fortune at festivals, including $5 million for *Tadpole* (Winick 2002), $6 million each for *The Castle* (Sitch 1997) and *Next Stop Wonderland* (Anderson 1998), and a stunning $10 million for *Happy, Texas* (Illsley 1999), all of which died grisly deaths at the box office (Harris and Dunkley). In theory, all of these films had the capacity to be indie hits had they been bought for realistic costs instead of at the end of bidding wars that put them under immense pressure to make back money for Miramax and Disney. While actual numbers always vary, a fairly solid formula in determining the success of a film is 3 to 1, meaning that if a film makes back three times its production costs, then it can be considered successful, though not necessarily profitable—as in the arcane practice of Hollywood studio accounting almost nothing is ever listed as having actually made a profit. When you're in a market niche that rewards prudence and foresight, paying $5 million for a film like *Tadpole,* which only cost $150,000 to make and was shot on DV and told the predictably noncommercial tale of a 15-year-old who falls in love with his stepmother, is financial suicide, and Miramax wasn't operating in a vacuum. For a while there in the 1990s and 2000s, seemingly all the movie companies, big and small, were often making what in hindsight seem like incredibly poor investment choices. So poor at times, in fact, that one wonders just who, exactly, was minding the store while the indie business spun out of control.

Again, Miramax upped the ante in the Oscar sweepstakes as well, investing millions in award campaigns in the hopes of nominations that, as Harvey Weinstein himself noted, could "make the difference between a movie grossing $5 million at the box office and a movie grossing $20 million" (Gumbel). Prior to the Weinsteins' revolutionary Oscar campaigns, jockeying for position, though it existed, was relatively staid. As John Horn notes, the Weinsteins changed all that by "establishing telephone banks to call awards voters, hiring outside awards consultants, spending small fortunes on trade and consumer advertising, and shipping thousands of free DVDs" to Academy members ("Best-Picture"). It's hard to argue with the Weinsteins' results at Miramax, for which they garnered 294 Oscar nominations and 54 wins, including their engineering of the legendary upset Best Picture win for *Shakespeare in Love* over *Schindler's List* (Spielberg) in 1998, before acrimoniously splitting with Disney in 2005, in part because the parent company claimed their spending was out of hand and needed to be reigned in (Eller and Munoz). Still, yet again other companies followed suit as "indie" became synonymous with "quality," in part because of Miramax's phenomenal success. While companies don't normally disclose the marketing costs of their awards blitz pushes—and in the rare cases they do, it's best to take the numbers with a grain of salt—it's safe to say that in some cases the award campaign costs can exceed a film's production cost, further damaging a film's chance of profitability. The Weinsteins believed a film didn't have to win an Oscar, that just getting nominated would boost its box office enough to make the campaign costs worth it, and when they were the only ones routinely operating under that assumption, they were probably right. But when everyone else joined the fray and the cost to direct a piece of the media spotlight on a film rose accordingly, that's when the already increasingly fragile indie business model began to break for good. But that's not the fault of Miramax; they were a smart business and they did things first, and it's only natural that other companies would follow their lead. As Lions Gate exec Tom Ortenberg says, "Miramax may have rewritten the book on awards marketing, but Miramax hasn't been alone in driving up the cost and spectacle of Academy campaigning" (Horn, "Best-Picture"). As Dade Hayes notes, until recently only a handful of companies chased awards, while most were happy to stay on the periphery. But that seems a long time ago, as currently there seems to be "a unanimous belief in the importance of awards" (Hayes), even though it can be argued that in a crowded marketplace the benefit of nominations no longer outweighs the costs required to earn them.

The rise in acquisition costs and the accompanying rise in Oscar campaigns was only a part of the blurring of the lines between Hollywood studio films and truly independent productions. Perhaps more damning was the wholesale move into production by the specialty arms of the major studios. The whole point of the indie acquisition and distribution model is that you didn't have to pay production costs and that films could often be bought comparatively cheaply. But the move into production changed all that. Specialty arms wanted to produce character-driven dramas in the *style* of indie films and that distinction is very important; because they were often using A-list Hollywood talent, the costs of the film would run well into the multiple millions. While the costs were sometimes low compared to those of their mainstream studio counterparts, truly independent filmmakers don't have access to multimillion-dollar budgets and A-list actors and professional crews, thus making it much harder for them to compete with the big boys. And just as occurred at Miramax when they were acquired by Disney, so too did the studios' backing of their specialty arms actually ratchet up the pressure on indie-style films to make money, as the huge multinational media conglomerates weren't looking to make artistic statements. As a result, the output of the specialty arms increasingly grew to look like that of their parent companies, which met with mixed box office results, especially given the ever-shrinking margins of indie-style films.

Take a film like *Brokeback Mountain* (Lee 2005), a film that structurally resembles the classic Robert Mulligan movie *Same Time Next Year* (1978), albeit with the twist of the trysters being gay. It's well scripted, acted, and directed and gives the appearance of being an indie film. Though it was made by major studio Universal's specialty arm Focus Features and had a production budget of $14 million, it has an indie feel to it and even won the Best Feature Award at the increasingly high-profile and unintentionally aptly named Independent *Spirit* (my emphasis) Awards. And despite what some saw as limited chances of financial success given its tricky subject matter, the film was a huge hit, grossing nearly $180 million in worldwide box office (*Box Office Mojo.com*). This would be an example of a specialty arm taking some risk that is rewarded handsomely. Just as often, though, the opposite happens, and it sometimes has less to do with a film's quality than it does its budget.

To whit, in 2007 Paramount Vantage backed Paul Thomas Anderson's *There Will Be Blood,* a brilliant but brooding, dark, and far from cheery film that was met with almost universal critical acclaim upon its release and garnered nominations and awards the world over, including a Best Actor Oscar for the critically revered Daniel Day-Lewis. In many ways this film is much more true to the indie spirit of the late 1980s and early 1990s; it's far edgier and less predictable and life affirming than what we normally currently see coming out of the studio specialty arms, but that darker tone does limit its commercial appeal. It's the kind of film that perhaps could have had niche success, but it cost $25 million to make; though there's no doubt that because of its being effectively put to use by Anderson and his cast and crew, the budget made the film better than it would have been otherwise. Still, that's a huge budget for a film with its subject matter and tone, which hamstrung its chances for box office gold from the start. It barely topped $76 million in worldwide receipts (*Box Office Mojo.com*), which, given what were likely large marketing and award campaign costs—the amount of which we don't know because, like Miller writes, "as with the majors, no specialty player will say on the record how much they actually spend on marketing; nobody wants to admit to overspending"—was at best a break-even proposition for its production company, Paramount Vantage. As Anne Thompson notes, the films produced by the specialty arms are increasingly moving towards the middle-budget area of filmmaking—between $20 and $60 million—and that budget range has proved to be a far more difficult one in which to make money, as the truly small-budget films need to make a lot less to turn a profit and the larger ones have less chance of failing if they're tent-pole productions based on presold properties, as they now almost always are ("Mid-Range"). Still, for most of the 2000s, the indie market was dominated by the output of the specialty arms, which churned out indie-style films because they believed they could make money on them, even though their doing so meant a dramatically shrinking marketplace for independent films actually produced outside of the system.

Just as the specialty arms were making more higher-budget, middle-ground films, many of the indies produced without the backing of a specialty arm were undergoing a transformation that brought them back towards the middle as well. It's very hard for studios to justify the expense required to buy and market a film featuring unknown talents, especially given the need for films to make money not just in America but also abroad. As Mark Gill, chief executive at the indie company The Film Department says, "The film with nobody in it, directed by someone you've never heard of, is dead on arrival overseas" (Dobuzinskis); so in order to get investors, it's important for filmmakers to get known faces in their films, and that's pretty tough for true outsiders to do. This has resulted in the production of films like *Little Miss Sunshine* (Dayton and Faris 2006), a blueprint indie-style crowd-pleaser if ever there was one, featuring as it does a combination of time-tested indie standards: the lovably quirky dysfunctional family and a road trip odyssey. At least it doesn't take place around a holiday gathering. Again, the film was celebrated in the press as an indie film and it won Best Feature, Director, First Screenplay, and Supporting Actor at the Independent Spirit Awards and Best Original Screenplay and Supporting Actor Oscars as well. But even though it wasn't produced by a major—after several specialty arms repeatedly passed on the project, it was largely financed by indie producer Marc Turtletaub—it definitely had a lot more going for it than something like *Clerks* or *El Mariachi.* For starters, Turtletaub's family used to own The Money Store, so he was able to secure the film's production budget of $8 million. Already, that takes it far beyond the realm of what truly independent folks would be able to raise in their wildest dreams. Still, the script was that of a first-time writer, former Mathew Broderick assistant Michael Arndt, and the directors, Jonathan Dayton and Valerie Faris, were feature first-timers as well, though they had extensive experience in commercials and music videos. But through judicious casting they were able to give the film appeal it might not have otherwise had. Though there are no A-list stars in the pic, Toni Collette, Alan Arkin, and Greg Kinnear were all previously nominated for Oscars, and Steve Carell was the breakout star of NBC's *The Office,* making it an exceptionally strong cast for an indie-style ensemble piece. The combination proved a success and immediately after its 2006 Sundance debut, a bidding war broke out for the film's distribution rights, which were ultimately won by Fox Searchlight in exchange for a reported $10.5 million plus 10 percent of the gross, the highest acquisition sum ever paid at Sundance (Waxman). The film grossed just over $100 million internationally, making it one of the more successful indies ever made (*Box Office Mojo.com*). But I would argue that it wasn't an indie at all, at least not in the way that indies were originally defined; instead, it was a comparatively expensive film with a studio friendly script, high production values, and a perfectly chosen cast. Technically, it was made outside of the system, but it was always meant to become a studio property, and where bets could be hedged to ensure that it would happen, they were. This is not to denigrate the film, which is an incredibly endearing and enjoyable movie; rather, it's meant to illustrate how much the meaning of "indie" has transformed in such a relatively short time period.

The allure of box office gold wasn't only of interest to the Hollywood studios. It was of great interest to Wall Street types as well, who viewed the industry (accurately) as a high-risk, high-reward venture in which they had the money to take part. So in addition to the advent of the specialty arms, in the early 2000s Hollywood also experienced a huge influx of cash from outside investors who had the liquid capital that gave them the financial wherewithal to invest in movies, and so they did, and in spades. Sometimes individual financiers invested in singular films, but what also frequently happened was financial groups investing in a studio's slate, which would spread the risk out over several films and/or years instead of all the money riding on the success or failure of a single film, which is an incredible risk. In exchange for their investment, companies stand to earn what Frank DiGiacomo writes is "a 5 to 25 percent return on investment [with] the high end of that range being more in line with typical equity investing" (123). So, for example, in 2007 Dresdner Kleinwort, an international financial services firm, committed $200 million to a slate of 20 or so films to be produced by Universal's specialty arm Focus Features (Zeitchik). Also in 2008, Relativity Media signed a $535 million, seven-year, multipicture slate deal to co-fund Universal's output and a similar $550 million deal with Sony (DiGiacomo 123). The principle behind the influx of Wall Street's Hollywood investments is quite simple: the risk is lessened (or hedged, to use the Wall Street parlance) by being spread out over a number of films co-financed by two or more firms, meaning the blow is dulled when a movie doesn't make money and everybody wins when a film profits. But what do these kinds of deals mean as concerns the kinds of films that are likely to get made? Well, Relativity's founder and CEO Ryan Kavanaugh summed it up nicely when he said that in considering the decision to make or not make a film, the quantitative analysis holds a lot more weight than the qualitative one: "If we creatively love a project, but the model says it's not going to work, we probably won't proceed" (DiGiacomo 126). Admittedly, if no attention were paid to a film's financial prospects, then the industry would be in worse shape than it is; that said, the influx of outside investment money has made studios even more cautious in their production choices. And ultimately, it's the audience who is left shortchanged as regards the quality of a movie. But you can't argue that it isn't a sound strategy when it works, and for a while it worked pretty well.

And as more and more money came into Hollywood, even more companies were created to meet the increased production demand, and many of these companies were well-funded, high-profile studio subsidiaries staffed by highly respected indie vets, a prime illustration of which is Warner's Picturehouse. At the time of Picturehouse's 2005 inception, Warner already had several in-house subsidiary studios, including one for non-indie, non-tent-pole films—New Line—and Warner Independent for their art house releases. But because they thought the demand was there, they allowed New Line to partner with another of their subsidiaries, HBO Films, to create Picturehouse, which essentially took the place of New Line's extant specialty arm, Fine Line Pictures. When indie veteran Bob Berney was hired to head Picturehouse and run it with some degree of autonomy, it looked likely to be a winning combination, as Berney had a strong indie reputation and track record. In his earlier posts at Newmarket Films and IFC Films, Berney had shepherded unheralded films like *My Big Fat Greek Wedding, Whale Rider* (Caro 2002), *Memento,* and *The Passion of the Christ* (Gibson 2004)—the last considered to be surefire box office poison by all save Berney—to huge returns on investment. The company made some interesting and successful films, including *Pan's Labyrinth* (del Toro 2006) and *La Vie En Rose* (Dahan 2007), but it didn't fully find its footing in those first few years, and that would signal its doom.

Everything that had been building for the previous decade came to a head in 2008. First, costs for specialty films continued to rise unabated. According to the MPAA, from just 2006 to 2007, the average cost for a specialty film had risen over 60 percent, to $49.2 million, and the average cost of advertising had increased 44 percent as well, to $25.7 million (Miller). At this point, the lines between studio films and the indies produced by their specialty arms were pretty much nonexistent. In many ways they were victims of their own success. As indie-style films began to earn good box-office and reap profits and the prestige of awards, more and more people crowded into the industry, which meant that to get your film noticed required more and more money. And the resultant glut also changed the landscape of opportunity for indies as well. When there were fewer films, indies had the chance to play for a while, and, if they were worth their salt, generate word of mouth buzz that would lead to a solid run. As Pamela McClintock writes, "The business model of all niche pics calls for a long and steady run, not a sprint. But with the flood of new equity money upping the number of indie titles . . . the playing field is more crowded." Indeed, as recently as 2003, there were only 455 films released theatrically in the United States, but that number had risen to 633 by 2008 (*MPAA.org*). And as then MPAA chairman Dan Glickman noted— positively at the time, although one doubts he feels the same way now—"All of that growth is in independent film" (Thompson, "Mid-Range"). This crowded marketplace made it harder and harder to secure a spot for an indie-style film. As Winter Miller quotes Berney himself as saying, "It's become more of a one-weekend business. That Friday night thumbs up or down decision that is the fate of a studio film. . . . It's become more like that with indie films, which is tough because it's more crowded." In order to make your film more likely to attract an audience, you have to make your scripts more commercial and secure the services of an A-list actor if at all possible, thus further muddying the lines between studio and independent films and creating a vicious circle of ever-escalating costs. Add to this the fact that the market was growing ever more saturated at a time in which the industry was facing additional pressure from the rise of new media that was in direct competition for their audience, and all the pieces for an industry shakeout had lined up neatly in a row. Accordingly, the specialty biz was already at a make or break juncture when the world-wide financial crisis struck in the fall of 2008. All that outside money that had been pouring into the industry in the few years prior to that point—it's estimated that hedge funds had invested as much $12 billion (Clark)—dried up as quickly as it had arrived. The era of independent film, which Simon Houpt describes as "a decade beginning in the early 1990s, [during which] commercially oriented independent film distributors were the cool kids in Hollywood, flooding festivals with cash and making big bets that often brought home Academy Awards," came to an abrupt and unceremonious close.

When the financial crisis hit the industry, it was clear that Picturehouse and other specialty houses, studio owned and otherwise, were in trouble and the shake-out that was inevitably going to happen finally did. At Warner Brothers, they first shocked the industry by folding New Line, which had a decades-long string of success under its belt, into the parent company. This left most industry insiders assuming that Picturehouse and Warner Independent Pictures (WIP) would merge to create a singular specialty arm, for which pundits wondered just who would be in charge. Picturehouse president Berney tried to negotiate the merger between his company and WIP. But his approach revealed as much about the current state of indies as it did of his own misreading of the industry. He wanted Warner to embark on a "more aggressive approach that could ride the waves with deep pockets, producing high-quality pics with stars, backed by robust marketing. He was afraid that a slate of small-budget, no-name films might not thrive" (Thompson, "Niche"). In other words, Berney wanted the revamped specialty arm to go even further in acting just like a major. But Warner even more clearly signaled what was coming in the industry by deciding that the best way to deal with the specialty business was to get out of it entirely, which they did on May 8, 2008, when they shut down both Warner Independent Pictures and Picturehouse and sold off the rights to all their remaining films, including, ironically, WIP's *Slumdog Millionaire* (Boyle 2008), a massively successful film that was subsequently distributed in part by Fox Searchlight. In the words of Warner's COO Alan Horne, "This was a difficult decision to make, but it reflects the reality of a changing marketplace and our need to prudently run our businesses with increased efficiencies" (McNary and Hayes).

It wasn't just the majors' specialty arms that felt the heat; as Manohla Dargis and A. O. Scott quote Kino International's Gary Palmucci as saying, "The current situation is a nightmare. The Cuisinarting of accelerated production, release schedules, critics buckling under the strain of reviewing them all, the commensurate effect on attention spans and priorities of various generations of filmgoers—it all adds up to a major migraine for the small, specialized distributor." And so the foreseen shakeout happened, and companies big and small began shutting their doors and the industry sought to the circle the wagons and retool. For *Vanity Fair*'s 2010 Annual Hollywood issue, Bruce Feirstein composed a chart that offers a joking comparison between 2000 and 2010 to illustrate just how much Hollywood has changed in only 10 years. Of particular note is the entry comparing the whereabouts of an "Independent Producer's Lair." In 2000, it was "Office on studio lot." In 2010? "Office in guest bedroom." While it was meant to be tongue in cheek, there's no shortage of accuracy in the comparison. Perhaps more telling is the entry noting which industry titan is most likely to be unknown by young Hollywood execs in 2010: "Harvey Weinstein" (103).

Conceptually, the companies left standing in the indie business are in a comparatively good position in that the competition has been winnowed down nicely. But with narrow profit margins becoming narrower still, "the good reasons for staying in this business have become harder to argue with fiscally demanding bosses [although the] advantages are clear for experienced indie execs . . . who understand the intricacies of the sector, which has been bloated with easy money and is now undergoing a harsh reality check. The downside of the well-run specialty labels is that their conservatism means they aren't taking the risks they once did" (Thompson, "Niche"). But perhaps the loss of so many indie houses is not such a bad thing. After all, there's only so much screen space and the glut of specialty movies being released simultaneously in the fall every year makes it hard to get a foothold. As Anthony Kaufman notes, "With fewer players, the release calendar will eventually loosen up, and when it does, Fox Searchlight's Steve Gilula says it will be a much-needed readjustment. 'It reduces some of the pressure in terms of spending money to be visible and will be easier for the public to absorb.'" But not everyone feels that way, as evidenced by Focus Features president James Shamus, who quips, "It's not like, 'Wow, all my competitors are gone.' It's like, 'Wow, there's less input into the culture.' If I was going out with a specialty film on Sept. 12, think about it: I have nothing to trailer on all summer long. They're not going to theaters. And once people get out of the habit, you have to work hard to get them back. For me, I like a pulse. If I'm competing against corpses, I have to start checking my own pulse pretty quick" (Kaufman).

Despite some mixed feelings, some industry watchers, such as *The New York Times*' Manohla Dargis, continue to hold out hope for studio indie production (a paradoxical idea if ever there was one, but one that's become accepted nonetheless): "I'm keeping my fingers crossed that more specialty divisions keep afloat. Without them it's hard to see how a modern masterwork like Paul Thomas Anderson's *There Will Be Blood,* which was released . . . by Paramount Vantage . . . will be made. Over the past few decades the studios siphoned talent from the independent sector, including independent filmmakers like Mr. Anderson and Mr. Nolan (late of *Batman* fame, but originally noticed on the heels of *Memento*), and went into the art-house business. I have deeply ambivalent feelings about how this incursion affected the independent world (it turned the Sundance Film

Festival into a frenzied meat market, among other unfortunate developments), but there's no question that American mainstream movies have been better for it" ("In the Big"). While I share her feelings as concerns *There Will Be Blood*, the irony of the subsequent dismantling of the company she lauds for producing it, Paramount Vantage, is hard to escape. In June 2008, not long after Warner shut down Picturehouse and WIP, Paramount Vantage was absorbed by its parent company, which meant, as put in prototypically canned corporate-speak by Paramount Pictures vice chairman Rob Moore, "The new corporate structure allows Paramount and Paramount Vantage to leverage the strengths and resources of a combined talent base, while minimizing redundancies and optimizing efficiencies" (Thompson, "Paramount"). Ugh. Perhaps even more ironic is the fact that Vantage's financial demise was blamed in part on the high cost of advertising their relatively noncommercial and expensive films. As noted in the *Canberra Times*, "One reason Vantage took a fall was that it had to spend so much to run Oscar Campaigns for *No Country for Old Men* and *There Will Be Blood*, the Best Picture nominees it co-produced with Miramax. Studio insiders say the two specialty divisions spent roughly $50 million marketing *No Country* alone, a healthy portion of that going to running a prolonged awards campaign for the movie" ("High Cost"). Nominations ensued, and *No Country* won Best Picture; the Coens won Best Director and Adapted Screenplay; and Javier Bardem won Best Supporting Actor, while *There Will Be Blood* won Best Cinematography and Best Actor for Daniel Day-Lewis. But at what cost? Similarly, when Dargis went on to optimistically note that "while independent distributors have taken plenty of hits, veteran outfits like New Yorker Films . . . and newcomers like Oscilloscope Pictures . . . are keeping the faith" ("In the Big"), how could she have known then that venerated New Yorker Films would go belly up just a few months later in the spring of 2009? A year later New Yorker Films was reincarnated, but who knows for how long?

Predictably, as noted by Hayes and Jones, while the studios stumbled in their attempts to make sense of the changing theatrical marketplace and the world's financial systems were hit by "the financial crisis of the fall of 2008, the festival system, once the place where deals were made, collapsed." Potential buyers, unwilling to sink their money into films on which they'd be taking a chance, just aren't buying. The heady days of bidding wars over minor films seem a long time ago indeed. And yet, because of the advent of cheap and widely accessible digital technology, more and more films are being made. To whit, according to festival director John Cooper, around 9,000 films were submitted for the 2010 Sundance Film Festival, 3,000 or so of which were features (Masters, "Here Comes Sundance"). As more films are made and submitted for festival consideration, the already statistically tiny chances of getting in a major fest go down concomitantly. For an independent film to get a distribution deal at a festival or a film market is only becoming more akin to winning the Powerball lottery. Make no mistake, the dream is alive and it can still sometimes happen, as it did in 2008 when

Chicago-based company Music Box Films hit gold with *Tell No One,* a little heard of French thriller they platform released to an American box office total in excess of $3 million. "'We saw an opportunity,' says Music Box's William Schopf. 'The beauty of independent film is that it's not about famous actors and multi-million dollar marketing budgets. It's about films that connect to the audience'" (Kaufman). While small, truly independent films making it big under the bright kliegs of Hollywood are the inspiring stuff of which legends are made, the fact is that based on the number of films that have followed such a rarified trajectory, for all intents and purposes it basically just doesn't happen. Ever. And those near impossible odds are only getting longer.

In a sign of the times that also neatly brings this tale almost full circle, in August of 2009 the Disney Corporation paid over $4 billion to acquire Marvel Entertainment. The purchase allows Disney to mine any of Marvel's 5,000 characters (save the ones about whom movies have already been made) in any way they choose. Disney's purchase further solidifies the industry's move towards even larger-scale productions and seems to have a lot of potential benefit for both companies. According to Marvel chief executive Ike Perlmutter, "Disney is the perfect home for Marvel's fantastic library of characters given its proven ability to expand content creation and licensing businesses. This is an unparalleled opportunity for Marvel to build upon its vibrant brand and character properties by accessing Disney's tremendous global organization and infrastructure around the world" (Goldman). But what did this mean for Disney's specialty arm? Doom, as in early 2010 the company announced that they had shut down Miramax, which proved to be a financial drain even in light of the streamlined makeover it was given after the Weinsteins' ouster. Disney initially tried to sell the company in two parts, the first being the Miramax library, which has upwards of 700 films in its catalogue (Smith). This is the only part of the company that has real value, although with the leveling off of DVD sales in recent years, nowhere near the reported $700 million initial asking price. They also tried to sell the Miramax name, which is a brand seemingly without value sans the accompanying library; hence no serious bidders emerged after the announcement, though one name kept surfacing in connection to the sale of the Miramax brand: the Weinsteins themselves. How interesting would it have been if they bought back the brand they had sweetly created from the amalgam of their parents' given names and went back to their indie beginnings? Alas, they didn't have the cash on hand to make the purchase, as credit was tight, especially given that upon their departure from Disney they kept in the production game, and their latest release prior to the putting of Miramax on the auction block, the critically reviled $80 million Rob Marshall musical *Nine* (2009), did its best impression of the *Titanic.* Unfortunately for the Weinsteins, not the movie but the ship. In the summer of 2010 Disney announced it had sold both the Miramax name and the accompanying library to a group headed by construction magnate Ron Tutor for $660 million, a far cry from its original hopes, but a lot better than nothing (Lowry).

The future of indies remains in a state of flux, caught as they are in what Emerging Pictures' CEO Ira Deutchman accurately calls the "post-studio, pre-Internet era," which has resulted in a distribution vortex (Rickey). More indies are being made than ever before. And while most probably don't deserve theatrical distribution and still others might be better served with another platform, whether it be VOD or DVD or via the Internet or some technology that's yet to emerge, surely there are films out there that would do well theatrically if they were handled correctly but aren't getting a chance as the industry is too spooked at the moment to move forward. As Manohla Dargis asks, "If the studios don't buy independent films, fewer investors in turn may be inclined to bankroll projects, particularly those with bigger budgets. . . . If the investors don't invest and the buyers don't buy, will the movies still be made, and what kind?" ("In the Snows"). Ty Burr suggests that as a result of the disappearance of medium-sized films, caused in part by the bloating that occurred with increasing competition within the film industry, "the extreme ends will most likely flourish: tiny art house offerings scrambling to be seen, and bloated 3D apocu-tainments that gobble up all the media oxygen." So with the flourishing era of independent filmmaking that began in the early 1990s now over and the industry perhaps moving towards bifurcation on opposite ends, what comes next?

When Martin Scorsese said in his 1990 Independent Spirit Awards keynote speech, "Being independent doesn't mean making low-budget films without studio backing . . . it is a way for being innovative out of inspiration as well as necessity," he wasn't wrong ("Spirit Awards History"). But the industry took the idea of making studio-funded independent films to the extreme, and their financial excesses ultimately resulted in indie films often being unrecognizable from their mainstream studio counterparts, thus removing any meaning from the term "indie," which was just as likely to be used in reference to the $83 million *Cold Mountain* (Minghella 2003) as it was to the $400 thousand *Napoleon Dynamite*. Yet the financial fallout may ultimately restore some common sense to industry practices, as it seems that a return to a more accurate, or at least more reasonable, definition of "independent" within the industry is afoot and smart investors know the score, not the least of whom is none other than former Picturehouse prexy Bob Berney. In the summer of 2009, Berney launched a new company, Apparition, which is a return to his roots in that rather than focusing on production, Apparition will instead try to fill its slate by taking risks and acquiring films on the festival circuit in the hopes that they have a chance to be financially successful, just as the indie companies of yore did before the entry of the studio specialty arms into the marketplace.

As Wade Bradley, chief executive of the IndieVest financing group posits, "Independent film will again be what it should have always been. It's essentially $12 million or less production budgets and outside the studio" (Dobuzinskis). A budget in the millions is still far beyond what a true independent filmmaker can hope to have, but the specialty arms' and Wall Street's film-investing schemes still exist, albeit in fewer numbers, and it's the films they support that are most likely to see the light of day as concerns theatrical distribution. And if the budgets go down, perhaps the pressure to get unrealistic box office returns on films that would be better off marketed towards niche audiences will ratchet down as well, and that might be just what the world of indie filmmaking needs. After all, as 20th Century Fox co-chief Tom Rothman, who started Fox Searchlight over a decade ago, observes, "The more fiscally conservative you are, the more boldly and radically creative you can be" (Eller and Munoz). We can only hope that in whatever new shape the industry ultimately takes, the more "boldly and radically creative" indies will still be able to get a chance to find an audience with which to connect.

## WORKS CITED

Biskind, Peter. *Down and Dirty Pictures: Miramax, Sundance, and the Rise of Independent Film*. New York: Simon & Schuster, 2004. While I don't cite this book in this chapter, it is the definitive book on Miramax's colorful history and a must-read for those interested in further information.

*Box Office Mojo.com*. "The Blair Witch Project." 1999.

*Box Office Mojo.com*. "Brokeback Mountain." 2005.

*Box Office Mojo.com*. "Clerks." 1994.

*Box Office Mojo.com*. "Little Miss Sunshine." 2006.

*Box Office Mojo.com*. "My Big Fat Greek Wedding." 2002.

*Box Office Mojo.com*. "Napoleon Dynamite." 2004.

*Box Office Mojo.com*. "Paranormal Activity." 2009.

*Box Office Mojo.com*. "Pulp Fiction." 1994.

*Box Office Mojo.com*. "There Will Be Blood." 2007.

Burr, Ty. "2008—The Year in Movies." *The Boston Globe*. Dec. 28, 2008. *LexisNexis Academic*.

Clark, Nick. "Movie Horror Stories." *The Independent* [London]. Jan. 28, 2009. *LexisNexis Academic*.

"Clerks." *viewaskew.com*. n.d.

Dargis, Manohla. "In the Big Picture, Big Screen Hopes." *The New York Times*. Dec. 21, 2008. *LexisNexis Academic*.

Dargis, Manohla. "In the Snows of Sundance: A Marked Chill in the Air." *The New York Times*. Jan. 23, 2009. *LexisNexis Academic*.

Dargis, Manohla, and A. O. Scott. "Uncertain Futures for Bounty at Cannes." *The New York Times*. May 14, 2008. *LexisNexis Academic*.

DiGiacomo, Frank. "The Theory of Relativity." *Vanity Fair,* March 2010: 122–28.

Dobuzinskis, Alex. "After Cutting Back, Independent Filmmakers Looking to Bounce Back." *The Boston Globe*. Aug. 21, 2009. *LexisNexis Academic*.

Eller, Claudia, and Lorenza Munoz. "Disney's Miramax Unit to Get a Makeover." *Los Angeles Times*. Feb. 22, 2005. *LexisNexis Academic*.

Feirstein, Bruce. "Downsized Hollywood." *Vanity Fair,* March 2010: 103.

Fonseca, Nicholas. "Inside the Story of 'Greek Wedding.'" *Entertainment Weekly.* Sept. 20, 2002. *LexisNexis Academic*.

Goldman, David. "Disney to Buy Marvel for $4 Billion." *CNNMoney.com*. Aug. 31, 2009.

Gumbel, Andrew. "How the Mogul of Miramax Made Winning Oscars into a Business." *The Independent* [London]. Dec. 20, 2003. *LexisNexis Academic*.

Harris, Dana, and Cathy Dunkley. "Little Heat after the Snow at Sundance." *Variety*. Jan. 24, 2004. *LexisNexis Academic*.

Hayes, Dade. "Battle of Boutiques." *Variety*. Dec. 18, 2007. *LexisNexis Academic*.

Hayes, Dade, and Michael Jones. "Biz's Big Fest Test." *Variety*. Dec. 8–14, 2008. *LexisNexis Academic*.

"The High Cost of Oscar Glory." *The Canberra Times* [Australia]. Oct. 11, 2008. *Lexis-Nexis Academic*.

Holson, Laura M. "How the Tumultuous Marriage between Disney and Miramax Failed." *The New York Times*. March 6, 2005. *LexisNexis Academic*.

Horn, John. "Best-Picture Shutout Ends Miramax's 11-Year Run." *Los Angeles Times*. Jan. 11, 2004.

Horn, John. "The Haunted History of 'Paranormal Activity.'" *Los Angeles Times*. Sept. 20, 2009.

Houpt, Simon. "Indie Boom Going Bust?" *The Globe and Mail* [Canada]. Sept. 6, 2008. *LexisNexis Academic*.

Kaufman, Anthony. "Second Coming: Burst of Life." *Variety*. Sept. 9, 2008. *LexisNexis Academic*.

Lowry, Tom. "Disney is Still Waiting for Miramax Money." *Variety.com*. Aug. 18, 2010.

Masters, Kim. "Here Comes Sundance." *KCRW's The Business Podcast*. Jan. 18, 2010.

Masters, Kim. "Paranormal Activity Gets Life." *KCRW's The Business Podcast*. Oct. 6, 2010.

McClintock, Pamela. "Screen Door Slams on Niches." *Variety*. July 16–22, 2007.

McNary, Dave, and Dade Hayes. "Warner Slams Door on Specialty Pix. *Variety*. May 9, 2008. *LexisNexis Academic*.

Miller, Winter. "The Gap Narrows." *Variety*. March 10–16, 2008. *LexisNexis Academic*.

Mohr, Ian. "Lost in Transition." *Variety*. May 22–28, 2006. *LexisNexis Academic*.

Rickey, Carrie. "Art Houses Are Empty—But It Is Summer; Indie-Film Distribution Is Changing: It's a 'Post-studio, Pre-Internet Era.'" *The Philadelphia Inquirer*. June 22, 2008. *LexisNexis Academic*.

Smith, Ethan. "Disney Seeks to Sell Miramax Label." *The Wall Street Journal.com*. Feb. 1, 2010.

"Spirit Awards History." *spiritawards.com*. n.d.

Thompson, Anne. "Mid-Range Meltdown." *Variety*. March 17–23, 2008. *LexisNexis Academic*.

Thompson, Anne. "Paramount Shrinks Vantage Arm." *Variety*. June 4, 2008. *LexisNexis Academic*.

Thompson, Anne. "Niche Distrib Crunch Claims Paramount Vantage." *Variety*. June 9–15, 2008. *LexisNexis Academic*.

Waxman, Sharon. "A Small Film Nearly Left for Dead Has Its Day in the Sundance Rays." *The New York Times*. Jan. 23, 2006. *LexisNexis Academic*.

Zeitchik, Steven. "Focus Gets Financing Pact." *Variety*. Jan. 25, 2007. *LexisNexis Academic*.

# Chapter 4

## SEX AND CENSORSHIP SINCE MONICAGATE: WHITHER THE ARTISTIC "X"?

On January 17, 1998, President Bill Clinton was deposed as part of Paula Jones' sexual harassment lawsuit against him. In something of an ambush—at least to the extent that he likely didn't know they were coming—Clinton was asked questions about the nature of his relationship with a young intern named Monica Lewinsky, which he categorically denied was sexual. On that same day, an unnamed intern was mentioned in connection with the president in a posting by online political gossip columnist Matt Drudge, who wrote that "at the last minute, at 6 P.M. on Saturday evening, *Newsweek* magazine killed a story that was destined to shake official Washington to its foundation: A White House intern carried on a sexual affair with the President of the United States!" The next day Drudge cited Lewinsky by name, and with that the dam broke and the mainstream press subsequently reported the story en masse, ultimately forcing Clinton, on January 26, 1998, to make his now famous public and false finger-waving declaration: "I did not have sexual relations with that woman, Miss Lewinsky."

Clinton's plight then dominated print media and the airwaves, becoming a seemingly never-ending story from which we just couldn't escape. As Mark Rozell and Clyde Wilcox note, "The Clinton scandal consumed the better part of a year of American public life" (xii). The scandal arguably created a conservative political backlash that would help George W. Bush win the first of two U.S. presidential elections in 2000. Through the clear lens of hindsight, one can argue that the astute political acumen of the political Right enabled them to opportunistically take advantage of the president's mistruths and turn the presidential race of 2000 into a referendum on the Left's ostensibly corrupt cultural values as epitomized by the indecency of then president Clinton's repeatedly receiving oral sex from Miss Lewinsky.

Indeed, there's no denying Clinton's signification as a child of the 1960s and all that is stereotypically associated with that decade, especially when it comes to the sexual satyrism with which Clinton has become irrevocably identified in the popular imagination. Clinton was young and hip, especially when compared to his predecessors—can anyone imagine Reagan or Bush Sr. playing the sax in public at all, let alone on *The Arsenio Hall Show*? It's now de rigueur for politicians to make such appearances, albeit normally sans instruments, but Clinton was the first. As Eli Zaretsky astutely observes,

> He had associated himself with the forces of cultural revolution, feminism, gay liberation and African Americans; he had fought for symbolic appointments (Janet Reno, Madeleine Albright, James Hormel), affirmative action, and abortion rights. His opponents strove to restore an older model of patriarchal authority against all that he represented. But that program could never have found conscious support among the American people who, overwhelmingly, if mostly tacitly, welcomed the cultural changes of the sixties, along with the further loosening of mores that accompanied globalization and economic growth. (26)

Despite the Right's painting of him as the worst kind of 1960s hedonist, Clinton's record as a liberal is at best a mixed bag, as he seemingly tried to disassociate himself from the accusation of liberalism by supporting a series of policies and decisions that could hardly be considered the product of a 60s liberal: the Personal Responsibility Act and its accompanying reform of welfare; the Defense of Marriage Act, which he signed into law; the firing of Jocelyn Elders for publicly discussing the benefits of masturbation; his "don't ask, don't tell" policy and the ensuing unprecedented numbers of gays and lesbians being booted from the military; and his signing into law the Communications Decency Act in 1996, which was determined to be so restrictive of Web users' First Amendment rights that it was declared unconstitutional by the U.S. Supreme Court in 1997 (Davis 89–90).

In spite of these actions, Clinton just couldn't escape his depiction in the media as a prototypical liberal. And although in some ways it likely helped him get elected, Clinton's swinging persona would also at least equally hurt him, not only with the Right but also with the traditional Washington media powers, who understood that "Clinton owed much of his victory to extra-Washington media such as *The Larry King Show*, MTV, and Hollywood. From the moment he arrived in Washington, the political pundits and the White House press corps regarded him as an interloper" (Zaretsky 20). When Clinton's relationship with Lewinsky—such as it was—went public, the press pounced and the door that his election had seemingly helped to slam on those on the conservative political Right who "strove to restore an older model of patriarchal authority against all that he represented" was suddenly once again ajar and they did not miss their chance. They kicked it wide open, and beginning in 2000 the Right controlled much of Washington's legislative priorities for the next eight years, even though they never had veto-proof majorities in the House and Senate.

The question, then, becomes this: What effect, if any, did the fallout from the Clinton/Lewinsky scandal have on the movie industry, which had so visibly supported his candidacy and his presidency? Or as Lauren Berlant and Lisa Duggan put it, "How does the intersection of sex and politics shape U.S. public culture? What can alternating waves of public obsession, revulsion, and boredom generated by this scandal of sex and justice tell us about the national interest?" (1). That the extracurricular sexual proclivities of a president might indirectly (at least) cast a shadow over the creative endeavors of the film industry isn't surprising, as since "the ascent of Reaganite conservatism, questions of the relation between a politician's moral and political character and that of the nation have been posed frequently" (Berlant and Duggan 2). As concerns the movies, those who wanted a return to the era of Reagan got their wish, but that doesn't mean that censorship came back into vogue in Hollywood, at least not the old school kind we normally think of when we think of the classical-era studio system. No, what happened instead is that violence came to the fore and sex went out of the public eye and into the home, helped in no small part by the Supreme Court's 1997 overturning of the Communications Decency Act, which allowed porn to continue its meteoric rise to Internet dominance. Also, as we'll later see in the case of Todd Solondz, filmmakers who wanted to make edgier fare, who earlier at least had the possibility of releasing a film as an NC-17, are now left with no choice but to revise their visions so as to be in accordance with a more financially amenable R rating or face almost certain exclusion from the industry.

There was a moment in the early 1990s when movies seemed ready to take the next step forward as concerns their treatment of sex and sexuality. A series of high-profile films, some good, some less so, ranging from works such as *Henry and June* (Kaufman 1990) to *Showgirls* (Verhoeven 1995), challenged the primacy of the Motion Picture Association of America's (MPAA) rating system, and they did it not so much by trying to go outside of the system as by trying to work within it. Prior to the establishment of the MPAA rating system in 1968, all films had to be submitted for approval to the Motion Picture Production Code's (MPPC) offices (early versions of the code—sometimes called the Hays Code after its original author Will Hays—first came into being in the late 1920s, but the code wasn't regularly enforced until 1934). When a film was approved, this meant that it was approved for *all audiences*—that the film was suitable for anyone at any age. Even today, it's hard to look back at films like Billy Wilder's *Double Indemnity* (1944) and *Sunset Boulevard* (1950) and think anyone ever thought they were appropriate viewing for a six-year-old. But regardless, that's the way it worked: you submitted your film at various points from script to completion and you made the required changes along the way to make sure that it ultimately earned the MPPC Seal of Approval, which you can typically see in the lower right- or left-hand corner of a film from the code era's opening credits.

Technically, you could choose not to submit your film for approval, but this was financial suicide. First of all, if you were working under the auspices of a studio, which you were if you wanted to get your film distributed and exhibited, they wouldn't allow you to release your film without the code's seal of approval (indeed, the code office would fine any company that released a movie without its approval and none of the dominant eight film studios was ever hit with a fine). If you tried to release your film yourself, no newspaper would advertise a film that didn't have the seal and no studio-affiliated movie theaters would play it. The exception to this was foreign films, which did not have to be submitted for code approval. While foreign films didn't (and still don't for that matter) usually play in the sticks, they did play in urban areas and college towns, and they enjoyed their largest screen share in the late 1950s and 1960s, in no small part because they enjoyed the freedom to be more sexual in nature than their American counterparts.

From its inception, filmmakers of all stripes challenged the code in whatever ways they could. As the industry moved into the latter half of the 1960s, these challenges intensified until the release of Mike Nichols's *The Graduate* and Arthur Penn's *Bonnie and Clyde* in 1967, both of which received the MPPC Seal of Approval. *Bonnie and Clyde,* with its over-the-top-violence, overtly randy female lead, and obvious homosexual undertones, is a film that no one in her right mind would have tried to make even five years earlier, as is *The Graduate,* which tells the tale of a young man's sexual affair with a much older woman who also happens to be his father's law partner's wife. But the culture—influenced by foreign films and witness to the brutal assassination of JFK, escalating violence in Vietnam, and the fruits of the burgeoning sexual revolution—had changed, and audiences, particularly younger ones, wanted more realism in their films and that meant more stark portrayals of sex and violence on-screen. And a production code that approved films for all audiences had clearly lost its teeth when it gave *Bonnie and Clyde* and *The Graduate* approval. So what next? The response was the aforementioned 1968 creation of the Motion Picture Association of America's new rating board, which would give a film not a seal, but a rating. This meant that a *range* of films could be approved, and this was an important distinction as it would allow filmmakers a lot more freedom to make the kinds of films they wanted to make.

It also, not surprisingly, resulted in an explosion of American exploitation films, in which low-budget movies prominently featured lurid sex and violence more because they could and audiences would pay to see it than for any artistic purposes. The initial rating system had three ratings, G (for general audiences), M (for mature audiences—this would quickly be changed to PG, meaning parental guidance suggested), and R (restricted to those under 17 without the accompaniment of an adult). Filmmakers loudly protested the fact that there wasn't another rating that would allow filmmakers to make movies for adults only. The MPAA, led by Jack Valenti, responded with the creation of the X rating, given to films for which no one under 17 would be admitted, period. While most films weren't rated X, that the rating existed meant that films such as *Midnight Cowboy* (Schlesinger 1969), *A Clockwork Orange* (Kubrick 1971), and *Last Tango in Paris* (Bertolucci 1972), all of which received an X rating (although *Midnight Cowboy* was suspiciously re-rated as an R after it won the Oscar for Best Picture), could be made and enjoy mainstream releases the same way as films with the other ratings could.

Sadly, this newfound artistic freedom would be a short-lived phenomenon never again seen in the film industry. The primary culprit in the demise of the X rating (or at least its use) was actually not internal but external. As Justin Wyatt observes, MPAA head Jack Valenti claimed that he intentionally did not copyright the X rating (all the other ratings were copyrighted) "to ensure that the new ratings system would not limit potential releases, a concern since the studios were making fewer and fewer films: 'We didn't copyright the X rating from a legal standpoint. It had to be open-ended so that if somebody doesn't want to submit a picture, they can use the X. Otherwise we could be challenged on First Amendment grounds'" (241). Whatever Valenti and the MPAA's intentions, the result was that folks outside the industry could co-opt the X rating with impunity as there could be neither legal nor financial repercussions for their having done so. Not long after the birth of the X rating, porn impresarios began giving their films an unauthorized X—after all, it's not like they were submitting them to the MPAA for a rating—as a way to advertise the graphic nature of their films. And as logically follows, they quickly realized that if one X was good, then three were great! Because of the ensuing confusion, films that weren't submitted to the MPAA and had an X (or XX or XXX) rating were conflated with those that had received a legitimate X from the MPAA. For a while this wasn't necessarily a huge problem for Hollywood filmmakers, and some unofficially X-rated films were released en masse along with their more mainstream counterparts, the most notable example of which is *Deep Throat* (Damiano 1972), the success of which started a very short-lived but famous era of porno chic, during which a number of porns were released theatrically in mainstream movie houses and garnered financial—though little critical—success.

But by the late 1970s the culture had shifted, and the conflation of legitimate and illegitimate X ratings in the public imagination had resulted in a de facto return to the code era in that just as films not submitted to the code office were destined for financial failure, so too were films that received an X rating from the MPAA. Rather than release a film with an X rating or with no rating at all, which meant most theaters wouldn't play it and most newspapers wouldn't advertise it, most filmmakers, even if they didn't want to, typically just made the cuts required to get the financially viable R rating. Such was the climate throughout the 1980s, the Reagan years, an era during which, as Steve Vineberg puts it, "the culture began to go haywire . . . moving backwards to a pre-Kennedy conservatism and proclaiming a wholesale embracing of American glory that denied history," the result of which was that "not only did our movies grow loonier (*Fatal Attraction* [Lyne 1987], *Field of Dreams* [Robinson 1989], *Dead Poets Society* [Weir 1989]), but the dissenting voices grew dimmer," and "as for acceptable sexual conduct on [the] screen, suddenly Hollywood was caught in what was practically a Hays Code mentality" (6–7). Filmmakers who wanted to make more adult fare, but not pornography, were in a bind as the X rating was a kiss of death. This was true not only of certain depictions of sex and sexuality, but in rarer instances in depictions of violence as well, as for example in the case of Brian De Palma's *Scarface* (1983), which initially received an X but was subsequently submitted to the MPAA repeatedly until they were finally satisfied enough with the cuts he'd made to give it an R rating.

While there were certainly some great films made during the 1980s, generally the decade is thought to be a qualitative low point in Hollywood filmmaking, in part because "in the Reagan era every movie, whatever its genre, was supposed to be a feel-good movie, a logical extension of Reagan's invocation to the American people to stand tall and feel great about our country" (Vineberg 9). This is not to say that there weren't filmmakers who wanted to make films that challenged the status quo, nor is it to say that there wasn't an audience hungry for films that did so; rather, the funding from the major studios that had so bravely funded landmark films such as *Network* (Lumet 1976) and *Taxi Driver* (Scorsese 1976) in the 1970s had dried up. It's essential to realize, though, that this wasn't necessarily simply a result of their responding to what was perceived as a cultural chill towards edgier fare. More likely, their decisions to fund particular films were based on sound financial reasons. Often lost in all the hullaballoo concerning the 1970s and the great studio films that came from the period is the fact that a huge number of the films revered by cineasts were financial flops. And this is perhaps the most important thing to remember when we talk about censorship in Hollywood and what films get made and those that don't.

In addition to veering towards the right of center with their content, mainstream Hollywood also spent the early part of the 1980s fighting the onset of VHS. Interestingly, Hollywood almost always fights that which can save it. If it wasn't for the industry's ultimate embrace of VHS tapes, and later DVDs, where would it be today? An unexpected beneficiary of the rise of the VHS was the other Hollywood, the porn industry. While the studios quibbled, the porn industry realized almost immediately that the backlash with which its theatrical releases ended up meeting in the latter half of the 1970s meant that theatrical release as an industry option was forevermore to be a nonstarter. Looking for an alternative means of distribution, the porn industry adapted to the videotape almost overnight, quickly converting to not only distributing on video tape but shooting on it as well, simultaneously dramatically lowering their production costs while increasing their market penetration. Whether spotted in a movie theater or an adult shop, there has always been a cultural stigma associated with being publicly seen as a consumer of porn. Home video took the ignominy out of the equation; mail order, in the form of discreetly wrapped packages, meant that folks with an interest in hardcore could have their needs satiated simply by placing an order, which would come directly to their door with no one the wiser. In a sense you could argue that the VHS sent porn underground in that it wasn't as readily available in publicly visible outlets in the same way it had been earlier, but the opposite is much more true; going into the living rooms of its consumers resulted in a porn explosion in the United States. In fact, it may have saved the industry, at least its harder variants, which were no longer subject to the gaze of folks who were in theory against it but in practice no longer saw it in their communities as they once did.

Whatever one's artistic desires, there was little *financial* incentive for studios to allow the inclusion of anything more than incidental or passing nudity—let alone graphic sexuality—in their films in the 1980s. Doing so could result in a rating not conducive to box office, and if people really wanted to see sex, they could do so in the comfort of their own homes; they didn't need to go out and see a mainstream movie to get their fill. As Stephen Vaughn writes, "The peak year for . . . the [MPAA's] X rating came in 1976 when sixty films were so classified, about 12 percent of the total number of pictures the rating board reviewed that year. During the next five years [the rating board] used the rating less frequently, assigning 22 Xs in 1978 and 34 in 1979. With the arrival of the video revolution, it all but abandoned the rating. Between 1982 and 1989, only 15 out of 3,339 films rated received an X" (70). Still, many filmmakers chafed at what they saw as the artistic censorship imposed on them by the MBA types making the financial decisions at the studios.

Yes, there were other avenues to reach an audience, such as the burgeoning festival circuit, but the end goal for most filmmakers was (and is) to get their films seen and to do that in any meaningful way as concerns the number of people you can reach, it's almost impossible not to have studio affiliation as they were—and are—the only companies that can effectively mass market and distribute a movie. Further, the big studios appear to be much more successful in persuading the rating board to give a particular rating than their smaller independent brethren. The conflict between filmmakers and the rating board came to a head at the end of the 1980s, during which three critically well-received films, *The Cook, The Thief, His Wife and Her Lover* (Greenaway 1989), *Tie Me Up! Tie Me Down!* (Almodóvar 1990), and *Henry: Portrait of a Serial Killer* (McNaughton 1989), were all initially given X ratings, much to the chagrin of Miramax Films, which was trying to distribute the former two movies, and Maljack Productions, which was trying to distribute the latter. It could be argued that the resultant hubbub was artistic, and it clearly was for Greenaway and McNaughton, who bravely released their films unrated. But for the small studios who had bought the films for distribution, despite whatever they said, the fact was that they had great financial incentive to argue against the rating (all three were ultimately financially successful, albeit very modestly).

While not without their disturbing elements, none of these films were anything even close to pornography (although *Henry* does at times resemble the mythical snuff film). Filmmakers throughout the industry called for a new copyrighted rating, something that would take the place of the X and allow the wide release of non-pornographic films geared for an adult audience, without the accompanying artistic and financial bugaboos associated with the old X. And so a new rating was born: the NC-17 (no children under 17 allowed). The first film to get this new rating was Philip Kaufman's *Henry and June,* about the relationship and resultant ménage à trois between Henry Miller, his wife, June, and his lover, Anaïs Nin. The new rating was met with applause by much of the above-the-line talent in Hollywood, and it was initially believed that the rating might breathe some life into the making of serious adult films. While the film generated enormous controversy—not always a bad thing for a movie—it didn't do much for the merits of the NC-17 rating. Rather, because of its subject matter and comparatively graphic sex, *Henry and June,* as well as the NC-17 films released in its wake (most famously and decidedly with *Showgirls,* which arguably put the final nail in the rating's coffin), quickly led to NC-17 films being just as stigmatized as the previous X movies were, in large part because major theater chains refused to play them, major newspapers refused to advertise them, and major retailers refused to sell the subsequent home video releases.

Interestingly, the release of *Showgirls* in 1995 and the adjacent backlash in some ways anticipated the moral furor aimed at Bill Clinton a few years later. I am not arguing a causal relationship here, but I am suggesting illustrative connections in that the vitriol aimed at Hollywood in the mid-1990s for its supposed promulgation of immorality would in part be transferred to the president himself once his infidelities were made public in 1998; this was perhaps not coincidentally due to the fact that Hollywood had almost quit making NC-17 films by that time. In 1990 there were 20 pictures released with an NC-17 and there were 21 more released in 1991. And that was the new rating's high point. Just as they had in the case of the X rating, in the early 1990s major retailers and media outlets once again began inexplicably equating the NC-17 rating with hardcore pornography. In 1991 Blockbuster, at that time the nation's largest video retailer, announced it wouldn't carry NC-17 titles—although they would ultimately carry unrated titles, but not in time to save the NC-17. Likewise, in 1992 K-Mart and Wal-Mart both announced they wouldn't carry NC-17 titles. Together, the two Marts and Blockbuster accounted for over half of all video sales (Vaughn 220). While their decision as concerns NC-17 films was an ill-informed knee-jerk reaction, it nevertheless put a serious damper on the intentional production of adult oriented films likely to garner an NC-17; indeed, for very real financial reasons, no studio exec in her right mind would give the go-ahead to a film that was *intended* to earn the dreaded rating. By 1995 only four MPAA-rated films had an NC-17 rating. In 1999 that number was two, neither of which was a major studio production (Vaughn 220–21). In light of the absence of Hollywood's very public product as a target for protest, the attentions of many of those who had railed against its output were turned elsewhere while Hollywood quietly backed away from its brief dalliance with edgier fare.

Again, in many ways it was *Showgirls* that closed the door on the NC-17. With its graphic and unintentionally hilarious over-the-top sex scenes it deserved the rating it received, but it was its tone and the leering way in which the sex was depicted that made it so damaging to the rating. Most earlier films with an NC-17 rating, whether one liked them or not, weren't exploitation films, and maybe that's part of the problem with the rating. Films that clearly had titillation as their primary intent—*Flesh Gordon Meets the Cosmic Cheerleaders* and the like— were given NC-17 ratings, despite their never being meant for cinematic distribution. It would be impossible for all but the worst ideologues and zealots to confuse the artistic intents of these kinds of films with those of their more representative brethren, such as *Clerks* (Smith 1994), *Kids* (Clark 1995), and *Crash* (Cronenberg

1996), all of which garnered an NC-17 rating. (*Clerks* was recut to receive an R, *Kids* surrendered its rating and was released unrated, and *Crash* was released with an NC-17.) So long as it could be reasonably claimed that the NC-17 was the equivalent of an art X, it was able to uneasily coexist with other Hollywood fare, though its bearers were shunted to the commercial margins. But when *Showgirls* was released in 1995, it had a lot more in common with *Flesh Gordon*–style films than it did with its more artistically inclined NC-17 counterparts. Already the rating was in trouble, and the furor surrounding this film about a Las Vegas stripper who works in a casino—and was played by former *Saved by the Bell* teen star Elizabeth Berkley—didn't help matters any. Also not helpful was the fact that its overbearing screenwriter, Joe Eszterhas, who claimed the movie's message was important in that it epitomized the axiom that selling your soul for success isn't worth it, was quoted as saying, "What I want to say to teenagers under 17 is, don't let anyone stop you from seeing this movie. Do whatever you've got to do to see it. Use your fake IDs" (Vaughn 219).

This is not an art film. It was a $45 million film bankrolled primarily by MGM subsidiary United Artists, which put the full weight of its marketing machine behind it and managed to get it released on 1,300 screens, still the highest ever number for an NC-17-rated film. Had *Showgirls,* by far the highest-profile NC-17 film ever released, reeled in big dollars at the box office then perhaps the fate of the NC-17 might have been different as studios will back what they think can make money. But it tanked at the box office (it is the highest-grossing NC-17 film of all time, but with a domestic gross of $20 million—less than half its production budget—that's small consolation for its investors ["All Time Box Office . . . NC-17," *Box Office Mojo.com*]). More important than its financial failure was that for the first time those from outside the industry who opposed the NC-17 rating and equated it with pornography could draw a reasonably straight line between *Showgirls* and NC-17-rated exploitation films such as *Fantasy* (Brown and Strahan 1991) and *Erotique* (Borden, Law, Magalhães, and Treut 1994). Both movies, incidentally, were recut to get a more favorable R rating for their video release, which was common. After the huge outcry of protest surrounding the mainstream debacle that was *Showgirls,* even defenders of the NC-17 rating were rendered silent, or were at least no longer heard. It wasn't that Hollywood wantonly gave up on edgier art; it's just that when a certain kind of art has no concomitant financial benefit, why would companies in the business of making money bother pursuing the defense of that kind of art? They wouldn't. After all, only 11 NC-17 films have ever made more than $1 million domestically at the box office, with only one other beside *Showgirls,* *Henry and June* at $11.5 million, making more than $10 million ("All Time Box Office . . . NC-17," *Box Office Mojo.com*).

Even before *Showgirls* the road to hoe for filmmakers with harder-edged visions was growing significantly more rocky, especially if they hoped to get any kind of mainstream distribution, which, as the term "mainstream" implies, requires studio affiliation and studios just weren't interested in releasing NC-17 films anymore (not that they were crazy about it to begin with—studios avoid controversy like the plague). Take, for example, the story of Larry Clark's *Kids*, released in the summer of 1995. The film was bought by Harvey Weinstein's Miramax division of the Walt Disney Company, reportedly for $3.5 million. Already, the original producers had a return on their investment, as the film had only cost $1.5 million to make. But the film, which features the recreational drug–fueled sex lives of a group of NYC teens, received an NC-17 from the rating board. Disney was not, and is not, in the business of sullying its brand and had a policy of not releasing NC-17 films, and so refused to release the film. Incensed, Harvey and his brother Bob bought the film back from Disney and released it themselves. In a rare instance of a company standing behind a filmmaker's vision, Miramax agreed to surrender the NC-17 and release the film unrated. Their integrity was rewarded handsomely when the film, despite a ton of negative outcry surrounding its treatment of its controversial subject matter, received mostly positive reviews and went on to gross over $7 million domestically and near $20 million total (*Box Office Mojo.com*). But *Kids* was the miraculous exception to the rule before *Showgirls*; after *Showgirls* there would be no such miracles forthcoming.

Perhaps the work of no post-*Showgirls* filmmaker is more important to consider than that of Todd Solondz, a bookish-looking, Yale-educated, New Jersey native whose mousy outward appearance belies a dark and often very disturbing worldview. Solondz made his first splash as a short filmmaker, which earned him a three-picture deal with 20th Century Fox, which wanted him to make *Revenge of the Nerds II*. (That he didn't is not surprising, though it is a little sad. Who knows in what direction he would have taken the franchise, especially given his much more interesting and tragic depiction of social misfits in his subsequent work?) Instead, Solondz wrote, directed, and starred in *Fear, Anxiety & Depression* (1989), a critically reviled film that even he's disowned. So despondent was he over the experience, he quit the business for a number of years, choosing instead to teach ESL to Russian immigrants. Of that period in his life, Solondz says, "I had no ambition. And it was the happiest time of my life. But I didn't want the first movie to have the last word" (Hirschberg).

And so as his first film never saw the light of day via any kind of wide theatrical distribution, Solondz sought to make a second first feature, only this time he very intentionally worked outside of the system, making the film for less than $1 million, which he raised from private investors. The result was *Welcome to the Dollhouse* (1995), which he reportedly originally wanted to call *Faggots and Retards*. *Dollhouse* recounts the travails of Dawn Weiner (Heather Matarazzo), a "self-righteous and unlikable" middle-schooler (Hirschberg). Still, upon its debut at the 1994 Toronto Film Festival, the film struck a chord, and a bidding war for its rights broke out, with Sony Picture Classics winning. The film went on to gross in excess of $4.5 million domestically, making it a modest hit (*Box Office Mojo.com*). More important, the film garnered Solondz the attention of the more powerful independent studios, one of which, Universal indie subsidiary October Films, signed on to produce his next film.

Xan Brooks notes that after *Dollhouse* and the film industry's subsequent re-embrace of Solondz, it was "tempting to frame Solondz's story as a classic redemption; a triumph over disaster; the bullied kid who gets even." But just because the film industry once again came calling doesn't mean Solondz was waiting at the door with open arms. Rather, he "believes filmmaking is a dreadful business" and says, "I think most filmmakers love what they do, and I wish I loved it more. I really do. But I don't like the stress. I don't. I can imagine just dropping out" (Brooks). Still, riding the wave of critical momentum, Solondz forged ahead with his next film, ultimately called *Happiness* (1998). But in the three short years since the release of *Dollhouse,* the landscape of American film had changed, resulting in things beginning to go horribly awry for Solondz, at least as concerns his ability to reconcile his admittedly offbeat artistic vision with the social mores and accompanying financial realities of Middle America and the mainstream film industry.

As Andrew Gumbel aptly puts it, "*Happiness* is the sort of film that ought to give independent cinema a good name. Its subject matter may lack that instant mass appeal that big studios crave—it dwells on the bleak emotions and furtive sexual appetites of a group of New Jersey suburbanites—but it's expertly crafted, beautifully acted, and uncomfortable enough to stay under your skin for days. Just the sort of film, in fact, one would expect to win plaudits at international film festivals, find a niche with a medium sized distributor and put in a healthy performance on the arthouse circuit and at more discerning big-city cinemas." And so it initially seemed this would be the case, as *Happiness* debuted at the Cannes film festival, where it received a lot of attention. Later it would play at Toronto, where once again Solondz proved to be a cause célèbre, his film voted by critics as the best of the 315 that played at Toronto that year (Dwyer). The film seemed poised to follow the now de rigueur path towards indie success: first playing at select elite festivals to glowing reviews, then a limited release in more accepting urban locales to further build a head of positive critical steam, an Oscar nomination or two (which *Happiness* didn't get, though it was nominated for a Golden Globe screenplay award and several Independent Spirit awards), and finally, a slow rollout release eventually blanketing the country and resulting in bona fide indie box office success. Alas, such was not to be the case with *Happiness,* primarily because one of the aforementioned New Jersey suburbanites, Bill Maplewood, wonderfully portrayed by Dylan Baker, is a pedophile who preys on his 11-year-old son's peers. And so *Happiness* would take a "rather different path to prominence, one that illustrates the precariousness of all independent productions and the ever more invasive influence of the big entertainment conglomerates" (Gumbel). Indeed, *Happiness* would end up being victimized not once but twice, even though it was never actually officially censored by the MPAA.

The first instance was a case of self-censorship from October's parent company Universal Studios. October had free reign to produce and/or acquire its slate of films so long as it stayed within the financial parameters put in place by its parent company. But after seeing the film at Cannes for the first time, Universal CEO Ron Meyer went ballistic, saying, "As long as I have the job and can throw my

body in front of something, I will. I don't want to understand the mind of a pedophile. I don't want that to be a part of this company" (Hirschberg). And so he
forbade October from releasing the film. Meyer's seemingly strong moral stand
belies the sensitivity with which Maplewood is depicted in the film. As Solondz
puts it, "When I thought of the paedophile [*sic*] story-line, I thought, what is the
most horrible thing, the greatest atrocity, that I could come up with, and yet at the
same time bring the audience in in a way that they would care? That was something of the challenge. The idea of softening the paedophilia [*sic*] seems to me an
obscenity. You try to look it in the eye as best you can. What makes his story tragic
is it's not that he's a monster but he struggles with that monster within, and he suc-
cumbs" (Rees). And when one understands the economic realities of independent
cinema and mainstream Hollywood, it's hard to take Meyer's stance at face value.
As Howard Feinstein writes, Solondz had "no illusions about Universal's decision,"
nor, frankly, should we. This wasn't moral censorship; it was economic, plain and
simple, a fact of which Solondz was all too aware: "It was just about money. . . .
*Happiness* is just a little movie. There was a lot of flak and controversy they weren't
anticipating. It didn't make it worth their while to attach their name to it. If they
thought it would make $100 million, then of course the movie would've been 'mor-
ally courageous.' Why go through all of the headaches with the stockholders? What
surprises him, however, is that people took a studio seriously when they said they
found the film 'morally objectionable.' The idea of attaching any morality to a
studio is naïve" (Feinstein).

It's hard not to see the merit in Solondz's point of view, especially given the
fact that two of the film's most notorious scenes revolve around the showing
of male ejaculate. But what was somehow reprobate in *Happiness,* not to mention on the infamously presidentially semen-stained Lewinsky blue dress, was
in the Farrelly Brothers' *There's Something About Mary,* in which semen is featured
as hair gel, deemed a hilarious use of bodily fluids. The intent was different to be
sure, but it's still not hard to see a double standard between the way *Happiness* and
the star-driven *Mary,* produced and distributed by 20th Century Fox, were treated
by the industry. Fox backed *Mary,* and with a $370 million cumulative box of-
fice take it was the third-highest-grossing film in the world in 1998 (*Box Office Mojo.
com*). As a result of Universal's financially motivated self-censorship, October was
forced to sell the film. In what initially appeared to be a stroke of good fortune, indie
distributor Good Machine bought the film from October for its $3 million pro-
duction cost. And then came the second wave of censorship, though again it was
never official.

Solondz is an admittedly iconoclastic filmmaker, "quirky and beguiling, with the
gift of an outsider: the ability to observe closely without courting acceptance. He's
interested in little but his vision, and that vision, while compelling, is also troubling"
(Hirschberg). He doesn't want to direct scripts other than his own and he's openly
contemptuous of the Hollywood system. This is in some ways admirable, but it's
also a tough sell and career self-sabotage. You can work outside of the system while

you're making your film, but once it comes time to get that film distributed, the participation of the greater Hollywood system is a virtually unavoidable requirement if you want your film seen. Even if you go with a so-called independent distributor, you have to understand that they almost always have distribution deals with the majors, otherwise they wouldn't be able to get films out across the country and world. But beginning with *Happiness,* Solondz has ignored that reality and made no concessions in his art, which has earned him respect but not dollars.

In the case of *Happiness,* it was an artistic victory for Solondz in that once he was dropped by Universal, final cut (the right to say what a film's final form will be) reverted to him and he reserved that right when he signed with Good Machine. But given the film's subject matter, the chance of ever securing anything but an NC-17 rating from the MPAA was seemingly infinitely less than zero. The problem with *Happiness* is that there's virtually nothing to cut as concerns its visual elements: there isn't really any graphic nudity and even the simulated sex (which is primarily masturbation) is comparatively chaste. No, the problems with *Happiness* are its tone and subtext, a result of Solondz putting "on film certain characters that might be normally deemed repugnant or freakish, and to somehow whittle away at those surfaces, so that the audience could sympathize with the unsympathetic and see that there was a richness of life there, and that the person wasn't just reduced to an obscene phone caller or a pedophile" (Gerstel). What people end up debating about the film wasn't "explicit violence or nudity, but something more complex: the filmmaker's attitude towards his characters" (Lacey). The totality of the sum of its parts equals a witch's brew of pedophilia and perversion, subjects forever taboo in American multiplexes. That Solondz handles his characters so deftly didn't matter a whit in the end. How, after all, can you recut a film to change the entirety of its tone, especially given that its tone is its power and message? Solondz, perhaps wisely, opted to not even bother submitting the film to the MPAA, choosing instead to release it unrated, which predictably led to financial disaster.

Once the decision was made to release the film unrated, even its distributor, Good Machine, chose to back off, realizing that given the film's limited opportunities for marketing and exhibition, there wasn't much point in sinking a ton of time and effort into the film. As producer Christine Vachon says, "Everyone was getting absorbed by their places in the Greek tragedy, Oh, how does this reflect on me? And no one was saying, There's this movie that has two years of life and blood in it, let's get the movie out! It was really rough. Good Machine had a horrible time doing it, it was a big money suck, a lot of work for a little return. We so could have had a screenplay nomination, and we maybe even could have gotten Dylan Baker a nomination, but we didn't do a real Academy push" (Biskind 336). And so one of the most critically lauded films of the 1990s crashed and burned, barely making back its $3 million cost and earning for Solondz around only $30,000 for two years' worth of writing and directing (Ibid.). *Happiness,* a brave and incendiary film, has taken its place in Hollywood lore, but not in the way that many film critics thought it might have when it first came to light. Instead, it's become a kind of

cautionary tale for film financiers. It doesn't matter how good a film is or how original a director's vision if said vision is likely to come into the crosshairs of America's
box office killing moral watchdogs. Like Universal, the other majors have chosen
to avoid involvement with anything that can bring them negative attention or any
kind of controversy, and subsequent independent distributors have learned from
Good Machine's experience and stayed away from anything they think can't be
recut for an R. It's self-censorship from both the upper and lower echelons of the
industry, and certain filmmakers either need to change what it is they do or get
stuck out in the cold.

Interestingly, Todd Solondz is a filmmaker who has steadfastly and stubbornly
stayed true to his vision. His subsequent film was *Storytelling* (2001), a diptych that
featured in its first segment a very extended, possibly nonconsensual anal sex scene
between a young white creative writing student and her much older Pulitzer Prize–
winning African American professor. The film was released with an R rating, but
only after concessions were made. Solondz knew the film was playing with fire,
so, as Simon Houpt writes:

> He ensured that his contract with Fine Line Pictures gave him the right to deal with
> objections from the MPAA . . . as he desired. Instead of trimming an objectionable
> scene, or cutting away from a vexing image to another shot within the scene, he
> reserved the right to insert "boxes, beeps or bars," over what he had shot. (When
> the studio head found out Solondz intended to actually exercise his right to use the
> box, he reportedly swore it would happen only "over my dead body." That execu-
> tive, however, remains alive and in good health.)

And so the offending sex scene was covered by a giant red box on-screen. Two years
earlier, there was a furor around Stanley Kubrick's posthumously released *Eyes Wide
Shut,* which in order to get an R rating in the States had to digitally obstruct
certain parts of its orgy scene. But the end results of the respective censoring of the
two films weren't similar, thus illustrating the differences between independent-
spirited movies and star-driven, studio-backed films. *Eyes Wide Shut* was a Warner
Brothers' film, and in addition to the Kubrick imprimatur it boasted the presence
of Tom Cruise and Nicole Kidman, two of Hollywood's biggest stars, who also
happened to be married at the time. And so the Warner machine was able to use
the required digitization to their advantage, flogging what they claimed was artistic
censorship in the press and heightening interest in an otherwise overwrought and
turgid film, which ultimately earned a worldwide gross of $162 million against its
$65 million production budget (*Box Office Mojo.com*). One assumes it earned a
tidy sum on the release of the unrated DVD as well. Coincidentally, *Storytelling*
was backed by Fine Line, like Warner Brothers also a subsidiary of Time Warner
Communications, one of the six largest media companies in the world. While they
may have contracted that Solondz had the right to visually obstruct certain scenes

(a clause that no one has earned since), they didn't contract having to market the film and so they didn't. In direct opposition to their backing of the comparatively big-budget, star-driven *Eyes Wide Shut,* rather than getting involved in the controversy, they realized that a film of *Storytelling*'s scope and stature had little chance of notable profitability anyway. So they cut their losses and barely released the film, which earned less than $1 million at the box office and reinforced the idea that MPAA censorship and the financial fate of a film differ dramatically depending on whether or not one has the backing of a major studio (*Box Office Mojo.com*). (In Kirby Dick's *This Film Is Not Yet Rated,* which is actually rated NC-17, Matt Stone, cowriter/director of *Orgazmo* [1997] and *South Park: Bigger, Longer and Uncut* [1999], unflinchingly details the ocean of difference in his dealings with the MPAA as an independent filmmaker—*Orgazmo,* a film about a reluctant Mormon porn star, received an NC-17 and was released to little fanfare by, coincidentally, October Films—and a studio filmmaker working for Paramount, which bankrolled *South Park,* which was offered extensive recutting suggestions by the MPAA to ensure its financial viability for Paramount. Not surprisingly, *Orgazmo,* though a beloved cult classic, barely made $500,000 at the box office, whereas *South Park,* which essentially mocks the validity of the MPAA rating system from start to finish, earned nearly $84 million worldwide [*Box Office Mojo.com*].)

As of 2010, Solondz has only made two more films. The first was the little-seen *Palindromes* (2004), which features a soccer mom who makes her 13-year-old get an abortion she doesn't want and a pro-life Christian family that cares for challenged children while also planning to murder abortion providers. The independently made film failed to be picked up by a major distributor and earned less than $750,000 worldwide (*Box Office Mojo.com*). His next film was *Life During Wartime* (2009), also independently produced, which picks up the lives of characters from *Happiness,* albeit with different actors. Despite playing at a series of prestigious festivals, including Telluride, Venice, Toronto, New York, and London, it received mixed reviews and didn't land a distribution deal for almost a year, and even then the distributor, IFC, barely released it at all. In discussing the career of Solondz, I'd be remiss not to point out the fact that a lot of people just aren't going to like his films. And even those that do sometimes have a hard time watching them. His is not easy or pretty art. But qualitative issues aside, Solondz is a case study of a truly independent spirit who, despite his uncompromising vision, likely would've been able to forge some sort of career had he been lucky enough to have been born earlier, so he could have either worked in the much more open-minded and freewheeling 1970s or during the independent boom that began in the late 1980s. But because he didn't hit his stride until 1995, the beginning of the end of the heady days of the American independent movement of the late 1980s and early 1990s, the market for a filmmaker of his ilk has simply evaporated, perhaps due to some change in cultural mores, and certainly as a result of the industry's realization that there simply isn't any money to be made in backing someone who won't even try to play along with the financial realities of dealing with certain subject matters in the contemporary film industry. As Solondz says,

> I don't know how much longer I can continue. There is no government subsidy process to sustain a career like mine. If I were Australian or European or Canadian, there are systems in place to support filmmakers like myself. That doesn't exist here in the U.S. It's solely driven by the marketplace, which is why so few American filmmakers can continue to have a career making art films. . . . If the movies made more money, I would be able to get more money, but they don't and because I deal with difficult subjects, it's that much more difficult. (Sutherland)

Of *Happiness* Lynn Hirschberg asked the question, "Can a work of art go too far?" It's a tough question in the abstract, but a stupidly simple one in the context of today's Hollywood: yes, unequivocally. Conversely, the opposite of this is true in the world of porn, where the answer is decidedly no. The death of the NC-17 as a legitimate rating for Hollywood adult films coincided with the explosion of pornography in American culture at the end of the 20th century. This is not to say that porn hasn't always had a ready audience of consumers, but the rising ubiquity of the Internet made porn much more accessible (if still not socially acceptable in all circles) than it had ever been before. And as it became more accessible, it also became much harder in nature than it had earlier been, at least as concerns the visibility of certain kinds of fetish porn, which have certainly always existed in some form or another, but in many instances weren't so publicly available. The consequence of this is that there's been a bifurcation between Hollywood and the other Hollywood: Hollywood has gone soft while porn has gone increasingly hard. If you have a fetish, porn is made to satisfy your fantasies, seemingly no matter what those may be. Anal sex, once considered the last sexual taboo, is almost austere in the current porn milieu. For those who are interested in exploring more outré activities, there's no shortage of rape porn, teen porn, bondage porn, foot porn, bukkake, gay porn, gang bangs, you name it.

Take, for example, the San Francisco–based kink.com, a fetish super-site that offers access to an array of sites in what the parent site dubs "the kink family," including Divine Bitches, 3D Kink, Kink Live, Everything Butt, Public Disgrace, Hogtied, F***ing Machines, Whipped A**, Wired P***y, Men in Pain, Water Bondage, Device Bondage, and TS Seduction to name just a few. And this is not skeezy 1980s-era video porn with unattractive actors and horrible production values; rather, it features comparatively very attractive folks and high-quality, aesthetically pleasing HD production values. These are inarguably very well made professional films. Regardless of one's tastes as concerns the content, it's top-notch filmmaking for its genre. And it's incredibly profitable; in fact, as concerns return on investment, porn is a moneymaker well beyond that of any Hollywood exec's wildest dreams. As Vaughn notes, "By the end of the century [porn] had become a $10 to $14 billion-a-year business, bringing in more money than all of professional baseball, football, and basketball combined, and more than the American public spent on mainstream movie tickets" (167). And while mainstream Hollywood has gone soft, the big six companies that control the industry—GE (which sold NBC/Universal to Comcast in 2010), Disney, Fox, Time Warner, Viacom, and Sony— couldn't help but notice the profitability of pornography and get involved in the gold rush. While none of these six are porn producers, that doesn't mean some of them aren't profiting from it in their role as distributors, specifically via their cable and satellite pay-per-view holdings, which offer porn on demand both in the home and at almost any hotel in the world with a TV. The money to be made is fabulous and requires no investment on the part of the mainstream media industry and there's no risk of financial failure. It's virtually foolproof for the industry and a no-brainer that they'd be involved. Conversely, why would any company back a Hollywood film with an NC-17 rating, which would almost certainly result in controversy and a serious hamstringing of a film's potential box office? Easy answer: they wouldn't.

So since those heady days in the early and mid-1990s when it seemed for a nanosecond that the NC-17 might gain a foothold in the American film industry, the rating has since faded into relative obscurity, even though it technically still exists. Contemporarily, it seems that the only real use for the rating is to hope that an early cut of a particular film gets an NC-17, which a company can then use to generate interest in their inevitably recut R-rated film. Films like *Bruno* (Charles 2009), *Team America: World Police* (Parker 2004), *American Pie* (Weitz 1999), *Saw* (Wan 2004), *Kill Bill, Volumes 1 & 2* (Tarantino 2003, 2004), and *Grindhouse* (Rodriguez and Tarantino 2007) were all initially rumored to have been given the NC-17 rating. But none of these films are anything close to a serious-minded adult film. It's hard to believe that the responsible studios remotely considered for even a second releasing any of these films with an NC-17. Why would they? They all had the potential to connect with teen audiences and make a big chunk of dough for their parent companies, which several of them did. You could even argue that it would be financial malfeasance on the part of a studio to even entertain the idea of an NC-17 release with these kinds of films. It's very difficult to rail against the industry's conservatism when trying to reconcile that with the fact that they are first and foremost in the business of making money, and "art for art's sake" is an awesome motto but a terrible business model, at least when it comes to the movies.

Even in cases in which an NC-17 is merited (arguably at any rate—it is all subjective), it behooves a studio to require a reedit, especially when not doing so can mean a great film that deserves a chance to find an audience might not get it. Kimberly Pierce's *Boys Don't Cry* (1999) immediately comes to mind. In *This Picture Is Not Yet Rated* she convincingly argues against the reasons her film received an NC-17 rating. That being said, the recut R-rated version earned a very respectable $11.5 million domestic box office return against a $2 million production budget, not to mention widespread acclaim for Pierce and a Best Actress Academy Award for Hillary Swank (*Box Office Mojo.com*). Conversely, the following year Darren Aronofsky's *Requiem for a Dream* (2000) was given an NC-17 and the filmmaker was allowed to surrender the rating, choosing instead to release it without one. While perhaps it was a better film than it otherwise would have been, releasing it sans rating meant that it wouldn't be played in most cities or advertised in most venues, which certainly played a large part in its sorry return of $3.6 million domestic against a $4.5 million production budget (*Box Office Mojo. com*). No amount of critical accolades and award nominations can make a film profitable if it doesn't get the distribution that allows people the chance to see it. In the virtually unheard-of contemporary instance in which a film is released with an NC-17, the circumstances are typically such that doing so makes virtually no difference, which is a rare happening indeed. Take, for example, the case of Ang Lee's *Lust, Caution* (2007), which was released with an NC-17. It also featured Mandarin as its primary language, meaning it wasn't going to play anywhere outside of America's big cities and art houses anyway. Its $4.5 million domestic gross against its $15 million production budget might seem like a disaster until one realizes it made over $62 million overseas (*Box Office Mojo.com*). But *Lust* is a remarkable exception to the rule. American art films, indie or otherwise, are so culturally specific that they just don't translate abroad in the same way as their high-dollar, action-oriented brethren do. There's very little audience. *Lust,* however, is an almost one of a kind film: an American art film best suited for foreign audiences. Barring the exceedingly rare exception such as *Lust,* it's no wonder studios are loathe to release NC-17 films. It just doesn't make financial sense.

And so here we are. The early years of the Clinton presidency coincided with a perceived move towards cultural liberalization at the expense of Reaganesque family values. And just as Clinton's rise to power ran parallel to this cultural shift as illustrated by the initial industry support of the NC-17 rating, so too did his later very public fall from grace signal the end of what in hindsight was a relatively brief moment in time, both in wider American culture and in the film industry in particular. While filmmakers still sometimes complain about what they see as artistic censorship, it really isn't artistic censorship at all; if the power brokers in the film industry thought for a second that they could turn a slick profit on NC-17-rated films, we'd never see the end of them. No, the self-imposed censorship prevalent in Hollywood is purely economic and for the good of the business if not necessarily the art form, the result of which really is the return of Reagan-era values to the American film industry, at least as concerns its treatment of sex and sexuality. And at the present moment, it's hard to envision the circumstances that might emerge in which that will change.

## WORKS CITED

Berlant, Lauren, and Lisa Duggan. "Introduction." *Our Monica Ourselves: The Clinton Affair and the National Interest,* ed. Lauren Berlant and Lisa Duggan, 1–6. New York: New York University Press, 2001.

Biskind, Peter. *Down and Dirty Pictures: Miramax, Sundance, and the Rise of Independent Film.* New York: Simon & Schuster, 2004.

*Box Office Mojo.com.* "All Time Box Office Domestic Grosses by MPAA Rating: NC-17."

*Box Office Mojo.com.* "Boys Don't Cry."

*Box Office Mojo.com.* "Eyes Wide Shut."

*Box Office Mojo.com.* "Henry and June."

*Box Office Mojo.com.* "Kids."

*Box Office Mojo.com.* "Lust, Caution."

*Box Office Mojo.com.* "Orgazmo."

*Box Office Mojo.com.* "Palindromes."

*Box Office Mojo.com.* "Requiem for a Dream."

*Box Office Mojo.com.* "There's Something About Mary."

*Box Office Mojo.com.* "South Park—Bigger, Longer and Uncut." 1999.

*Box Office Mojo.com.* "Storytelling."

*Box Office Mojo.com.* "Welcome to the Dollhouse."

Brooks, Xan. "It's My Film And I'll Cry If I Want To; Todd Solondz, Director of *Happiness,* Says Success Hasn't Changed Him. He Was Miserable Before. He Still Is." *The Independent* [London]. April 15, 1999. *LexisNexis Academic.*

Davis, Simone Weil. "The Erotics of Hypocrisy in the White House Scandal: The Door Ajar." In *Our Monica Ourselves: The Clinton Affair and the National Interest,* ed. Lauren Berlant and Lisa Duggan, 86–101. New York: New York University Press, 2001.

Dick, Kirby. *This Film Is Not Yet Rated.* Independent Film Channel, 2006.

Drudge, Matt. "Newsweek Kills Story on White House Intern." *The Drudge Report.* Jan. 17, 2002.

Dwyer, Michael. "Too Hot to Handle." *The Irish Times.* Oct. 3, 1998. *LexisNexis Academic.*

Feinstein, Howard. "A Tender Comedy About Child Abuse? What Is Todd Solondz Up To?" *The Guardian* [London]. March 26, 1999. *LexisNexis Academic.*

Gerstel, Judy. "*Happiness* Is in the Eye of the Beholder." *The Toronto Star.* Sept. 17, 1998. *LexisNexis Academic.*

Gumbel, Andrew. "How *Happiness* Won: Letter From Hollywood." *The Independent* [London]. Oct. 25, 1998. *LexisNexis Academic.*

Hirschberg, Lynn. "Crabgrass Gothic." *New York Times.* Sept. 27, 1998. *LexisNexis Academic.*

Houpt, Simon. "Censored and Proud." *The Globe and Mail* [Canada]. Feb. 15, 2002. *LexisNexis Academic.*

Lacey, Liam. "A Director's Disturbing Vision of *Happiness.*" *The Globe and Mail* [Canada]. Sept. 15, 1998. *LexisNexis Academic.*

Rees, Jasper. "The Suburban Horror of One Man's *Happiness.*" *The Evening Standard* [London]. April 15, 1999. *LexisNexis Academic.*

Rozell, Mark J., and Clyde Wilcox. "The Clinton Presidency and the Politics of Scandal." In *The Clinton Scandal and the Future of American Government,* ed. Mark J. Rozell and Clyde Wilcox, vii–xxii. Washington, D.C.: Georgetown University Press, 2000.

Sutherland, Claire. "Act of Todd." *Herald Sun* [Australia]. Aug. 25, 2005. *LexisNexis Academic.*

Vaughn, Stephen. *Freedom and Entertainment: Rating the Movies in an Age of New Media.* New York: Cambridge University Press, 2006.

Vineberg, Steve. *No Surprises, Please: Movies in the Reagan Decade.* New York: Schirmer Books, 1993.

Wyatt, Justin. "The Stigma of X: Adult Cinema and the Institution of the MPAA Ratings System." In *Controlling Hollywood: Censorship and Regulation in the Studio Era,* ed. Matthew Bernstein, 238–63. New Brunswick, NJ: Rutgers University Press, 1999.

Zaretsky, Eli. "The Culture Wars of the 1960s and the Assault on the Presidency." In *Our Monica Ourselves: The Clinton Affair and the National Interest,* ed. Lauren Berlant and Lisa Duggan, 9–33. New York: New York University Press, 2001.

# Chapter 5

## GENRE GOES PASTICHE: GENRE IN CONTEMPORARY HOLLYWOOD

At the beginning of Robert Altman's 1992 film *The Player*, there's a deservedly famous scene in which the audience is privy to a gloriously long take featuring assorted Hollywood folks, some real, some fictional, pitching projects to studio execs of varying levels. They range in type and scope, from "*The Graduate, Part II*," featuring Julia Roberts as the recently graduated from college daughter of Ben and Elaine Braddock to a Goldie Hawn vehicle called "*Goldie Goes to Africa*," that's both like *The Gods Must be Crazy*—"except the coke bottle is an actress"—and a combination of "*Out of Africa* meets *Pretty Woman*." There's even a pitch for a Bruce Willis movie, a "psychic, political, thriller comedy with a heart" that's "not unlike *Ghost* meets *Manchurian Candidate*." Coming as it does from one of the more renowned stalwarts of the heady days of 1970s American filmmaking, the point of Altman's piquantly hilarious send-up is sharply wrought: whereas in previous eras of Hollywood filmmaking there were always pockets of resistant filmmakers who could make movies that went beyond the pale of conventional commercial filmmaking and still hope to be able to secure some sort of studio financing and theatrical distribution for the work, by the end of the 1980s that hope was seemingly dead, replaced instead by the creative and fiscal realities of a new corporate Hollywood dominated by risk-averse Ivy League MBAs in positions of decision-making power who were loathe to make anything they couldn't sell to an audience as a recognizable text. Ironically, right as *The Player* was coming out, Hollywood was enjoying the nascence of what was arguably its greatest era of independent filmmaking, though, as illustrated in chapter 3, it would prove to be short-lived and lead back to even more difficult realities for artistic-minded filmmakers. In hindsight it's clear that Altman's comic point has, in fact, turned out to be remarkably prescient, as what was a highly exaggerated insiders' joke in 1992 has since become gospel in contemporary Hollywood. While much has changed in Hollywood since the late 1980s, one thing has remained constant, and that's the role genre plays in filmmaking, especially as concerns the studios and what they choose to fund, which has increasingly become films that are easily recognized and categorized by audiences.

Contemporarily, genre is more important in the industry than perhaps at any other point in its history. What comprises an individual genre is open to debate, and in some cases, such as in that of film noir, genre theorists argue over whether or not something is a film genre or a type of film. On a more artistic level, genre is a kind of classification that allows us to put films in a grouping based on certain stylistic and/or narrative traits, just as we would with any other kind of art form. So just as we can classify certain paintings in accordance to their characteristics as being impressionist, realist, surrealist, modernist, or abstract impressionist, so too can you look at the tropes present in films and identify them as westerns, gangster pics, musicals, sci-fi films, and so forth. But on a more practical level, that which is justifiably practiced by the studios, films genres are simply the formulae used in making popular films, thus allowing them to be more easily sold to the public and also, at least illusorily, allowing studio accounting types to estimate the likely success of a new film based on how films of a similar type have done in the past.

By design, film genres are a little different than genre categories in other art forms as concerns how they're judged qualitatively, in that the kinds of things that might be considered negatives when talking about things like novels or plays—patently predictable plots, static heroes, repetitive generic iconography, and so on—are essential elements of film genres' narrative systems. Because a film's genre identification also plays a role in how it's marketed by a given studio, the goal is not to make something new and original and unrecognizable; rather, as parodied in *The Player*, it's to make something with which the audience is highly familiar and comfortable, which presumably makes them more likely to want to pay to see it. On occasion filmmakers are able to do interesting things within a given form, but it's rare that a filmmaker can ignore form completely. In fact, regardless of genre, the overwhelming majority of films feature a goal-oriented protagonist. The generic protagonist is introduced, as is his or her generically appropriate goal, and the rest of the story centers on he or (more rarely) she overcoming the obstacles in the way of achieving said goal. Most films resolve with the goal being reached, although once in a while they don't.

Film genres may be time-tested marketable formulae, but that doesn't mean they're stagnant. Indeed, one of the great pleasures of film genres is that they have an interestingly incestuous relationship with their audience, both reflecting the social and aesthetic sensibilities of their audience and also shaping it. By necessity then, film genres evolve. At the simplest level, genre films exist because they make money. But they evolve because the same film can't keep making money, at least not forever. We don't want to see the same film, but we want to see the same form. Each genre film poses to its audience the same central question: "Do you still want to believe this?" Or, more succinctly, "Do you still like me?" Popularity, and sequels, occurs when the audience says, "Yes." When the audience says, "No, no we don't," evolution eventually results and we get new variations of the form. Individual occurrences within specific genres have the ability to change a genre as a whole. So, for example, you get a film like *Avatar* (Cameron 2009). Based on

*Avatar*'s massive worldwide success, it's safe to argue that because of the amazingly convincing way James Cameron uses technology to create an alternate future universe, all subsequent makers of science fiction films will likely have to take this into account, as it has changed audiences' expectations of what a futuristic film will look like. Indeed, *Avatar* is the film that has proven the new 3D technology viable, as already a number of high-profile blockbuster event pictures have been announced as 3D projects, and a number of films already in the can, most notably *Clash of the Titans* (Leterrier 2010), have been converted to 3D after the fact. Similarly, cultural circumstances can change a genre, an example of which is seen in the case of westerns, which were once by far the most popular kind of American film. But around the time of the Vietnam War, a culturally hegemonic genre that has its roots in the myth of American exceptionalism lost its luster and audiences couldn't stomach seeing the cowboys overrunning the Indians, and the genre took a nosedive from which it never really recovered.

As film moves increasingly into the digital age, genre films have as strong a presence as they ever have in the American cinema, in part because of the rise of sequels and remakes in the past 30 years of Hollywood filmmaking. In looking back over this period and observing the continuing evolution of and notable films produced in the traditional genres—noirs, romantic comedies, biopics, teen films, horror movies, gangster films, westerns, and so on—as well as looking extensively at the ubiquity of several previously less utilized forms, including but not necessarily limited to comic book films of the superhero variety, the adaptation of graphic novels, movies based on TV shows, remakes of old movies, remakes of foreign films, franchise films and their sequels—we can see the large-scale industrial changes that have taken place writ large on the silver screen (or the iPod touch screen, as it were). All of this points to the increasing incidence of films that aren't so much genre films as they are genre pastiches, films that include the most marketably palatable tropes from a wide array of genres so as to best appeal to the largest number of people, perhaps best evidenced first by the unbelievable $1 billion+ box office of James Cameron's *Titanic* (1997)—a historical-recreation-action movie-teen romance-disaster film, and his next film, *Avatar*—a science fiction–themed Vietnam/Iraq war movie with parallels to classical westerns and the creature films of the 1950s and 1960s (Gross)—which is the apotheosis of genre pastiche films.

While all genres continue to be made, though surely some more than others, several genres in particular have experienced a flowering of sorts over the past several decades, perhaps none more so than action movies, which Jeannette Catsoulis describes as "the generic brutishness that Hollywood grinds out more efficiently than any other trope." Their rise is not particularly surprising, given that many films now reap more box office overseas than they do in the United States. In fact, a number of films initially widely derided as box office flops in the end weren't, in large part because of their ability to make money overseas. Take films like Universal Pictures' *The Last Action Hero* (McTiernan 1993) and

*Waterworld* (Reynolds 1995) for example. As soon as it was announced, *The Last Action Hero* was a widely anticipated film, featuring the teaming of Arnold Schwarzenegger and veteran *Die Hard* (1988) director John McTiernan (*Box Office Mojo.com*). However, it was beset by a troubled production, as was widely reported at the time and later chronicled in chapters in Nancy Griffin and Kim Masters' *Hit and Run* and James Robert Parish's *Fiasco: A History of Hollywood's Iconic Flops.* Its release was met with poor reviews, perhaps fueled in part by the negative press stemming from the production difficulties (sometimes the media smells blood with certain movies), and followed by poor word of mouth. Additionally, the following week Steven Spielberg's *Jurassic Park* came out and crushed everything in its path at the box office, including *The Last Action Hero,* which would ultimately gross only $50 million domestically, which against its $85 million production budget was apparently poor showing indeed. Even so, *The Last Action Hero* grossed another $87 million internationally, bringing its total take to $137 million (*Box Office Mojo.com*). While the film profited when measured against its production budget, it almost certainly lost money when prints and advertising are taken into account. Still, when taken in the context of the gamut of all Hollywood releases, *The Last Action Hero* was far from the massive bomb it's still purported to be. It certainly wasn't a failure of epic proportions like, say, *The Adventures of Pluto Nash* (Underwood 2002), the $100 million Eddie Murphy vehicle that grossed less than $8 million domestic and international combined (*Box Office Mojo.com*). Many films every year lose a far greater amount of money percentage-wise. It's just that in the early 1990s, the media didn't report overseas grosses in the same way they contemporarily do, which certainly permanently colored the perception of *The Last Action Hero.*

Likewise, the Kevin Costner vehicle *Waterworld* was a Universal Studios film that was beset by an arduous production and grave cost overruns. The initial production budget was set at $100 by the studio, but it was ultimately rumored to have cost in the neighborhood of $175 million, which is a lot for a film even now and was a fortune then. When adjusted to today's dollars, the film still ranks as among the most expensive ever made. The on-set difficulties resulted in the press dubbing it "*Fishtar,*" a reference to the notorious Warren Beatty/Dustin Hoffman flop *Ishtar* (May 1987), before it was even released (Kempley). While the film wasn't met with the same kind of abysmal reviews as *The Last Action Hero,* it was still not well reviewed, and audiences that had been primed for a disaster for months by the press predictably didn't turn out in the hoped-for numbers, resulting in a domestic take of a disappointing $88 million. But the film went on to earn an additional $175 million worldwide, bringing its total box office take to a very respectable $264 million (*Box Office Mojo.com*). Even adding in prints and advertising, given its decent home video sales, *Waterworld* likely lost little if any money for Universal, even though it too ended up sharing a chapter with another Costner film, *The Postman* (1997), in Parish's *Fiasco.*

Not all failures are equal, especially when taking into account worldwide grosses. Even though the press wasn't reporting them in the early 1990s the way they are now, you can bet the studios were acutely aware that the rise in overseas box office, which had always been strong, had grown to the point where you could use your guesstimation of a film's likely foreign take to hedge your bets on deciding what to make. Certainly, there are plenty of films with horrible reputations that were also box office flops precisely because they didn't make anywhere near enough overseas to recoup their disappointing domestic grosses—*Cutthroat Island* (Harlin 1995), *Showgirls* (Verhoeven 1995), and *Battlefield Earth* (Christian 2000) to name just a few. But there was a clear lesson to be learned from the overseas grosses of films like *The Last Action Hero* and *Waterworld,* and it was that action movies can and often do gross decidedly more overseas than domestically. The Hollywood response was predictable, and, frankly, appropriate. Critics often lament that smart, adult-oriented pictures are a dying breed in the landscape of contemporary Hollywood, and while that's to some extent true, it belies the fact that the companies that make movies are in the business of making money, and smaller, less expensive films, which tend to rely on character interaction instead of visual spectacle, are often by design more culturally specific than their big-budget counterparts, which can severely limit their ability to cash in at the box office internationally. Accordingly, it's smart business to make broad, visually engaging movies that don't require much nuance on the part of the viewers to understand. Top-notch visual effects, and broad physical humor for that matter, are thrilling and funny the world over and they can make even the worst films almost critic proof.

The golden goose for contemporary Hollywood is the tent-pole film that can be the centerpiece of your business plan over time and spread out over various other subsidiary companies in the form of ancillary products, such as video games, toys, DVDs, theme park rides, and so on. And the best kind of tent-pole film is one that is based on a presold property, that is, an extant text or toy or icon of some kind with which large numbers of people would already be familiar. Sometimes a film is so successful in its own right that it has the effect of becoming a presold property for sequels, such as in the case of the original *Indiana Jones* or *Die Hard* movies, both of which resulted in long-running franchises. It's not like these films were wholly original—after all, they were pretty recognizable genre films—but they were original enough to do the trick. But more common is the optioning of a presold property to be adapted for the big screen, which can be wildly successful, like in the cases of the *Harry Potter, Lord of the Rings, Spider-Man,* and *Twilight* films. And it doesn't have to be a book. It can be anything, from a toy (G.I. Joes or Transformers) to a videogame (*Lara Croft: Tomb Raider*). While movie sequels and presold properties have a long history—think about the monster movies of the 1930s and 1940s, not to mention serials and the like—the modern version of this trend began in the 1970s with the *Star Wars* and *Jaws* franchises and has grown to dominate world film culture. When looking at a list of the top 20 films in the history of international theatrical box office (as of 2010), one can't help but notice the commonalities between the movies making up the list. As the list isn't adjusted for inflation, that most of the films are recent is to be expected. But more interestingly telling is the *kind* of films that are on the list:

1. *Avatar* (Cameron 2009, Fox) at $2.7 billion. At first look this might seem like an exception to the rule in that it's not based on a presold property, nor was it meant to be the first film in a new franchise (though talk of a possible sequel started circulating almost immediately upon its ridiculously successful release [Ditzian]). But its story is overwhelmingly familiar and it expertly mixes the conventions of several genres and utilizes bleeding-edge 3D visuals, putting it right in line with the rest of the films on the list.
2. *Titanic* (Cameron 1997, a joint production between Fox and Viacom subsidiary Paramount) at $1.8 billion. While technically not based on a presold property, it is based on a widely known true story (it's not like anyone was surprised when the ship sank) that's been repeatedly chronicled in print and film over the years, and, like *Avatar,* also has the elements of several genres and stunning cutting-edge (at the time) special effects.
3. *The Lord of the Rings: The Return of the King* (Jackson 2003, New Line Cinema, a subsidiary of Time Warner) at $1.1 billion. The third and final film of the series based on J.R.R. Tolkien's much-loved classic fantasy trilogy. As of 2011, *The Hobbit,* Tolkien's predecessor to *The Lord of the Rings,* is in production and plans are to take the book and split it into two movies, so as to maximize its financial potential. The same profit maximizing strategy is also being used in the filmic adaptations of the final books in the *Harry Potter* and *Twilight* series, each of which will also result in two movies.
4. *Pirates of the Caribbean: Dead Man's Chest* (Verbinski 2006, Buena Vista, a subsidiary of Disney) at $1.06 billion. The second installment of the movie based on the classic Disneyland ride.
5. *Alice in Wonderland* (Burton 2010, Buena Vista, a subsidiary of Disney) at $1.02 billion. Based on Lewis Carroll's classic children's book, which has been adapted repeatedly in a variety of media over the years. Also the sixth Tim Burton film in which Johnny Depp has starred.
6. *The Dark Knight* (Nolan 2008, Warner Brothers) at $1 billion. This was the second of three planned Nolan-directed films in a franchise reboot, which features the relaunch of a character that still had many extant DC comic book titles; several earlier TV shows, both live action and animated; and a number of previous movies, including a five-film franchise for the same studio that was kicked off with Tim Burton's *Batman* in 1989.
7. *Harry Potter and the Sorcerer's Stone* (Columbus 2001, Warner Brothers) at $974 million. This is the first installment of the franchise based on J. K. Rowling's wildly successful book series.
8. *Pirates of the Caribbean: At World's End* (Verbinski 2007, Buena Vista, a subsidiary of Disney) at $961 million. The third installment of the *Pirates'* franchise.

9. *Harry Potter and the Order of the Phoenix* (Yates 2007, Warner Brothers) at $938 million. The fifth film in the *Harry Potter* franchise. Of special note here is the fact that the six films in the series to date have had four different directors, whereas other recent film franchises such as *Pirates, Star Wars, Spider-Man,* and the new *Batman,* feature a single helmer guiding the series' direction from film to film. This indicates that in this instance the property is more important than the talent, at least behind the scenes (though to be fair, David Yates directed both parts of the final installment as well). Conversely, at this point it would be almost impossible to replace Daniel Radcliffe, Emma Watson, and Rupert Grint as Harry, Hermione, and Ron.

10. *Harry Potter and the Half-Blood Prince* (Yates 2009, Warner Brothers) at $934 million. The sixth film in the series.

11. *The Lord of the Rings: The Two Towers* (Jackson 2002, New Line Cinema, a subsidiary of Time Warner) at $925 million. The second film in the trilogy.

12. *Star Wars: Episode I—The Phantom Menace* (Lucas 1999, Lucasfilm and Fox) at $924 million. While technically a prequel to the anachronistically released previous three *Star Wars* films, episodes IV through VI, it had been so long since the release of *The Return of the Jedi* (1983 Marquand, Lucasfilm), that for all intents and purposes, this essentially served the same function as a franchise reboot. It's unique in that it's kind of an independent film, although George Lucas's Lucasfilm has a long-standing distribution agreement in place with Fox, so it was never a film in search of a purchaser; it was always positioned as a high-powered box office behemoth, which it was.

13. *Shrek 2* (Adamson and Asbury 2004, DreamWorks and DreamWorks Animation) at $919 million. The second film in the animated franchise based on William Steig's children's book *Shrek.* DreamWorks and DreamWorks Animation were owned by the media mogul triumvirate of David Geffen, Jeffrey Katzenberg, and Steven Spielberg, making it not quite a major, but close. It's been called a mini-major in the same way that Summit and Lions Gate have. What separates them from the true majors is that they aren't owned by one of the six major media conglomerates, although they do enter into distribution agreements with them, much as Columbia, Universal, and United Artists used to do with the big five studios—MGM, Fox, Warner Brothers, Paramount, and RKO—back in the heyday of the classical studio era. And even with the huge industry clout and pocketbooks of its founders, Dream-Works has had a hard time staying independent. To whit, DreamWorks Animation has an exclusive distribution deal with Viacom subsidiary Paramount. And the DreamWorks live action studio, after supposedly nearing bankruptcy more than once, was purchased by Paramount in 2006, where it remained until 2009 when it broke off again with the help of the monetary investment of India's Reliant Media Group and an exclusive distribution deal with Disney, proving that even the media's apparent big boys aren't so big when competing against the mighty powers of a worldwide media conglomerate (McClintock).

14. *Jurassic Park* (Spielberg 1993, Universal) at $914 million. The first film in the *Jurassic Park* trilogy based on the Michael Crichton novel *Jurassic Park.*

15. *Harry Potter and the Goblet of Fire* (Newell 2005, Warner Brothers) at $895 million. The fourth film in the series.

16. *Spider-Man 3* (Raimi 2007, Sony Pictures subsidiary Columbia) at $890 million. Based on the iconic Marvel comic book hero of the same name.

17. *Ice Age: Dawn of the Dinosaurs* (Saldanha and Thurmeier 2009, Fox subsidiary Blue Sky Studios) at $884 million. The third film in the animated franchise. The first movie was based on an original story, but the next two (to date) were the result of the success of the first one, which makes them based on a presold property. Also, it's important not to underestimate the allure of animated films, which kids and parents tend to flock to, seemingly with little regard for the quality of either the animation or the narrative.

18. *Harry Potter and the Chamber of Secrets* (Columbus 2002, Warner Brothers) at $876 million. The second film in the series.

19. *The Lord of the Rings: The Fellowship of the Ring* (Jackson 2001, New Line Cinema, a subsidiary of Time Warner). The first film in the trilogy.

20. *Finding Nemo* (2003 Stanton and Unkrich, Buena Vista, a subsidiary of Disney) at $864 million. This film was based on an original story, although it's not quite that simple. Pixar has been unprecedented in its string of successes in creating animated films that appeal to people of all ages. So much so, that I would argue that after its first couple of films, the company name has become the presold property in that people are excited when a new Pixar film comes out, much in the way they used to be when a new Disney animated movie came out. So it makes sense that Disney would purchase Pixar outright and make it its primary animation arm, which they did in 2006, thus allowing them to get more of the profits than they did when they were just distributing Pixar movies and also perhaps allowing Pixar a little more financial flexibility as well, although that was supposedly going to be the case when Disney bought Miramax, and that certainly didn't end well (Hof). Also, *Nemo* definitely adheres to the long-running orphan/dead parent(s) motif that runs through Disney's animated films. Interestingly, despite its massive success, Pixar has chosen, with the exception of the *Toy Story* films, to eschew sequels and instead concentrate on original stories, all of which to date have been remarkably lucrative and well reviewed (with the exception of *Cars,* which was a box office behemoth but not a critics' darling). That said, the enormously successful *Toy Story 3* came out in 2010 and sequels to *Monsters, Inc., Finding Nemo,* and *Cars* are being discussed so what Pixar does in the future will continue to be interesting to watch. (*Box Office Mojo.com,* "All Time")

The list is instructive in that it shows the contemporary dominance of generic big studio franchise films in international box office. In a strange kind of inverse logic, in a lot of ways it makes more sense for a company to invest a couple of hundred million or more dollars in the production of a presold property than it does to spend $30 million to make and distribute a movie based on an original script, as the higher budgeted film might actually have less risk involved in the investment. In fact, in perusing the top 500 films in all-time international box office, what becomes clear is that the previous illustrative exercise could literally go on with little variance over the course of the list's entirety, as the vast majority of these films are readily identifiable genre films based on presold properties, whereas critically revered art films—not to mention films not produced in the United States—just aren't on the list. The numbers speak for themselves.

The template for a franchise film—or a one-off à la *2012* (Emmerich 2009) for that matter—that can do well at the box office internationally tends to be an adaptation of a presold property that can be visually spectacular and not too culturally specific. This more often than not lends itself to an action-oriented and/or science fiction film, which can be somewhat critic proof as tons of mediocre—or worse—films of this style have gone on to enormous box office returns. But it's dangerous to get too caught up in critical response to a film anyway, as from a business point of view the only real barometer for a film's success or failure is the bottom line. It's fun to argue the merits of particular films, but in the end it's strictly bar talk for aesthetes. And if box office returns tell us anything, it's that most people aren't going to the movies for a museum experience or a poetry reading or any other kind of high art exposure—they want to be entertained, period. If the two happen to intersect now and again, then so be it, but it's certainly not required or overtly desired by the lion's share of consumers of Hollywood's annual output.

Repetition is essential to all genre films, not just franchise or tent-pole films that can be spun off into multiple installments, but even to films that aren't intended to have sequels. To sell, genre films still need to be recognizable to the audience, which means, just as *The Player* suggests, that they're best served slightly warmed over. Perhaps no genre does this more successfully than romantic comedies, which can come in a number of varieties, although the most high profile tend to be star vehicles, which means that in the case of romantic comedies, it's the genre and its stars that are the presold properties. And whereas it's men who are most often associated with action and science fiction films, more often than not romantic comedy is a genre for which women become known. So even though some men are associated with romantic comedies—Hugh Grant, for example—when most people think of romantic comedies, they often don't even think of the films so much as they do the female stars: Meg Ryan and Julia Roberts or, more contemporarily, Drew Barrymore, Sandra Bullock, Renée Zellweger, Reese Witherspoon, and so on. Their star personas are a huge part of a given film's appeal and they are marketed accordingly, which can result in the creation of not just a singularly successful film, but a franchise in its own right. Examples include Zellweger's *Bridget Jones* movies (Maguire 2001, Kidron 2004) based on the novels and columns of Helen Fielding, Bullock's *Miss Congeniality* films (Petrie 2000, Pasquin 2005), and Witherspoon's two *Legally Blonde* films (Luketic 2001, Herman-Wurmfeld 2003), which not only made Witherspoon a star but also went on to spawn a made-for-TV movie and even, inexplicably, a hit Broadway musical! And much more rarely are instances in which a man is in a romantic comedy that's so popular it spawns a franchise, as is the case with Ben Stiller's *Meet the . . .* series of films (Roach 2000, 2004; Weitz 2010). Romantic comedies don't do as well as the aforementioned tent-pole films overseas in that they don't normally make way more abroad than they do at home, but then again they don't cost nearly as much either, which means that they don't have to. Still, based on the draw of their stars, they often make almost as much as overseas as they do in the States, which has made them traditionally very profitable and a large part of the bedrock of the foundation upon which Hollywood studios have built their business, which they're likely to remain forever.

But even a genre as time-tested and somewhat intractable as romantic comedies can evolve, as romantic comedies have done with the rise of the so-called bromantic comedies (also known as dick flicks or frat pack movies) highlighted by the work of those affiliated with Judd Apatow's Apatow Productions. These films are in some ways generic hybrids in that they clearly stem from male-dominated teen films along the lines of the *American Pie* series, but the premise—what happens when these teens become 20-, or 30-, or 40-somethings?—is a smart take on an old form that has resulted in a not so subtle reworking of the traditional romantic comedy in which our romantic couple has changed from a man and a woman to a man and a man, or, in some instances, a man and his men. While there are certainly homoerotic undertones to these films, the men aren't overtly gay; they just don't know how to grow up and they are loathe to leave the safety of boyhood friendships behind. Just as there are in straight romantic comedies, there is normally a love triangle; it's just that rather than a good guy and a bad guy fighting for the affections of a woman it's a man fighting against his desires to both be with a woman and remain a boy, which often results in surprisingly sweet stories, despite the Apatow Productions' tendency towards verbal crudity. The actors associated with these films include Luke and Owen Wilson, Will Ferrell, Seth Rogan, Paul Rudd, Vince Vaughn, Jonah Hill, Michael Cera, Jason Segel, and others. A number of directors have tackled the form, including Judd Apatow with *The 40-Year-Old Virgin* (2005), *Knocked Up* (2007), and *Funny People* (2009); Todd Phillips with *Old School* (2003) and *The Hangover* (2009); Greg Mottola with *Superbad* (2007); and Nicholas Stoller with *Forgetting Sarah Marshall* (2008), which was written by veteran Apatow player Jason Segel.

Among other traditional franchises that continue to flourish are horror films, for which there are a lot of reasons. At the root of the genre's appeal is an eons-old appeal to myth and the human subconscious in which we are haunted by our dreams of imagined monsters of all shapes and sizes. For a lot of people, being scared is a ton of fun and going to do it at a movie theater, where you can be truly scared but are in actuality totally safe, is an incredibly satisfying experience. And there's a lot of appeal for people in the business of making movies as well. In the early era of the studio system, Universal made a mint making horror films, including such classics of the genre as *Dracula* (Browning 1931), *Frankenstein* (Whale 1931), and *The Mummy* (Freund 1932), and all of the many sequels. As a minor studio (a studio that didn't own and control the means to exhibit its own product), it was very difficult for Universal to make the high-budget star vehicles of its major counterparts. Instead, Universal found gold by making movies out of presold properties based on monsters, which could be made fairly cheaply and quickly. In order to keep costs down, Universal directors would sometimes even use darkness and smoke to avoid having to build whole sets! These films made stars out of Boris Karloff and Bela Lugosi, but even that wasn't an issue back then as they were under studio contracts and the costs of their labors were relatively fixed, unlike contemporarily when a star can ask for a lot more money for a sequel.

And the attraction of horror films remains just as strong for the contemporary film studios and probably always will. The beauty of them is they can be made comparatively cheaply, and they have a predictable built-in teen audience that does a lot to offset potential financial risk. They aren't globe-trotting films that require extensive or elaborate location shooting and they aren't normally star vehicles either. In fact, in many ways, that's the genius of these films; the monsters are the stars and, as such, if you cover the actor's face it's possible that someone different can play the lead in every film. So, for example, psychotic hockey-mask-clad Jason Vorhees of the *Friday the 13th* series, which has been going strong since 1980, has been played by multiple actors, as has the serial-killing Michael Myers, who has been killing oversexed teens since the first *Halloween* film way back in 1978. Sometimes, however, an actor becomes synonymous with a role—as did Lugosi and Karloff—and his presence becomes essential to the series' success, as was the case with Robert Englund's repeated turn as Freddy Krueger in the long-running *Nightmare on Elm Street* film series (after nearly 30 years he finally ceded the role to Jackie Earle Haley in 2010). As for the supporting casts, which are essentially victim fodder for the killer, they routinely consist of highly unknown but very attractive young actors. Some of them, Jamie Lee Curtis, Kevin Bacon, and Johnny Depp to name a few, rise from obscurity to become stars, but most simply endure their gruesome but creatively done executions and then remain forevermore in the trash bin of Hollywood obscurity. If a movie does well and sequels are made, then you just get a new group of youngsters and kill them off as well, which you can do pretty much infinitely.

A tent-pole film—a film the you can build your entire production slate around—is in some ways a relatively new concept, but a franchise film is not. To whit, when a horror film is a huge hit, it can very quickly spawn a franchise, which, going back to the aforementioned Universal films, has always been the case. Indeed, Universal's *Dracula, The Mummy,* and *Frankenstein* all spawned multiple sequels. While horror films don't normally make enough money to be tent-pole films in that a studio can't build their business around them, they are the definition of franchise films in that they become a formulaic blueprint that can be made repeatedly and, for the movie business, a reliable income generator. So, for instance, when Miramax's Harvey Weinstein began taking higher risks on bigger-dollar productions, it was his brother Bob's subsidiary company Dimension Films that put the most coin in their coffers by making comparatively low-budget and profitable genre films, including the multiple films in the *Hellraiser, Scream,* and other horror franchises. Not surprisingly, in this era in which franchises are highly sought-after commodities, horror films, historically the most successful genre at generating franchises, have flourished, resulting in the establishment and continuation of loads of franchises, including *The Mummy* (the story of the first of which was based on the same story as that of the 1932 Universal version), *Underworld, Saw, Final Destination,* and *Resident Evil* series. Additionally, there's even been horror franchise crossovers such as *Freddy vs. Jason* (Yu 2003), *Alien vs. Predator* (Anderson 2004), and *Alien vs. Predator: Requiem* (Strause and Strause 2007). This might seem like franchise genre filmmaking taken to the nth degree, a new and unprecedentedly cynical exercise in cold and calculated blatantly commercial filmmaking. While it is some of those things, what it's not is new. Again, going back to Universal, which unapologetically made films such as *Frankenstein Meets the Wolf Man* (Neill 1943) and *Abbott and Costello Meet Frankenstein* (Barton 1948)—which also featured Bela Lugosi as Dracula and Lon Chaney Jr. as the Wolf Man—this kind of thing has been around in Hollywood forever.

Indeed, it sometimes really does feel as though there's nothing new under sun. As a young and very impressionable college student in the mid-1980s, I remember taking an Introduction to Fiction class from an ancient but marvelously distinguished and courtly professor who had trained in the New Criticism with the Fugitive Poets at Vanderbilt University in the 1930s. That first day of class he told us, "There are no new stories, as all stories can be categorized as being about either love, death, or war. But when someone finds a way to tell one of the old stories in a new way, well then that's what makes art." It stuck with me and I still believe that in a lot of ways that wily old teacher was right. And since that time, I've repeatedly been struck by how often filmmakers find amazing new ways to tell the same old stories, even within the confines of genre filmmaking, and that has prevented the movies from ever growing stale for me. This remains true and I'm pretty optimistic that it always will. That said, in the movie business at the moment, seemingly everything old is new again. Only it's not really new. It's just repackaged as such but it's not new at all. Nowhere is this more true than in the areas of remakes and adaptations of TV series. Adapting a presold property to the big screen, say in the case of *Lord of the Rings* or *Harry Potter,* is all well and good and that sort of thing has been done forever. But making a TV show into a movie is another thing entirely. In the rare instance that it's a loose adaptation and advances the source material in another direction in an interesting way—as in something like the knowingly wry *Addams Family Values* (Sonnenfeld 1993) or *The Brady Bunch Movie* (Thomas 1995)—then that's one thing. But too often Hollywood makes crass films that make it seem simultaneously bereft of new ideas and ridiculously hard up for presold properties. Did they really have to make films based on TV shows like *Scooby Doo, The Flintstones, Land of the Lost,* or *Bewitched?* Or worse, any number of third-rate *Saturday Night Live* skits? Yeah, I liked *Wayne's World* (Spheeris 1992 ) too, but *It's Pat* (Bernstein 1994) or *A Night at the Roxbury* (Fortenberry 1998)? C'mon.

Not content to mine TV shows for story ideas—although are they really ideas if you're just cribbing for the big screen?—Hollywood also remakes its own films on an increasingly regular basis. And I'm not sure what's worse, the remaking of films that weren't that great to begin with—think something like *The Island of Dr. Moreau* (Taylor 1977, Frankenheimer 1996), *Doctor/Dr. Dolittle* (Fleischer 1967, Thomas 1998), and *Around the World in 80 Days* (Anderson 1956, Coraci 2004)—or the desecration of classics remade for a contemporary audience, à la *The Women* (Cukor 1939, English 2008), *The Getaway* (Peckinpah 1972, Donaldson 1994), *Planet of the Apes* (Schaffner 1968, Burton 2001), *Willy Wonka/ Charlie and the Chocolate Factory* (Stuart 1971, Burton 2005), *King Kong* (Cooper 1933, Jackson 2005), *Charade/The Truth About Charlie* (Donen 1963, Demme 2002), *Mr. Deeds Goes to Town/Mr. Deeds* (Capra 1936, Brill 2002), *The Manchurian Candidate* (Frankenheimer 1962, Demme 2004), and so on. Horror films in particular seem prone to remakes, although perhaps this is less surprising, as in addition to the idea that the killer's rampage is somehow a punishment for the real or imagined sins of society, so too is the seemingly immortal recyclable killer a generic hallmark. And thus in recent years we've had new versions of *The Texas Chainsaw Massacre* (Nispel 2003), *Dawn of the Dead* (Snyder 2004), *The Amityville Horror* (Douglas 2004), *The Fog* (Wainwright 2005), *The Hills Have Eyes* (Aja 2006), *Halloween* (Zombie 2007), *Friday the 13th* (Nispel 2009), and *A Nightmare on Elm Street* (Bayer 2010).

Perhaps the aforementioned horror films aren't so much remakes as they are franchise reboots, itself an interesting phenomenon. When a successful franchise gets tired and loses its financial luster, why kill it off? Why not just go back and start over? After all, the James Bond films have been doing this forever, rebooting the series every time they bring a new Bond on board, which has resulted in the longest-running Hollywood film franchise. While this didn't work so well for Warner Brothers when they tried to restart the once mighty *Superman* movie franchise with *Superman Returns* (Singer 2006), it worked out fantastically when they let Christopher Nolan reboot their ailing *Batman* series, which he did with *Batman Begins* (2005). Indeed, rather than concede the point following the relative failure of the latest *Superman* movie, WB instead retrenched and dug in, handing the reigns over to Nolan, who will produce the sequel to the reboot in the hopes of capturing lightning in a bottle twice. Nolan is an amazing talent and his hiring is about the best WB can hope to do in avoiding the same kind of poor showing Universal had with its failed attempts to first start—*Hulk* (Lee 2003)—and then restart—*The Incredible Hulk* (Leterrier 2008)—a franchise around Marvel Comics' Hulk character.

Additionally, in its insatiable appetite for recyclable generic material, Hollywood has increasingly looked outside of America's borders for films to remake. This has resulted in all kinds of English-language films being remade, although most of them are based on somewhat older films, such as *Alfie* (Gilbert 1966, Shyer 2004), *The Ladykillers* (Mackendrick 1955, Coen Brothers 2004), *The Stepford Wives* (Forbes 1975, Oz 2004), and *The Italian Job* (Collinson 1969, Gray 2003). The original films are old enough that younger audiences likely won't have heard of them much less seen them, and older audiences aren't nearly as big a demographic target of interest for Hollywood so their possible familiarity with the originals is a negligible concern. They've also taken to remaking foreign-language films in English for contemporary audiences, such as *Spoorloos/The Vanishing* (Sluizer 1988, Netherlands; Sluizer 1993), *La Femme Nikita/Point of No Return* (Besson 1990, France; Badham 1993), *Abres Los Ojos/Vanilla Sky* (Amenábar 1997, Spain; Crowe 2001), *Ringu/The Ring* (Nakata 1998, Japan; Verbinski 2002), *Infernal Affairs/The Departed* (Lau and Mak 2002, Hong Kong; Scorsese 2006), *Let the Right One In/Let Me In* (Alfredson 2008, Reeves 2010), and *Bangkok Dangerous* (1999, Thailand; 2008), in which Danny Pang and Oxide Pang Chun, like Sluizer, direct the English-language remake of their own foreign-language movie (Willmore). That some of these remakes are themselves excellent films belies a somewhat ugly implication underlying the remaking of foreign-language films, and that's the tacit assumption that American audiences are too unwilling and/or stupid to go see a subtitled movie. This might be true when it comes to niche-type art films such as the *Three Colors* series (*Blue, White,* and *Red* [Kieslowski 1993, 1994, 1994]), but the same can be said for the English-language equivalent, films like David Lynch's *Inland Empire* (2006) and Gus Van Sant's *Paranoid Park* (2007). They just aren't mainstream films and they weren't intended to be. They're adventurous films made for an audience looking for an alternative to mainstream fare, the same audience that finds itself frustrated when trying to find foreign films in the theaters, as they play on very few American screens, the majority of which are either in big cities or college towns. They are increasingly hard to find in part because of the rise of what Therese Guirgis, head of independent film distributor Wellspring Media, calls "'mini-major pseudo indie productions' . . . which are distributed by divisions of the major Hollywood studios, but compete for the same art house space as foreign titles" (Kaufman). Yet one can't help but wonder, what if the original versions of *Ringu* or *Infernal Affairs* got some sort of wide release? The reason Hollywood adapted them in the first place is that they were akin to that which they normally make, and hence might meet with some success in the market. And they did and then some. But might not the original versions have done well given the chance to do so? We'll never know, and that's a shame. In addition to remaking foreign films, the lure of Hollywood, with its huge budgets and international marketing machine, has proven quite strong for a number of foreign filmmakers, who have jumped at the chance to work under its auspices, among the most successful of whom have been the Mexican-born trio of Guillermo del Toro, who has directed both *Hellboy* (2004, 2008) movies; Alfonso Cuarón, who directed an installment of the *Harry Potter* series, *Harry Potter and the Prisoner of Azkaban* (2004), and

*Children of Men* (2006); and Alejandro Iñárritu, who directed *21 Grams* (2003) and *Babel* (2006).

Even with country of origin becoming much harder to nail down in this age of multinational financing, foreign-language films are the kiss of death in American cinema, which is interesting given that in most of the rest of the world you'll be able to see more movies from Hollywood than from whatever country you happen to be in (Tuttle). And in most countries where this isn't the case (China and North Korea come to mind), it's government intervention that keeps Hollywood voices from dominating the screen, but thriving DVD black markets still give the people what they want. Or else there's infrastructure issues, as in India, which has been a tough market for Hollywood to crack, although that's now changing with an influx of multiplex construction in recent years. Conversely, even though India's Bollywood film industry routinely puts out more films per annum than Hollywood, there's virtually no space for their films in American movie theaters (*India Today*). In fact, the best-known Bollywood film in the States—*Slumdog Millionaire* (2008)—isn't a Bollywood movie at all, but a film financed by a number of U.S. and foreign companies, directed by Scotsman Danny Boyle, and released primarily by Fox Searchlight after WB shut down their boutique Picturehouse division. The big six media companies have a stranglehold on distribution and exhibition that they aren't likely to lose any time soon, if ever, which means that American movies will continue to dominate the world's screens, which is a shame because America certainly doesn't have a lock on original and innovative filmmaking talent. But alas, until the system changes, the Abbas Kiarostamis, Wong Kar-wais, Jacques Audiards, Michael Hanekes, and Joon-ho Bongs of the world will remain unknown in the States by all but the most obsessive cinephiles.

Two warhorse genres remain as popular and successful as they ever have, and that's biopics and literary adaptations. They are both by definition based on presold properties, and that's especially appealing to contemporary Hollywood studios. As for biopics, the personalities depicted are normally already famous and so are properties unto themselves, and further adding to the value is that many biopics are themselves based on best-selling books. Additionally, Oscar loves a good biopic, so they are often award fodder as well—in perusing a list of biopics of the past 20 or so years, one can't help but notice how many of them have been serious major award contenders and/or winners. If the person is also a writer or a musician and the film can result in an increase in ancillary book and/or record sales, then all the better. And larger than life figures are best played by larger than life figures, so the plumb parts tend to go to A-list actors, making most biopics star vehicles as well. Hence, biopics of note in recent years include films such as *Braveheart* (Gibson 1995, also starring Mel Gibson), *Erin Brockovich* (Soderbergh 2000, starring Julia Roberts), *A Beautiful Mind* (Howard 2001, starring Russell Crowe), *Ali* (2001, starring Will Smith), *Finding Neverland* (2004, starring Johnny Depp), *Catch Me If You Can* (Spielberg 2002, starring Leonardo DiCaprio), *The*

*Aviator* (Scorsese 2004, starring Leonardo DiCaprio), *Ray* (Hackford 2004, starring Jamie Foxx), and *Walk the Line* (Mangold 2005, starring Reese Witherspoon and Joaquin Phoenix). More independent-minded biopics still often attract the attention of A-listers wanting the challenge of bringing to life an offbeat story, as in the case of George Clooney directing and cowriting the Edwin R. Murrow film *Good Night, and Good Luck* (2005) and Sean Penn taking on the role of murdered San Francisco politician and gay rights activist Harvey Milk in *Milk* (Van Sant 2008).

Similarly, literary adaptations are often star-driven Oscar bait as well, which looking at a list of them from the past 20 years or so also aptly illustrates. Stereotypical examples include *A River Runs Through It* (Redford 1992, starring Brad Pitt), *The Age of Innocence* (Scorsese 1993, starring Daniel Day-Lewis), *The English Patient* (1996, starring Ralph Fiennes and Juliette Binoche), *Cold Mountain* (Minghella 2003, starring Renée Zellweger, Nicole Kidman, and Jude Law), *Mystic River* (Eastwood 2003, starring Sean Penn, Tim Robbins, and Kevin Bacon), and *The Curious Case of Benjamin Button* (Fincher 2008, starring Brad Pitt and Cate Blanchett). While the aforementioned films are straightforward adaptations, sticking relatively close to their source material, every once in a while a different tack is taken, which can result in some neat and unexpected twists. So, for example, you can get literary adaptations disguised as romantic comedies, as in the cases of *Clueless* (Heckerling 1995), an adaptation of Jane Austen's *Emma* set in a contemporary Los Angeles high school; and *10 Things I Hate About You* (Junger 1999), a remake of Shakespeare's *Taming of the Shrew* set in a contemporary Seattle high school that includes a star-making musical number of "Can't Take My Eyes Off of You" featuring Heath Ledger; or some other sort of innovative reinterpretation of the source material, such as Baz Luhrmann's *Romeo + Juliet* (1996), which retains Shakespeare's dialogue but anachronistically updates the setting to contemporary Verona in which the Montagues and Capulets are akin to warring youth gangs.

Despite the occasional radical reworking of a classic, traditionally the idea of a literary adaptation has been somewhat specific. Many movies are adapted from books, but when you call a film a literary adaptation, you're usually referring to source material that's the kind of stuff that would be taught in high school or college English courses. So cinematic versions of a Shakespeare play or a novel by Jane Austen or Graham Greene are literary adaptations, whereas films based on the novels of John Grisham or Dan Brown are just movies based on books. It's kind of a pretentious way of categorization, but that's just the way these things have historically been thought of, even though the definition of what makes something "literature" or not is pretty vague. After all, who decides? Why aren't the filmic adaptations of the work of Stephen King or Raymond Chandler or Elmore Leonard typically referred to as literary adaptations? And why not comic books, which are certainly considered in the same breath as canonical novels by their legions of fans? Maybe it's because they are so often easily identifiable as genre pics, à la *The Devil Wears Prada* (Frankel 2006, starring Meryl Streep), *The Da Vinci Code* and *Angels & Demons* (Howard, 2006, 2009, starring Tom Hanks), and the *Chronicles of Narnia, Twilight,* and *Harry Potter* films. And it's not like adaptations of serious literature aren't identifiable by their own generic conventions as well. And what about all the adaptations of Stoker's *Dracula* and Mary Shelley's *Frankenstein*? While the sources are reputably literary, it seems whether the movie versions are considered horror films or not has to do with the adaptors. So while the Universal adaptations of Dracula and Frankenstein are blueprint generic horror movies, Francis Ford Coppola's *Bram Stoker's Dracula* (1992) and Kenneth Branagh's *Mary Shelley's Frankenstein* (1993) are typically thought of as literary adaptations despite having all the conventions of a horror film. Perhaps putting the name of the author of the original text in the title was by design so as to avoid the delineation of genre.

At any rate, whether you think their sources are literary or not, one thing that has come to the fore in recent years is movies based on comic books and graphic novels, which in some ways has resulted in their own subgenre. Superhero films have flourished since *Superman* back in the 1970s, and they're well loved by the industry as their success by definition almost guarantees a franchise, but as it turns out, there are only so many iconographic heroes, so currently more comparatively obscure heroes are beginning to get their own movies, which as of yet hasn't proven to be surefire at the box office. That Batman, Superman, and Spider-Man are franchises is no surprise, nor was the attempt to do the same with the Hulk, who is well known despite the apparent difficulty of bringing him to the big screen. That Iron Man and The X Men have done well is also not totally unexpected, as they're well loved within the comic book fanboy community and some of the films were well made. But then so too were *Daredevil* and *Catwoman* and neither of those adaptations were particularly successful, but that they were given a shot doesn't seem unusual. But Hellboy or the Punisher? Ghost Rider? Jonah Hex? Surprisingly, the Hellboy films were both hits, but not so much with the latter films. It appears that there is a finite number of superheroes that are commercially viable, but what that number is remains uncertain. So the practice of bringing comic book superheroes to the big screen looks to continue unabated in the near future. In addition to the aforementioned second attempt at a franchise reboot for Superman and upcoming new installments in the Batman and Iron Man series, movies featuring Captain America, Thor, and The Avengers are also in the pipeline (Graser).

Also of note is the adapting of graphic novels to the big screen, examples of which include *Ghost World* (Zwigoff 2001), *Road to Perdition* (Mendes 2002), *A History of Violence* (Cronenberg 2005), *Sin City* (Miller, Rodriguez, and Tarantino 2005), and *Kick-Ass* (Vaughn 2010). For a lot of reasons, not the least of which was the Comics Code that prevented mainstream comic books from having too much edgy or explicit content, the graphic novel in its current long form didn't much exist prior to the 1980s, at which time independent comic companies began publishing graphic novels that offered an alternative to the mainstream. Like more traditional comic books, the fact that they are storyboarded narratives makes them perfectly suited for cinematic adaptation, even if they don't always feature superheroes and are often much darker in nature and characterized by more complex narratives, which can complicate their journey to the big screen. Indeed, arguably the best-known superhero-based graphic novel is *The Watchmen* (Snyder 2009), Alan Moore's depiction of an alternative universe in which superheroes are banned. The graphic novel is huge and dense and multilayered, in the same way the best literary novels are, and it proved hugely difficult to bring to the screen. Finally, after years of stops and starts, director Zack Snyder, fresh off of directing *300* (2006), a hugely successful adaptation of Frank Miller's graphic novel of the same name, was able to bring the film to the big screen. It was released in the spring of 2009 to lukewarm reviews and disappointing box office ($185 million worldwide against a reported $130 million production budget). It's not a bad movie per se, but the lesson of it is perhaps that while graphic novels are seemingly tailor-made for cinematic adaptation, they don't have the same kind of presold property recognition as their more mainstream comic book counterparts. This doesn't mean they shouldn't be made, it just means that studios should think long and hard before making one with a $100 million+ budget.

As culture changes, so too do audiences' tastes. Additionally, what's going on in the industry can also affect what studios choose to make. So while all genres have always been made by all studios, the frequency with which various genres get made varies a lot over time. While westerns were by far the most popular and oft-made genre films in their heyday, by the late 1960s, they had fallen out of vogue. As mentioned earlier, this was due in part to the cultural reaction to the Vietnam War; a genre that featured cultural imperialism as a recurring key element just didn't have the same appeal for the audience as it did in the afterglow of World War II. Add in the fact that the disassembly of the old studio system meant that studios no longer had the infrastructure (horses, contract players, sets, props, etc.) for westerns housed on their lots, which made westerns more expensive to make, thus further limiting their production and making the comparatively few that were made markedly revisionist of the genre's earlier form. Similarly, the demise of the studio system also made musicals much more expensive to make, as all that talent that's required to do the set-piece scenes we associate with classical Hollywood musicals was no longer on the lot and under contract. And again, with the heightening of the Vietnam War, people just didn't appear as willing as they once did to suspend their disbelief and accept a world in which people spontaneously break out into song and dance. So too did war movies change. In addition to being made less frequently than they had been during the 1950s, their tone underwent a dramatic shift. Gone were the celebratory gung ho pictures along the lines of *Sands of Iwo Jima* (Dwan 1949), and in their place came films that were often quite critical of American action abroad, such as *The Deer*

*Hunter* (Cimino 1978), *Apocalypse Now* (Coppola 1979), *Platoon* (Stone 1986), and *Full Metal Jacket* (Kubrick 1987). War films are certainly still made—*Saving Private Ryan* (Spielberg 1998), *Inglourious Basterds* (Tarantino 2009), and *The Hurt Locker* (Bigelow 2009), for example—but much less frequently and with tonal differences. Musicals and westerns are still made as well, but the same rings true for them, as evidenced by revisionist westerns such as *Unforgiven* (Eastwood 1992) and musicals like *Hedwig and the Angry Inch* (Mitchell 2001), *Moulin Rouge!* (Luhrmann 2001), *8 Mile* (Hanson 2002), and *Chicago* (Marshall 2002).

And while some genres have faded for now, still others come and go, ebbing and flowing with the cultural mood of the country, perhaps no better example of which is film noir. In its classical incarnation, noirs flourished in the immediate post–World War II era. With its dark themes, antiheroes, paranoid tone, and often nihilistic themes, it was seen as a response to the cultural xenophobia that alarmed many of the foreign-born directors of noirs who had immigrated to the United States to escape the rise of European fascism or the native-born directors who were interested in exploring the nooks and crannies of the lives of cultural outsiders. That many of these films were B movies means that they weren't given the same kind of Hays Code scrutiny as their big-budget counterparts, which perhaps allowed their writers and directors to push the boundaries of acceptability more than they otherwise could have. When rebellion slowly began to become mainstream in the late 1950s and early 1960s, film noir's major cycle came to a close as well. Interesting, in the early 1990s, noir—or neo-noir—experienced a mini production boom. Fascinatingly, noir, which is typically critical of mainstream cultural mores, seems to flourish in what are normally seen as good times rather than bad, hence their coming to the fore in the heady days of the *Leave It to Beaver* and *Ozzie and Harriet* nuclear family, with three kids, a dog, and a white picket fence, of the late 1940s and early 1950s, in which American culture was enjoying the fruits of the beginnings of the longest-sustained era of economic growth in American history to that time. As unrest became the norm, or at least much more common, in the 1960s, the genre went dormant with the exception of the occasional one-off success such as *Chinatown* (Polanski 1974). But after the turmoil of the Vietnam era and financial uncertainty of the late 1970s and 1980s, things began to change for the better. Unemployment was low, interest rates were down, and the stock market was on the rise, and beginning in the early 1990s, America was once again in the midst of a sustained economic boom and there was a lot to feel good about. Interestingly, it was in 1989, just as the Berlin Wall was falling and things were beginning to feel as though they were changing for the better, that a new cycle of neo-noir was kicked off by the first of John Dahl's neo-noir trilogy, *Kill Me Again,* which he followed up with *Red Rock West* (1993) and *The Last Seduction* (1994). The time was right and history repeated itself, resulting in a series of pessimistic noirs released against a backdrop of growing cultural optimism, including films such as *After Dark, My Sweet* (Foley 1990), *The Grifters* (Frears 1990), *Barton Fink* (Coen Brothers 1991), *Dead*

*Again* (Branagh 1991), *One False Move* (Franklin 1992), and *Reservoir Dogs* (Tarantino 1992). Like many of their classical predecessors, these were comparatively low-budget films, and as such they could feature the kind of masochistically minded themes that didn't translate to high dollars at the box office and still be relatively financially successful, although that doesn't mean some of them weren't able to be both profitable and very dark. The climax and conclusion of this particular noir cycle was roughly 9/11. Once everything seemingly went black and a lot of people began to question a lot of things, noirs, minus the occasional one-off like David Fincher's *Zodiac* (2007), ceased to be made seemingly overnight, although not without a heaving dying breath that included *American Beauty* (Mendes 1999), *Fight Club* (Fincher 1999), *Memento* (Nolan 2000), *Requiem for a Dream* (Aronofsky 2000), and *Mulholland Drive* (Lynch 2001). Since 2001, America has been constantly embroiled in war and in financial crises and the production of noirs has slowed considerably, thus the implication perhaps is that when times are so obviously bad, who needs a reminder?

Conversely, some genres are always in vogue, an example of which is science fiction, which has pretty much been with us consistently from when the Méliès Brothers made *A Trip to the Moon* way back in 1902! As society has grown more and more technology dependent, the appeal of the technological dystopias often depicted in sci-fi films has only grown stronger. And the fact that the very technology that's used in making movies has increasingly become digitized, thus making the alternate worlds created therein ever more believably fantastical, has only strengthened their appeal. But technological changes can go both ways. The advent of relatively inexpensive, lightweight professional cameras and desktop nonlinear editing systems has been a boon for documentarians, who have been able to make high-quality films on the cheap. But it hasn't often translated into industry opportunities. Documentaries are in many ways niche films, and their mass release is rarely, if ever, rewarded with huge box office. So while films such as *Fahrenheit 9/11* (Moore 2004)—the first and only documentary to gross more than $100 million at the box office—and *March of the Penguins* (Jacquet 2005) enjoyed critical and financial success, the truth of the matter is that they're at best blips on the radar. Only 11 documentaries in film history (4 of which were made by the aforementioned Michael Moore) have made more than $10 million, thus making them an unattractive proposition for studio investment ("Documentary Movies . . . ," *Box Office Mojo.com*). In reality, $1 million is actually a good return for a documentary, and even that's hard to get, as evidenced by 2007 Best Documentary Oscar winner *Taxi to the Dark Side,* which earned only $275,000, or Errol Morris's highly acclaimed Abu Ghraib doc *Standard Operating Procedure* (2008), which grossed an even more disappointing $209,000 (Ansen). The digital boom has in some ways made the situation worse, as too many documentary films are fighting for too few slots for theatrical distribution. So while it's in some ways the golden age of documentary filmmaking in that more good docs are being made than at any other point in history, it hasn't translated to box office success as documentary is a genre that hasn't proven to be financially viable theatrically; more docs being made hasn't resulted into more docs being seen, at least on the big screen.

Digital technology, though, has allowed for a rebirth of animated movies. There's never been a lot of them, as in their classical incarnation they were incredibly labor intensive, requiring thousands and thousands of individually hand drawn cells. It's the classical-era Disney films that were the best known and most revered of this kind (*Snow White and the Seven Dwarfs* [Hand 1937], *Pinocchio* [Luske and Sharpsteen 1940], *Bambi* [Hand 1942], *Cinderella* [Geronimi, Jackson, and Luske 1950], etc.), but over time the movie industry grew to believe animated films to be too time intensive and expensive to bother with. In *The Little Mermaid* (Clements and Musker 1989), Disney made a triumphant return to animated filmmaking, but it was their follow-up, *Beauty and the Beast* (Trousdale and Wise 1991), that would prove even more auspicious, as it was the first Disney animated film to use digital processes in its making, even if it was only for a small part of the ballroom sequence as the technology was still relatively primitive. Still, it was a hint of what was to follow. Computer-generated imagery (CGI) began to evolve quickly, and in 1995 Pixar Studios released *Toy Story* (Lasseter), the first all-CGI animated film, and with that, animated filmmaking entered a new era. Compared to a genre like romantic comedy, there's not a lot of animated films made as they're still quite labor intensive and time consuming to make. But what they have going for them is that they are kid friendly—a desired demographic in that you can get the parents' dollars too as they frequently accompany their kids—and also lend themselves to franchises (e.g., *Shrek, Toy Story, Ice Age,* and *Madagascar*) and concomitant ancillary revenue with toys, video games, coloring books, and the like, which makes animation a highly desirable genre in which contemporary movie studios like to invest.

No genre is more indicative of just how important genre films are in the Hollywood cinematic firmament than are genre parodies. After all, they only work if the audience is familiar enough with the conventions of a particular genre to appreciate the jokes, and make no mistake, as the name implies, they're almost all comedies, even when, or maybe especially when, the genre they parody is often serious, such as the case with the mockumentaries of Christopher Guest, which include *Waiting For Guffman* (1996), *Best in Show* (2000), *A Mighty Wind* (2003), and *For Your Consideration* (2006). While mockumentaries and other kinds of parodies have been made for a long time in Hollywood—consider films like *Take the Money and Run* (Allen 1969), *Airplane!* (Abrahams, Zucker, and Zucker 1980), any number of Mel Brooks films, and the *Naked Gun* films—the fact that more and more of them are being made points to the ever-increasing dominance of genre in Hollywood filmmaking, which is saying something because it's not like genre filmmaking is anything new. It's just that as the inherent financial risks of producing and releasing films has become increasingly expensive, studios have become even more loathe to release films that aren't recognizably generic. Qualitatively, genre parodies can vary widely, from films like *Scream* (Craven 1996), *Talladega Nights* (McKay 2006), *Tropic Thunder* (Stiller 2008), and *Zombieland* (Fleischer 2009), which even while they make you laugh still offer incisive and engaging commentary on that which they are sending up, to films like *Scary Movie* (Wayans 2000), *Meet the Spartans* (Friedberg and Seltzer 2008), and *Disaster Movie* (Friedberg and Seltzer 2008), which are more crass examples of purely commercial genre filmmaking, which is ironic in that's what they're supposed to be making fun of, although perhaps not as ironic as the fact that many of these films—*Scream, Scary Movie,* and the *Date/Disaster/Extreme/Superhero Movie*—have themselves turned into lucrative generic franchises, which seems to me to render their parody moot. How can you make fun of that which you've become, when what you've become is what you set out to parody? This philosophical conundrum has yet to slow the production of genre parodies.

Which brings us back to Altman and *The Player* and James Cameron's *Avatar,* a film that is representative of where we are in contemporary filmmaking. There's always been generic crossover in filmmaking in that you can often see elements of multiple genres in a given film. It's nothing new. But the crossover seems to have reached new heights of which *Avatar* is the pinnacle (or the nadir, depending on your point of view). Actually, though more high profile because of its writer/director, *Avatar* is not really any different than something like the various entries in the *Blade* series, which are vampire/horror/action/sci-fi/superhero movies that are based on the Marvel Comics' character that itself was modeled after the heroes of the black action films (better known as "blaxploitation") of the early 1970s. Altman was a wily movie vet who was able to do some of his best work during the silver age of American cinema in the 1970s, in which directors were able to get studio funding for films that had little or no chance at financial success, of which Altman's own *McCabe and Mrs. Miller* (1971) and *Nashville* (1975) are prime examples—and they are also both genre films, a western and a musical respectively, albeit of the highly deconstructive and incendiary kind. But to Altman and others, it was naively just as much if not more about the art as the money, and they believed that if they were just allowed to make what they wanted and their films were nurtured and released, then audiences would find them, which didn't exactly turn out to be true and is certainly a lousy practice upon which to base an industry. And so the executives Altman so despised took back the industry, and the kinds of films that are able to get funding inside the Hollywood mainstream have been permanently altered, despite the blip of independent cinema in the mid-1990s. *The Player,* with its famous send-up of genre pastiche in the opening scene and soulless lead character, Griffin Mill (Tim Robbins), a mid-level movie executive who's never seen *The Bicycle Thief* (De Sica 1948), parodies what in Altman's eyes Hollywood had become, a seething morass of hucksters, grifters, and players, all of whom want to make the biggest deals most likely to bring in the highest grosses. Despite his cynicism, I doubt if in his wildest dreams Altman thought the exaggerated world he depicted in *The Player* would come to pass. But it has, and then some. This is meant more as an indictment of Hollywood than it is of genre. There's nothing wrong with adapting a formula in the hopes of achieving a desired result, especially when there's so much money on the line. The problem arises when the formula becomes invariable and results in the same stories time and again rather than spicing things up on occasion and trying to tell an old story in a new way. Genre is basically a filmic recipe, and with just a little inspiration, a subpar recipe can be made good and an average recipe can be made great. As Martin Scorsese once said about the genre films of yesteryear, "Genre films remind me of Jazz. They allowed for endless, increasingly complex, sometimes perverse variations, and when these variations were played by the masters, they reflected changing times. They gave you fascinating insights into American culture, and the American psyche" (*A Personal Journey*). And the best ones still do.

## WORKS CITED

*A Personal Journey with Martin Scorsese through American Movies.* Dir. Martin Scorsese & Michael Henry Wilson. Miramax, 2000. DVD.

Ansen, David. "Multiple Choice: How Much Did 'Taxi to the Dark Side' Earn at the Box Office?" *Newsweek.* July 14, 2008. *LexisNexis Academic.*

*Box Office Mojo.com.* "The Adventures of Pluto Nash."

*Box Office Mojo.com.* "All Time World Wide Box Office Grosses."

*Box Office Mojo.com.* "Documentary Movies at the Box Office."

*Box Office Mojo.com.* "The Last Action Hero."

*Box Office Mojo.com.* "Waterworld."

Catsoulis, Jeanneatte. "When 'Predators' Attack (And Abs Fight Back)." *NPR.org.* July 9, 2010.

Ditzian, Eric. "James Cameron Confirms 'Technical' Discussions about 'Avatar' Sequel." *mtv.com.* Feb. 4, 2010.

Graser, Marc. "Whedon to Head *Avengers.*" *Variety.com.* April 13, 2010.

Griffin, Nancy, and Kim Masters. "How They Built the Bomb." In *Hit and Run: How Jon Peters and Peter Guber took Sony for a Ride in Hollywood,* 362–85. New York: Simon & Schuster, 1996.

Gross, Terry. "James Cameron: Pushing the Limits of Imagination." *NPR's Fresh Air Podcast.* Feb. 18, 2010.

Hof, Rob. "Who Wins the Most as Disney Buys Pixar?" *BusinessWeek.com.* Jan. 24, 2006.

*India Today.* "The All New Hollywood Effect." *Hollywood News-Yahoo! India.* March 8, 2010.

Kaufman, Anthony. "Is Foreign Film the New Endangered Species?" *The New York Times. com.* Jan. 22, 2006.

Kempley, Rita. "Waterworld." *The Washington Post.com.* July 28, 1995. *LexisNexis Academic.*

McClintock, Pamela. "Reliance, DreamWorks Close Deal." *Variety.* Aug. 17, 2009. *LexisNexis Academic.*

Parish, James Robert. "*Last Action Hero* (1993)" and *"Waterworld* (1995) and *The Post-man* (1997)." In *Fiasco: A History of Hollywood's Iconic Flops,* 190–210, 249–69. Hoboken, NJ: Wiley, 2006.

Tuttle, Harry. "Foreign Film Friendly Audiences—World Cinema Stats." *screenville.blog spot.com.* Jan. 19, 2010.

Willmore, Alison. "Remaking Your Own Foreign Language Film." *ifc.com.* Oct. 9, 2008.

# Chapter 6

## NAVIGATING THE CONTEMPORARY HOLLYWOOD BUSINESS MODEL: DIRECTORS IN THE DIGITAL AGE

In January of 1954 François Truffaut published an article in the then little-known French film journal *Cahiers du Cinema* titled, "Une Certaine Tendance du Cinéma Français" (a certain tendency in French cinema), in which he argued for what he saw as the superiority of directors who were able to rise above the assembly line nature of commercial filmmaking and put a personal artistic stamp on their work. From this seemingly innocuous beginning was born the auteur theory, which basically considers the "best" directors the primary authors of the movies they direct. As a result, so goes the argument, when watching a series of films by a singular director, one can gain insight and understanding into his or her cardinal themes and obsessions. This point of view gained a lot of currency in film criticism and came to dominate academic thought until the mid-1970s, during which time it became increasingly challenged by those who thought the theory too restrictive and hopelessly flawed in its failure to properly acknowledge filmmaking's inherently collaborative nature, which justifiably resulted in a rich plethora of other ways of looking at cinema coming to the fore. Martin Scorsese, for example, is a well-respected auteur, but can we consider his body of work without exploring his artistic relationship with longtime editor Thelma Schoonmaker? Likewise, James Cameron is a contemporary auteur, but look at the closing credits of *Titanic* and *Avatar.* Thousands of people other than him worked on those films. Cameron had to sign off on things, but despite his deserved reputation as a maniacal perfectionist, there's no way he could have personally taken part in more than a tiny fraction of the countless thousands of hours of work that it took to bring those films to life.

The auteur theory no doubt leaves a lot to be desired, but the thing about it is that when it works, it works really well. You don't have to be a formally trained film scholar to be able to watch five Woody Allen (or Coen Brothers or Wes Anderson or Quentin Tarantino, and on and on) films and tell that they're the work of the same artist. Further complicating the issue is that in that first article, Truffaut right away conflated recurring artistic signatures with quality when he wrote, "There are no good and bad movies, only good and bad directors." The problem with this is that just as you can look at many great directors through the lens of auteur theory, so too can you look at those who are less artistically successful (this is of course subjective), such as Ed Wood and Michael Bay, and still see their auteurist characteristics; their films are recognizably *theirs*. And what about directors generally considered to be working at a high level to whom the theory doesn't apply, in that from film to film they don't seem to have the same visual style, narrative approach, or cardinal themes? Could people who didn't already know watch *Angels With Dirty Faces* (1938), *The Adventures of Robin Hood* (1938), *Yankee Doodle Dandy* (1942), *Casablanca* (1942), *Mildred Pierce* (1945), and *White Christmas* (1954) and know that they were watching films by the same artist, in this instance Michael Curtiz? Or for that matter, what are the chances of a person who didn't already know watching *The Color Purple* (1985), *Empire of the Sun* (1987), *Hook* (1991), *Jurassic Park* (1993), *Schindler's List* (1993), and *Catch Me If You Can* (2002) and knowing that they were all directed by the same person, Steven Spielberg? It's not for nothing that these guys aren't exactly considered hacks. But they aren't auteurs in the way Truffaut saw the "good" directors, as they don't write their own scripts and they don't seem to imprint their style on the films they make; rather, they let the stories they choose to direct (or, in Curtiz's case, were assigned by the studio) dictate style and form, which makes them much harder to pin down in the taxonomic way that auteurist critics often look at filmmakers.

Still, the auteur theory, despite repeated attempts by its detractors to kill it once and for all, remains very much alive. Like all approaches, it's got its strengths and weaknesses and is probably best used as one of an array of approaches to get at the heart of a particular matter. That said, it's hard to know how to talk about a film when referring to its creators. Does one refer to the director? The actors? The studio, which most likely owns the film in the technical sense of the word? And what about the screenwriter(s), without whom no basis for a movie would exist? For ease, its become protocol that when a film is first listed in a text, it typically has the director's name and the year of release in parenthesis after it, although it doesn't necessarily mean the whomever is writing the text considers the director as the film's primary author. In the case of the particular book you're now reading, though the author adheres to the accepted academic norm of noting a film's director as needed, he does so in a kind of shorthand, choosing to use the director's name as a kind of captaincy for the endeavor but understanding that it's just the lead name in a collaborative cast of many, rather than an attribution for a sole author. And yet this chapter purports to look at directors; isn't this adhering to old-school auteurism? Yes and no.

While I'll by design be discussing certain directors, I'll be doing so in a somewhat different way than is the norm in studies of this nature. First off, for the purposes of this book I'm not hugely interested in the quality of a director's work, which already moves this out of the realm of Truffaut's good directors/bad directors dichotomization. While I'm not shy about positing my point of view as to the qualitative merits of a person's body of work, there are a seemingly limitless supply of auteurist-minded articles and books about contemporary films and filmmakers. What I am interested in is a look at some of the directors whose work to date either is or will prove to be among the most uniquely influential in a widespread way as we move deeper into the digital age. So, for example, Wes Anderson is certainly one of the most influential directors of the past decade. This becomes painfully obvious to any habitués of film festivals, at which one can see, repeatedly, other directors emulating his distinct visual style and quirky fragile characters to varying degrees of success. That said, though it pains me to leave out a more intensive study of a director whose films I adore so much, there's no place for him in this chapter, as while he's influenced a generation of would-be auteurs, he hasn't made much of a ripple in the industry outside of his own circle. Indeed, it is often the box office success of a movie in the global market that results in the widespread emulation of a filmmaker's work that makes it much more important in a recounting of industry practices than a film's perceived quality. This is certainly the case as concerns the directors looked at in this chapter,[1] a claim that is especially true when considering the work of George Lucas.

I think few folks with more than a fan boy's appreciation of cinema would want to engage in a philosophical argument as to the cinematic artistic merits of George Lucas's *Star Wars: Episode One—The Phantom Menace* (1999), especially when considering it was released in the same year as Woody Allen's *Sweet and Lowdown,* David Fincher's *Fight Club,* David Lynch's *The Straight Story,* P.T. Anderson's *Magnolia,* Kimberly Pierce's *Boys Don't Cry,* Sam Mendes's *American Beauty,* and Spike Jonze's *Being John Malkovich.* And while I would argue that 1999 was qualitatively as good a year as any in American film history, the big story is still *The Phantom Menace,* the year's highest-grossing film, the first live-action film that was shot entirely in a digital format, a prequel to three other highly successful films, and made by a director with his own movie studio and all the rights to all the characters in all his films.

A long time ago, in a different Hollywood that seems far, far away, George Lucas presciently saw the future of the film industry, at least as concerns the possibilities of his own work. When contracting to make the original *Star Wars* (1977) film, *Episode IV—A New Hope,* Lucas negotiated a small up-front salary and an additional percentage of the net profits, which by Hollywood standards basically meant that due to the Byzantine nature of Hollywood accounting, he was forgoing salary (always go for a percentage of the gross, which is guaranteed). But what he also did was negotiate ownership of the ancillary rights to the entirety of the *Star Wars* universe and to any and all sequels. The studio felt that they were getting the better end of the deal, as they didn't foresee the film being a hit, and at that point in time, no one outside of the Disney company worried much about the money to be made in ancillary sales. Likewise, Lucas was secure in knowing that if the movie was successful, then he'd be in a position to make another film ("How

George Lucas . . ."). But even he didn't initially fully understand the financial mag-
nitude of what he'd negotiated. Nothing having anything to do with *Star Wars* gets
made without George Lucas' approval. And nothing gets sold without his receiving a piece of the pie, usually twice—first in the form of up-front cash payments
and then as a percentage of the gross on subsequent sales. This has proven to be
an enormously successful financial arrangement, as sales of merchandise from the
*Star Wars* universe totaled $4.5 billion *before* the release of the first prequel in
1999 (Brand)! After the release of the first *Star Wars* film in 1977, Lucas was able
to achieve the dream that had been a glint in many a Hollywood creative type's
eyes since at least as far back as when Charlie Chaplin, Douglas Fairbanks, and
Mary Pickford combined forces to form United Artists in an attempt to gain
independence from the Hollywood studios. From humble beginnings in 1971,
Lucasfilm, Ltd., has grown into a multibillion-dollar company in its own right,
with huge complexes in Marin County, California, and at the Presidio, a former
military base in San Francisco, and several subsidiary companies, including Lucas
Digital Ltd., LucasArts Entertainment Co., Industrial Light & Magic, and Sky-
walker Sound. Lucas' companies are important in their own right for having both
advanced digital special effects and sound technology.

But it's the marketing schemes that started with the original *Star Wars* trilogy
and continued on in the second that have had the most profound influence in the
industry. Prior to the start of production of the first prequel, *The Phantom Menace*
(1999), Lucas had negotiated $600 million in guaranteed money from Hasbro for
the rights to make toys and another $2.5 billion from PepsiCo. for the rights to
use the characters in their advertising over the lifespan of the new trilogy (Brand);
accordingly, Lucas initially chose not to advertise the film at all, other than via
traditional cinematic trailers—relying instead on the free advertising resulting
from the fast food promotions that accompanied the film's release. By the time
of the second trilogy, other companies had taken to making tent-pole films with
presold ancillary tie-ins that could be marketed and sold by subsidiary companies
or through licensing agreements with third parties. But Lucas took it to a whole
new level, which has been emulated as best as possible by every company since,
becoming par for the course in the contemporary industry that is now dominated
by blockbuster filmmaking at the top end. Lucas might be associated with the film
school generation of 1970s filmmakers, but he was way ahead of his time as concerns the way he approached the business of filmmaking.

Though a comparatively narrative-minded, lo-fi filmmaker, another hugely important player in the early years of the digital age has been Judd Apatow, whose
Apatow Productions has produced some of the most influential of the so-called
frat pack films and also those that he has directed himself, *The 40-Year-Old Virgin*
(2005), *Knocked Up* (2007), and *Funny People* (2009), which has made Apatow
one of the most powerful players in contemporary Hollywood.[2] This is interesting because his huge influence has nothing to do with technology or marketing
and is instead a result of the kinds of narratives his company supports. In fact,

Apatow and crew are very traditional filmmakers. While he is presently hard to avoid, he didn't become a mogul overnight. Like so many before him, he started out doing whatever he could, learning the different jobs essential to production along the way. His first big break came with *The Ben Stiller Show* (1992–1993), a short-lived but well-respected sketch comedy show for which he wrote, directed, produced, and occasionally even acted (frustratingly, "short-lived but well-respected" applies to all of the TV shows Apatow's worked on, with the notable exception of *The Larry Sanders Show* [1993–1998], for which Apatow sporadically wrote and produced). From there he went on to don multiple hats on a number of critically revered shows, including *The Critic* (1994–1995), *The Larry Sanders Show, Freaks and Geeks* (1999–2000), and *Undeclared* (2001–2002).

In addition to learning the ins and outs of production firsthand during this pre-superstardom era, in 1999 Apatow also founded Apatow Productions, which started out in TV, producing both *Freaks and Geeks* and *Undeclared.* The company's first feature film, *Anchorman: The Legend of Ron Burgandy* (McKay 2004), was a modest hit, grossing more than $90 million internationally, but it was the company's second film, *The 40-Year-Old Virgin* (Apatow 2005—nearly $180 million in worldwide box office), that thrust Apatow into the pop cultural limelight (*Box Office Mojo. com*). Surprisingly, given his ubiquity in popular culture and all the press attention he's received, Apatow hasn't done much movie directing at all. In fact, *Virgin* was his cinematic directorial debut, and as of 2010, he's only directed two other features, *Knocked Up* (2007) and *Funny People* (2009). And this is where the significance of Apatow's achievement gets even more unusual and interesting. He's done what few before him have and made the jump from a writer/director/producer to an independent studio mogul who has created his own narrative brand with which he is at the moment inextricably intertwined, even if he sometimes has nothing to do with the products with which he is identified. To whit, Greg Mottola has good naturedly spent the past few years of his life telling people that it was he, and not Judd Apatow, who directed *Superbad* (2007) (Ramos). But at least Apatow's production company did in fact produce the film. One wonders if Mottola's good nature extended to his next feature, *Adventureland* (2009), which was also routinely noted for its Apatow connections, even though Apatow and his company had nothing to do with the film, which was written and directed by Mottola and produced by Miramax (Dwyer, "Adventureland").

Similarly, reviews of *I Love You, Man* (Hamburg 2009) invariably mentioned Apatow, even though neither he nor his company were involved with the film. Like Charlie Chaplin, Apatow has become a movie impresario who has created his own brand. But unlike Chaplin, Apatow's brand revolves around narrative recurrences instead of a beloved recurring character. So while Chaplin's brand was rightfully forever identified with The Little Tramp, Apatow's is the lingua franca of contemporary Hollywood romantic comedy, allowing him to transcend the hallowed auteur status normally granted exclusively to directors and to receive credit for work with which he literally has no connection. As Sean Dwyer notes in his review of

*I Love You, Man,* "Although they've been repackaged and renamed, the buddy comedy has been around for decades as an outlet to express the feelings that men have for each other but are too macho to say in real life. Judd Apatow didn't invent the idea, but he has found the sweet spot for balancing manly heartfelt moments with laughter, and presenting them in a way that attracts both male and female audiences." Apatow makes movies about men who are neither supermen nor even all that celebrated. They are, instead, normal guys: a bit schlubby, neither particularly smart nor ambitious, but generally well meaning and harmless, even though they have yet to learn to act like grown-ups. Instead, these guys have chosen to remain in an extended adolescence. They are not quite fully functioning adults and the pack they run with—the group that tends to stand in for family and heterosexual relationships—contributes to their lifestyle ruts. Apatow manages to both capture the dynamic of male friendship while offering an idealized version of male-male interaction. His characters create a boys' club—a space where the male characters can be men together. In many cases, the Apatow canon is about the bittersweet moment of reaching adulthood—however belatedly—and the heteronormative societal forces that ultimately drag boys kicking and screaming toward greater maturity. For Apatow, women often act as the catalyst that allow these boys to grow into men, following a long tradition codified and immortalized in both film and print in which women act as civilizing forces in the lives of male protagonists. In all of these cases, though, it is the sociability with other men that makes them feel safe, helps them develop, and prepares them for the fully functioning adulthood they will embrace when faced with their catalyst. Current American culture, as reflected in and driven by popular film, espouses a standard of schlubby masculinity in protracted adolescent boy-men who are either civilized by women or eschew relationships with women altogether in favor of close male friendships, and perhaps no one is more responsible for this than Judd Apatow Productions' revised take on romantic comedies.

It's interesting that Apatow is considered an auteur with so few films directed under his belt—and comedies at that. But given the success of his production company and those who he's worked with, it's more telling than surprising that in contemporary Hollywood this particular filmmaker is more than just a writer, a director, and a producer, but a brand unto himself, and many a filmmaker and production company are trying to copy his formula for success (Aftab). But when one thinks of American auteurs in the old-school-as-defined-by-Truffaut-way of thinking about it, it's Martin Scorsese whose name most often comes up, and not without good reason. So many of the acknowledged important directors from the halcyon days of the new American cinema of the 1970s crashed and burned under the weight of their own hubris and the changing structural realities of the industry. Coppola, Bogdanovich, Michael Cimino—all of whom are still alive as of this writing and totally irrelevant in the contemporary industry—come to mind. Certainly Spielberg continues to work in an extraordinarily prolific way, but he, along with George Lucas, is often credited (unfairly and erroneously) as having helped to kill the auteur-driven 1970s with the success of *Jaws* (1975) and *Star Wars* (1977). And still others, such as Woody Allen, Roman Polanski, Brian De Palma, and Robert Altman (before his death in 2006), continue to work with varying levels of financial and critical success. But no one has made the transition from the days of auteurs making highly personal and not-necessarily-likely-to-turn-a-profit films to the contemporary high-stakes poker table of contemporary Hollywood more successfully than Martin Scorsese.

By the end of the 1970s, Martin Scorsese had already established himself as one of the great American directors, having already directed such classics as *Mean Streets* (1973), *Taxi Driver* (1976), and *Raging Bull* (1980). *Taxi Driver* (#47) and *Raging Bull* (#24) are on the American Film Institute's 100 Greatest Films List. Another thing the films share in common is that despite their hallowed critical reception in film history, none of them were exactly huge hits. Scorsese was making films that the critics liked a lot more than audiences did. This was okay for a film like *Mean Streets,* which only had a $500,000 production budget, or *Taxi Driver,* which grossed a very nice $28 million against its $1.3 million production budget, but not so much in the case of *Raging Bull,* which managed to make only $23 million against its $18 million cost (*imdb.com*; *Box Office Mojo.com*). Furthermore, as very small culturally specific films, blueprints, really, for what would ultimately come to be known as independent-style productions, they had little success in the overseas markets. People often point to the fiasco involved in the making of Michael Cimino's *Heaven's Gate* (1979) as the film that really killed the auteur era in American cinema, and while that's not wrong, *Raging Bull* deserves some credit as well, albeit for different reasons. The sad truth is that it doesn't matter how much critical cachet a film generates—if it doesn't make money, studios won't want to make more like it. *Raging Bull* is often seen as the pinnacle of 1970s filmmaking, but a more cynical observer would also note it was the era's death knell as well, a great movie that was also the last of a long line of critically acclaimed auteurist films that failed to ignite at the box office.

Entering the 1980s, this left Scorsese at something of a crossroads—he was a well-regarded director who made films that didn't make much money. And unlike, say, Woody Allen, he didn't make films for a consistent price, nor did he have a built-in audience that would consistently come out to see his films, thus ensuring their profitability. But he kept working, and constantly, though he did continue to make films in his own uncompromising way and with his trademark stylings. Examples of these films include *The King of Comedy* (1982), a caustic comedy about stand-up comedian Rupert Pupkin (Robert De Niro); *The Color of Money* (1986), a sequel of sorts to the classic film *The Hustler* (Rossen 1961), in which Paul Newman reprises his role as Fast Eddie Felson; the highly controversial *The Last Temptation of Christ* (1988); *GoodFellas* (1990), #94 on the aforementioned AFI list, making Scorsese one of an elite group with three films on the list (only Alfred Hitchcock and Billy Wilder, with four each, had more); *The Age of Innocence* (1993); *Casino* (1995); and *Bringing out the Dead* (1999), as well as a number of documentaries and other films. He continued to grow in stature as an auteur, but the kind of commercial success that comes part and parcel with blockbuster filmmaking eluded him.

It's hard to imagine Scorsese ever making a film like *Spider-Man* (then again, who saw Ang Lee making *Hulk* [2003]?); he's certainly not averse to adapting pre-sold properties, but his sensibility is a few degrees off of the blockbuster mentality. He veers left when he should go right, he leaves the audience in the dark too often, and he certainly doesn't go for the pat Hollywood ending, happy or otherwise. In fact, often in his films there's no real closure at all, which is anathema in the industry. And yet, seemingly against all odds, Martin Scorsese has made the transition from 1970s auteur to a director of great clout in contemporary Hollywood. (Lucas has clout too, but he's stuck with *Star Wars,* whereas Scorsese can make anything he wants.) But how? This is an interesting question not readily answered by a singular thing. Even though Scorsese's made films in a wide variety of genres—from a straight literary adaptation like *Age of Innocence* (1993) and music documentaries like *The Last Waltz* (1978) and *No Direction Home* (2005) to a noirish remake of the B-movie classic *Cape Fear* (1991)—he nevertheless has a particular sensibility and style that's present from film to film. After all, it's this persistence of vision and stylistic tendency that goes a long way in getting someone labeled an auteur to begin with. And I would argue that Scorsese hasn't compromised his vision much at all. But what he has done is change the scope and scale of what he does. He's always made films rife with grand ambitions as concerns their philosophical content, but in the context of Hollywood, his films have been very modestly budgeted, until more recently anyway. Prior to 2001, his film with the highest budget was *Casino,* at an estimated $52 million (*imdb.com*). While some of his films turned a nice profit when taking overseas box office into account, none of them even came close to breaking the $100 million mark domestically, which was okay; he didn't make the studios a fortune, but he didn't cost them one either. Furthermore, he was a filmmaking eminence and he brought prestige and award cachet to the projects he made and the studios that funded them. And then in 2002 something changed when he made *Gangs of New York* for Harvey Weinstein and Miramax.

The film is epic in scope and scale, a blueprint big-budget pic in every way. Its published budget is normally put at around $100 million, which is $30 million or so larger than it was originally intended to be and likely a lot less than it actually cost (Holson). In addition to having to manage a large cast and a sprawling script and choosing to film much of the film at the legendary Cinecittà movie studio in Rome, Scorsese had to deal with Weinstein's attempts to help shape the film's content, which wasn't at all unusual for Weinstein, whose postproduction changes to films purchased or financed by Miramax had long before earned him the moniker "Harvey Scissor-Hands" (Auletta). Their battles raised a lot of eyebrows in Hollywood as Scorsese was thought to have reached a level of prestige that would keep meddling studio heads off the lot and out of his editing booth.

But Weinstein was no ordinary studio exec, and he and Scorsese spent the better part of a year after principal photography was completed wrangling over the film's final form, with Weinstein pushing to make it a shorter, more audience-friendly blockbuster and Scorsese fighting to keep his more ruminative take intact.

The finished product leaves something to be desired, feeling oddly clipped in places and containing montages that look like amalgams consisting of pieces that were perhaps taken from longer sequences. But we'll never know for sure, as Martin Scorsese has remained the picture of professional decorum about his experience at Miramax, both at the time and since, although it's perhaps worth noting that he hasn't worked with Weinstein again. While it was released to largely mixed reviews, *Gangs* wasn't a total disaster. In fact, it became his biggest hit to that point, earning almost $80 million domestically and close to $200 million total (*Box Office Mojo.com*). While it's not a hit along the lines of the loose 3 to 1 return on investment rule by which Hollywood measures hits (at least in part), it did put Martin Scorsese into a new category, which is rather remarkable given that he was 60 years old at the time of its release. It's been said that in Hollywood you can fail upward, meaning that you can move ahead just by illustrating you can do something, even if that something doesn't result in profits. And Scorsese certainly hadn't failed. The film earned multiple awards and nominations and wasn't a total disaster at the box office, and by not speaking poorly of Miramax, Scorsese, already a well-liked and much-respected figure in Hollywood (though not exactly an insider either, in part because his films didn't make money), only grew in stature.

But perhaps the most important thing to come out of all this was the formation of Scorsese's relationship with Leonardo DiCaprio, which would dramatically change the way Scorsese was able to work in Hollywood. Scorsese had worked with big movie stars in the past, notably Paul Newman and Tom Cruise in *The Color of Money* and Robert De Niro in several pictures. But Newman was on the downside of his box office appeal and Cruise wasn't quite yet what he'd come to be as a star, and De Niro never really has been a movie star, though he's certainly a famous actor. But a star, in the box office way of thinking about it, is a person whose very presence can first get a film bank rolled and then almost guarantee a certain amount of box office just because he (or, more rarely, she) is in the movie. In other words, people are going to go see the movie just because he or she is in it, regardless of reviews, genre, costars, director, or anything else. As *Sunset Boulevard*'s Norma Desmond (Gloria Swanson) says, "No one ever leaves a star. That is what makes one a star!" And with Leonardo DiCaprio, Scorsese was able to hitch his wagon to one of the brightest stars in the Hollywood firmament.

At the time of the production of *Gangs of New York*, it was surmised that DiCaprio's presence helped Scorsese secure more funding when he went over the initial budget. While the reasons for granting additional expenditures to a movie once production has commenced are varied and rarely publicly explained—and even if they were no one would ever say "we're increasing the budget because Leo is in the movie"—DiCaprio's presence almost certainly played some role in it. It's not that the studio necessarily wants to make him happy so much as it is that his presence makes the likelihood of a return on investment much higher than it would be otherwise. There's a reason big-budget movies don't star people the audience has never heard of. And a movie star's attachment to a project can get almost any movie made; in fact, it's much more likely that a movie studio will go ahead with a trite star vehicle than a sharply written film featuring a cast of unknowns. And once a movie star has signed on, it's incredibly rare that the plug is pulled on production. A rare exception to this occurred in 2009 when on the eve of production Sony pulled the plug on the Brad Pitt film *Moneyball*, an adaptation by Steven Zaillian and Steven Soderbergh, who was also slated to direct, of Michael Lewis's book of the same name (Bart and Fleming). But what should be noted here is not that the plug was pulled, but that the film was ever green-lighted at all, as it's about the Oakland Athletics, a small-market baseball team that in the early 2000s maximized market inefficiencies in an attempt to keep up with high-dollar, big-market teams like the Red Sox and the Yankees. No, what should be noted here is that the film was ever slated to be made at all. And there's no doubt it wouldn't have been were it not a Brad Pitt vanity project. Tellingly, the film is once again slated for production with a new, more audience-friendly script penned by Aaron Sorkin and a new director, Bennet Miller. But not a new star; Brad Pitt loves this property, hence it's once again in the production pipeline.

The mutually beneficial relationship between DiCaprio and Scorsese is likely more a matter of serendipity and personal chemistry than a calculated business relationship. Scorsese just hasn't shown himself to be the kind of person who would compromise his values and standards to get a film made. Similarly, DiCaprio's experience as Jack in *Titanic* (Cameron 1997) and the accompanying meteoric rise to superstardom caused him to reevaluate the kinds of films he wanted to make, which eventually resulted in his determining to act only in films in which he believed he could be challenged artistically. In working with Scorsese, DiCaprio can do just that, and for Scorsese, DiCaprio's attachment means that just about anything they agree to do together will likely get made. Accordingly, the follow-up to *Gangs* was *The Aviator* (2004), an ambitious period piece biopic with one of the more disturbing endings in recent mainstream Hollywood movies. In addition to garnering strong critical reviews, the film grossed $102 million domestically and $213 million total against a $110 million budget (*Box Office Mojo.com*; *imdb. com*). It was the first Scorsese film to gross $100 million domestically, undoubtedly in no small part because of the box office appeal of Leonardo DiCaprio. But despite its high production budget, the film doesn't hedge its bets by making sure the content is audience friendly in the same way a lot of other high-budget Hollywood films do. It's a recognizable genre pic, but its subject, Howard Hughes, is a very dark personage. There are no phoenix moments in which the likable main character rises from the ashes to assume his rightful place in the pantheon of American legends à la *Walk the Line* (Mangold 2005) or *Ray* (Hackford 2004). In fact, at the film's end, right after what should be a moment of great triumph for Hughes, Scorsese instead leaves his audience with a disturbing portrait of Hughes's obsessive compulsion, risking possible alienation of mainstream audiences that so often seem to prefer pat Hollywood endings. It's risky filmmaking, especially in that economic stratosphere, but it worked.

Next up was *The Departed* (2006), a remake of the Hong Kong film *Infernal Affairs* (Lau and Mak 2002). The budget was in the $90 million range, which is actually somewhat small given the huge star power of this ensemble cast, which in addition to DiCaprio included Matt Damon, Jack Nicholson, Alec Baldwin, Martin Sheen, and Mark Wahlberg (*imdb.com*). It's a readily recognizable cops and robbers film, pitting good cops and bad cops against each other and the mob, but that's where it ceases to be the norm. As in his earlier gangster classics *Good-Fellas* and *Casino*, the characters in *The Departed*, sans Jack Nicholson's Frank Costello, are morally ambiguous and deeply divided in their sense of right and wrong. And even Costello adheres to a moral code, albeit a gangster's. Yet even the worst of the lot are likable in some ways, or at least incredibly enjoyable to watch. And the movie is anything but predictable, killing off major characters seemingly on a whim and with no warning. Further, the deaths don't involve soliloquies or noble last words or promises of vengeance. People are just shot in the head and drop dead in their tracks. Like *Gangs* and *The Aviator*, in a lot of ways *The Departed* again pushes the boundaries of its genre in unexpected and surprising ways. And audiences lapped it up, with the film earning $132 million domestically and $289 million total, his highest-grossing film to that point (*Box Office Mojo.com*). It also won the Academy Award for Best Picture and a Best Director statuette for Scorsese.

Following *The Departed*, Scorsese and DiCaprio teamed up for a fourth film, *Shutter Island* (2010), another period piece, this one based on a Dennis LeHane novel of the same name. Of the four films they've made together, this $80 million movie is the most generically straightforward of the bunch, a noirish thriller that meets the expectations of its genre expertly, but doesn't push them in any particular way (*imdb.com*). That said, what it does it does extremely well, and it's a lot of fun to watch, an assessment audiences the world over agreed with, which resulted in a domestic gross of $128 million and $294 million total (*Box Office Mojo.com*).

Martin Scorsese is arguably the most influential director of the past 30 years; countless would-be auteurs have become filmmakers after falling under the stylishly hypnotic sway of his work. But the change in status within the industry he's been able to undergo as a result of his relationship with Leonardo DiCaprio is nothing short of remarkable; in fact, the industry has changed so much during his career that his evolution is equivalent to that of the relatively few directors who enjoyed box office success and critical accolades in both the silent and sound eras. He was a hugely respected artist with a handful of classics under his belt, but he was still somewhere in the middle. He got good budgets to work with on the basis of his deserved reputation, but he didn't get the huge budgets some of his dream projects would require, with *Gangs* being at the top of the list, because he had no track record of success in the context of the financial paradigm of the contemporary industry, in which high-dollar films are expected to gross in the hundreds of millions of dollars to make a decent return on their investment. It's very hard to imagine a filmmaker like Martin Scorsese making a *Harry Potter* movie or a superhero flick (although I'd like to see him try!); he's just interested in a different kind of fare. But he solved a career puzzle by teaming up with Leonardo DiCaprio in that he was able to get much bigger budgets than he previously had. Yet he was also able to do so without compromising the fundamentally dark nature of his vision, and this is surely because he had the support of DiCaprio, as financiers will support a less apparently mainstream film if a star is on board. The results are big-budget films that allowed Scorsese to relay his obsessions to audiences on a far grander scale than he had previously been able to do. But he did it without compromise, thus illustrating to other filmmakers that with the attachment and support of the right star(s), large-budget films can still be consistently personal, unyielding, and financially successful, which wasn't always entirely clear in the landscape of contemporary Hollywood prior to his four-film stint with DiCaprio. That Scorsese reinvented himself in a young person's world while in his 60s makes his accomplishment and the reach of his influence all the more remarkable. It'll be interesting to see if other filmmakers follow suit (it's hard not to notice that Christopher Nolan's first post–*Batman Returns* movie, the complex and concept heavy *Inception* [2010], also stars Leonardo DiCaprio). But whether they do or not, Scorsese has shown that not all high-budget films need to be tent-pole films based on well-known, presold properties to be successful.

Another filmmaker who has proven to be seriously influential while remaining staunchly iconoclastic is Steven Soderbergh. Soderbergh was arguably the poster boy for the American independent scene of the early 1990s, in some ways having kicked it off by winning the 1989 Cannes Film Festival Palme d'Or for *sex, lies, and videotape,* a low-budget, character-driven film he wrote himself and filmed in Baton Rouge, Louisiana, where he had grown up. The future seemed bright for Soderbergh, especially given what was at the time a reasonable climate for securing financing for edgier, more challenging fare. But Soderbergh stumbled, at least financially, directing a series of relative flops including *Kafka* (1991), *King of the Hill* (1993), and *The Underneath* (1995) before tucking tail and leaving Los Angeles for another return to Baton Rouge to shoot the ill-fated *Schizopolis* (1996), in which he stars as a man whose marriage is in dissolution. That his wife was played by his actual ex-wife, whom he had earlier divorced, only added to the self-referential, reflexive, and complicated narrative. It was filmed for nothing, $250,000, but it wasn't able to get a distributor and was never widely released theatrically (*imdb.com*). That it has since undergone a kind of critical resuscitation is beside the point; at the time, it was a disaster and considered evidence of a filmmaker whose career was in a nigh-irreparable state of disarray.

Steven Soderbergh was between a rock and a hard place and it was up to him to restart his career. Part of the problem was that the films he'd made to that point just weren't ever going to be commercial. It's not like they were all bad; some of them, especially *King of the Hill,* were well regarded. But audiences just weren't interested. If we lived in a perfect world, filmmakers would get to make what they want, but we don't, and therefore filmmakers must reconcile their visions with the realities of the commercial marketplace if they want to make films that audiences will pay to see. Soderbergh is a filmmaker of undeniable talent, but he's also got a quirky sensibility and would be the first to admit his tastes don't always match up to those of the mainstream audience. Still, if he was to continue working in the industry, a reinvention was in order. So after a brief hiatus, Soderbergh turned to the one thing that has remained a viable commercial constant in filmmaking since its inception, and that's genre films. The resultant film was *Out Of Sight* (1998), a critically acclaimed, highly stylized neo-noir adaptation of an Elmore Leonard novel. Modestly budgeted at $48 million, the film did less than $80 million worldwide, which is not exactly setting things afire, but it didn't tank, was extremely well respected, and put Soderbergh back on the map (*imdb.com*; *Box Office Mojo.com*). The other thing it did was legitimize George Clooney as a movie actor; he was a star based on his TV work on *ER,* but he'd previously been horribly miscast in *Batman & Robin* (Schumacher 1997) and *The Peacemaker* (Leder 1997), which were both high-profile disappointments. In *Out of Sight,* playing opposite Jennifer Lopez, Clooney was able to play an edgy, lovably wry ne'er-do-well, which is a type he's since played repeatedly and to great success.

Soderbergh followed *Out of Sight* with *The Limey* (1999), which stars Terrence Stamp as a dangerous and volatile ex-con named Wilson who goes to LA to investigate the death of his young daughter. Like *Out of Sight,* it's once again a kind of neo-noir, only this time the editing is highly anachronistic and the action is scant compared to most films of this kind, instead meditatively focusing on the cloudier inner problems of its characters. Soderbergh also incorporates clips of Stamp from *Poor Cow,* a 1967 Ken Loach film, the doing of which lends an eerie veracity to the film's flashback sequences. Somewhat akin to his earlier work, *The Limey* is in a much more experimental vein than *Out of Sight.* Perhaps not unsurprisingly, given its non-mainstream nature, it didn't even make back its $10 million production budget (*imdb.com*; *Box Office Mojo.com*). But it was a much-adored film, and a movie that costs $10 million and doesn't do well is a whole different ball game than a movie that costs $60 or $70 million or more and fails. Soderbergh had re-established himself as a director with clout and he used it to his advantage, making three huge films in a row, *Erin Brockovich* (2000), *Traffic* (2000), and *Ocean's Eleven* (2001).

All three of the aforementioned films are relatively modestly budgeted star vehicles that went on to make at least $205 million each in international box office, with the last of the bunch bringing in a monster $450 million total (*Box Office Mojo.com*). The biopic *Brockovich* featured Julia Roberts in the title role, for which she won a Best Actress Oscar, while *Traffic,* an Altmanesque ensemble piece adapted from a highly respected BBC mini-series of the same name, starred Michael Douglas,

Benicio del Toro (who won the Best Supporting Actor Academy Award, while Soderbergh won the Oscar for Best Director, beating out, well, himself among others, as he was also nominated for *Brockovich*), Catherine Zeta Jones, and others. *Ocean's Eleven,* a remake of the 1960 heist film that featured the original Rat Pack (Sinatra, Martin, and Davis Jr. et al.), this time starred George Clooney, Brad Pitt, Julia Roberts, Matt Damon, and a whole host of highly recognizable others. With this trilogy of films, Steven Soderbergh conquered Hollywood, rescuing his career from the scrap heap and reinventing himself as a highly sought-after studio director who could bring home big box office numbers and critical acclaim while directing the biggest names in Hollywood. He could have done anything he wanted to do. And what he did was return to his independent roots.

Soderbergh had no problems making the films he'd just finished making. He enjoyed the process, making a ton of money, establishing a series of important relationships with A-list actors and studios types, and getting a reserve of clout that afforded him some level of freedom as to his future choices. But in addition to a more Hollywood style of movie production, Soderbergh still had a fiercely independent streak and wanted to make smaller movies with his own imprint, the kind that had once almost cost him his career. But the earlier failures provided a valuable lesson in the financial realities of Hollywood, teaching him that in order to make the films he especially wanted to make, he also had to keep making more successful mainstream films as well. And as for his small films, they had to remain truly, or at least comparatively, low budget so that if they didn't recoup their investment, the losses were such that they could be overlooked in light of the return of his more mainstream films. This resulted in a "one for them, one for me" mentality, which has long been a dream for filmmakers in Hollywood, though no one in the contemporary era has pulled it off quite as spectacularly as Steven Soderbergh.

His first film after *Ocean's Eleven* was *Full Frontal* (2002), a very experimental and largely improvised ensemble piece shot on the fly and on the cheap on digital video. The film only cost $2 million to make, rendering moot the fact that it was received lukewarmly and only grossed $3.4 million (*imdb.com; Box Office Mojo. com*). Next up was *Solaris* (2002), a remake of the 1972 film by Russian director Andrei Tarkovsky. The original, though critically admired, was little seen, making it unlikely that Soderbergh could have gotten this project off the ground without the track record he'd recently established. That and the participation of George Clooney, who was now an A-list movie star in his own right (although that's complicated, as you'll read in chapter 7). *Solaris* failed to make back its $47 million budget by $15 or so million, but it kept Soderbergh and Clooney happy, as did their HBO series *K Street* (2003), an improvisational 10-part TV series they coproduced (along with others), and the episodes of which were directed by Soderbergh (*imdb.com; Box Office Mojo.com*).

After once again acquiring a reputation as a maverick, Soderbergh and Clooney then teamed up for their next film together, *Ocean's Twelve* (2004), the sequel to *Ocean's Eleven,* which grossed over $360 million worldwide (*Box Office Mojo.*

*com*). And then Soderbergh made a tiny HD film called *Bubble,* which featured no professional actors and was made for less than $2 million dollars (*imdb.com*; *Box Office Mojo.com*). That the film was poorly received and grossed less than $300,000 worldwide certainly didn't matter in the context of Soderbergh's career. But what is interesting is that *Bubble,* released to little fanfare on January 27, 2006, seemingly an innocuous Friday, might end up being one of the most important films of all time, one upon which we'll look back in the future and say its release began the inexorable movement towards the tipping point that changed forever the way movies are distributed and exhibited.

Soderbergh had previously struck up a friendship with Marc Cuban, publicly best known as the owner of the National Basketball Association's Dallas Mavericks, but in the business world much better known as the billionaire innovator of on-line endeavors such as Broadcast.com. Cuban is also the owner of HDnet, a pay TV channel that shows movies and sports in HD. Prior to *Bubble*'s production, he had purchased Landmark Cinemas, a nationwide theater chain with theaters in many metropolitan areas. Soderbergh read about this acquisition and a light went off in his head. So he arranged a meeting with Cuban and he pitched him an idea: "You already own a TV channel, and you own a ton of screens, and you have a lot of money, so why don't you start a DVD distribution business? Then I'll make you some movies and you can release them simultaneously in your theaters, on your TV station, and via DVD." The block to simultaneous multi-platform distribution has been competitive as concerns different companies owning different things. In this case, it was one company that owned everything so there was no competition, as they'd get all the profits from the film, which made it an attractive proposition to Cuban. That the film failed and his partnership with Soderbergh would ultimately be amicably dissolved is beside the point. It's only a matter of time before all films are released on multi-platforms simultaneously, and the world of movies as it's existed since the 1920s will be forever changed, and it was Steven Soderbergh who was the first to make this happen.

Next up was *The Good German* (2006), another moderately budgeted film ($32 million) featuring George Clooney (*imdb.com*). Comparatively, this did much worse at the box office than *Solaris,* earning less than $6 million worldwide, which probably didn't make the primary producing studio, Warner Brothers, too happy (*Box Office Mojo.com*). But the blow was undoubtedly lessened by the $311 million box office of *Ocean's Thirteen* (2007), the next Soderbergh film, which Warners also produced, as it had the first two (*Box Office Mojo.com*). And then came *Che* (2008), Soderbergh's critically divisive but ambitious $58 million (or more) two-part biopic starring Benicio del Toro (Barnes). Because Soderbergh, in pursuit of veracity, insisted the movie be made in Spanish, the film wasn't a major studio project (it was funded by a conglomeration of outside investors), and it never received widespread distribution in America by its rights owner, IFC, owing in part to its collective 4½–hour run time, which makes it quite possibly the longest-running commercial film in U.S. history (Corliss, "Guerilla"). It's a complicated film and it doesn't precisely follow the linear narrative that is part and parcel with standard Hollywood biopics. It mostly confounded the few American audiences that saw it and it perplexed a lot of critics as well, but it did so at least in part because it didn't follow the time-honored linear storytelling structure of Hollywood biopics. Time will tell how this film is regarded, but for now, it's the box office that tells the tale and it's a horror story: less than $1.5 million domestically and a little over $30 million total (*Box Office Mojo.com*; Barnes).

Undeterred, Soderbergh made his next feature, *The Girlfriend Experience* (2009), quick and inexpensively ($1.7 million), shooting the film on a Red One, a high-end but very light and—compared to film—dirt-cheap camera (*imdb.com*). Additionally, the film, about a high-priced call girl, features real-life porn star Sasha Grey in the lead role, which called attention to the film that it might not otherwise have garnered. While the film is about a sex worker, there's not a lot of actual sex in the movie. Still, its subject and lack of mainstream star power certainly played a role in its not getting wide theatrical distribution and earning less than $1 million total (*Box Office Mojo.com*). But the lesson from *Che,* which Richard Corliss calls—"a halfway movie: too expensive (reportedly $61 million) to be relegated to art houses, too stiff and forbidding to appeal to any part of a mass audience"—seems to have reminded Soderbergh that its perfectly okay to fail, so long as you fail *small* ("Guerilla"). Had Soderbergh made *Che* as his second or third feature he may have had trouble in the future. As it is, with all the huge hits he has under his belt, he's got a little leeway he wouldn't otherwise have. Wisely, Soderbergh followed up *The GFE* with *The Informant* (2009), a mainstream biopic about a very nontraditional corporate informant, played by Matt Damon, who runs afoul of the law while informing on others. The $21 million Warner Brothers' film earned $42 million worldwide and a lot of positive press for Soderbergh and Damon (*imdb.com*; *Box Office Mojo.com*).

It's rather remarkable to consider how varied Steven Soderbergh's career has been when one looks back over his output since his breakthrough with *sex, lies, and videotape* (1989). As Corliss writes of him,

> Among all contemporary American directors, he has the most restless ambitions. His interests range far and wide, across different genres but, more important, different kinds of movies: the indie romantic comedy (*sex, lies, and videotape*), the all-star action spectacle (*Ocean's*) and the defiantly obscurantist conundrum (*Schizopolis*). His films can toady to an audience's prejudices (*Erin Brockovich*) or virtually say, "Don't watch me" (*Bubble*). He has the clout to get his projects off the ground and the work ethic to make them quickly: *Che* is his ninth feature this decade, not including shorter films and the TV series *K Street*. And he doesn't just direct his own films, he photographs them (under the pseudonym Peter Andrews). Yet Soderbergh seems defined more by these giant, wayward ambitions than by a discernible authorial personality. If his name were taken off his films, sophisticated viewers would be hard pressed to locate a visual or thematic through-line. ("Warrior Auteurs")

Despite an arguable absence of the kind of authorial watermarks ascribed to other directors, Steven Soderbergh is a singularly diverse artist, as comfortable working with an Arriflex 35-mm camera under the bright klieg lights of a mainstream big-budget studio set as he is with a handheld digital camera on a dingy location with a skeleton crew and amateur actors. He can make a film as grand as Christoper Nolan or more quirkily than Sofia Coppola and either way, he's bound to make something that gets people talking. He's a unique artist who has managed to carve out a sizable commercial niche while simultaneously working on the fringes. It's surely a remarkable career path others will try to follow, but it remains to be seen if anyone will be quite as successful on it as Soderbergh has.

In these nascent moments of the digital age, it's impossible to talk about film-makers of influence over the past 20 years without discussing Canadian-born writer/director James Cameron and his influence on the industry, which is all the more remarkable given the fact that since 1990, he's only made four fictional nar-rative feature films. Regardless, his contribution to the industry in the area of spe-cial effects is huge, and may prove to be only more so in the coming years of the digital age as the industry moves more and more towards 3D production.

James Cameron's breakthrough film as a director was *The Terminator* (1984), a dark, effects-laden $7 million sci-fi movie in which Arnold Schwarzenegger stars as a terminator, a cyborg sent from the future by robots to kill Sarah Connor, the mother of the as yet to be born John Connor, the man who would otherwise lead the human race to defeat the robots' effort to rule the world (*imdb.com*). In ad-dition to adding the line "I'll be back" to the pop culture lexicon, the film made Schwarzenegger an A-list action movie star and put Cameron on the map as a visionary sci-fi director, which landed him a gig writing and directing *Aliens,* the sequel to Ridley Scott's legendary *Alien* (1979). This film was also a critical and financial success, and it put Cameron in new territory as a director, allowing him as close to carte blanche as to what he would direct next as anybody in Hollywood ever gets.

Cameron chose to make *The Abyss* (1989), a $70 million film about the at-tempted rescue of a nuclear submarine stranded in deep water and the complica-tions that arise when they run afoul of the aquatic extraterrestrials that are also in the abyss (*imdb.com*). Though well reviewed, the film underwhelmed at the box office, and it also went a long way in establishing Cameron's reputation as something of a prickly personality and an on-set tyrant, which may or may not be totally true; what is true is that he's a perfectionist, an insanely driven artist who controls as much of the filmmaking process as he possibly can and for whom "good enough" isn't. As Cameron told then Fox president Leonard Goldberg just prior to beginning production on *The Abyss,* "I want you to know one thing— once we embark on this adventure and I start to make this movie, the only way you'll be able to stop me is to kill me" (Goodyear). For a Cameron film to see the light of day, every aspect of the product must meet with his approval, which is not an easy thing and has sometimes resulted in long shoots and even longer periods of excruciatingly exacting postproduction. But the results are inarguably visually spectacular; whether or not one likes the scripts and the storytelling, it's hard not to appreciate how great his films look, and that's in no small part because of his attention to detail. In particular, the rippling swells of the water column in *The Abyss,* made possible by Cameron's deft manipulation of the digital technology available at the time, still have the power to awe. That said, *The Abyss* was at the time the most ambitious underwater movie ever attempted, and beleaguered crew members took to calling the film "The Abuse" (Goodyear). And this was just a prelude with what would subsequently come with *Titanic.*

But before he made *Titanic,* Cameron made two other films, *Terminator 2: Judgment Day* (1991) and *True Lies* (1994), both of which were critical and financial hits. In addition to the cultural touchstone of Arnold uttering, "Hasta la vista, baby," *T2,* which was the most expensive ever made at the time, remains famous for what is arguably the signature special effect of the 1990s, the repeated morphing of Robert Patrick's molten-silver T-1000 robot into different guises, an effect that would become ubiquitous but that was pioneered by a collaboration between Cameron and the team at George Lucas's Industrial Light & Magic. It's the special effects, far beyond what had previously been done in Hollywood film before, that drove the production cost so high, a reported $102 million or more, much of which went into research and development and the purchase of hardware and software required to get things just as Cameron envisioned (*imdb.com*). For the most part, the film was well reviewed and it was the highest-grossing film of that particular year. But it wasn't seen by all as having good effects on movie culture, with David Foster Wallace being among the most eviscerating of its critics when he wrote that its release was responsible for the rise of what he called the "F/X porn" of the 1990s:

1990s moviegoers who have sat clutching their heads in both awe and disappointment at movies like *Twister* and *Volcano* and *The Lost World* can thank James Cameron's *Terminator 2: Judgment Day* for inaugurating what's become this decade's special new genre of big-budget film: Special Effects Porn. "Porn" because, if you substitute F/X for intercourse, the parallels between the two genres become so obvious they're eerie. Just like hard-core cheapies, movies like *Terminator 2* and *Jurassic Park* aren't really "movies" in the standard sense at all. What they really are is half a dozen or so isolated, spectacular scenes—scenes comprising maybe twenty or thirty minutes of riveting, sensuous payoff—strung together via another sixty to ninety minutes of flat, dead, and often hilariously insipid narrative.

    . . . Think of the scenes we all still remember. That incredible chase and explosion in the L.A. sluiceway and then the liquid metal T-1000 Terminator walking out of the explosion's flames and morphing seamlessly into his Martin-Milner-as-Possessed-by-Hannibal-Lecter corporeal form. The T-1000 rising hideously up out of that checkerboard floor, the T-1000 melting headfirst through the windshield of that helicopter, the T-1000 freezing in liquid nitrogen and then collapsing fractally apart. These were truly spectacular images, and they represented exponential advances in digital F/X technology. But there were at most maybe eight of these incredible sequences, and they were the movie's heart and point; the rest of *T2* is empty and derivative, pure mimetic polycelluloid.

Whatever one thinks of the movie and the kind of movies it may have spawned in its wake, *T2* definitely raised the stakes in Hollywood filmmaking. Once audiences see a film's special effects look a particular way, they won't accept anything less believable in subsequent works, so all films most follow suit, which they did, and so the budgets of blockbusters, already huge, continued to jump accordingly.

After *T2* Cameron made *True Lies,* a remake of the French film *La Totale!* (Zidi 1991). True to form, Cameron adapted the small film about a secret agent who lies to his wife about his profession into a $120 million special effects extravaganza that climaxes with a nuclear explosion (*imdb.com*). That said, it's the closest thing he's made to a comedy, and Schwarzenegger and Jamie Lee Curtis received some of the best reviews of their careers for their self-deprecating turns in what Richard Corliss and Jeffrey Ressner describe as a James Bond thriller "welded" to a romantic comedy. Once again, the production received a lot of attention due to its cost, about which Schwarzenegger said, "The press thinks movie studios should be reviewed like the government—as if public money were spent and a crime committed. Well, it's not their money, it's the studios' money. Sometimes money is spent wisely, sometimes not. But it's like that in every business." As for Cameron, he succinctly summed up his thoughts on the furor by saying, "I like to keep challenging myself . . . so I try different things. And a lot of the things I like to try are expensive. I will say what I say about every budget: the price of a ticket is $7.50 [it was 1994, remember], and you're getting a lot of movie for it. End of story" (Corliss and Ressner). And there's little doubt audiences agreed, resulting in a healthy worldwide gross of almost $380 million (*Box Office Mojo.com*).

Next for Cameron came *Titanic,* which during its production many assumed would be an enormous flop, once again due to its having the biggest budget of any film ever made (upwards of $200 million or more), which marked the third time in a row a Cameron film had that distinction (*imdb.com*). The film is different than some of his other works in that at its heart it's a straight up love story. That said, it's still a special effects movie as that ship has got to sink and audiences paid to see it go under. The studio, Fox, took the unprecedented step of building a special studio in Mexico from scratch just for this production, to the tune of $57 million dollars. The pièce de résistance was an almost to scale cross section reproduction of the ship, which measured 775 feet long and 10 stories high and was outfitted so as to be as exact a replication of the actual ship as possible. For the water sequences, they built a 19-million-gallon-capacity tank, the largest ever constructed for a movie. These two things, in combination with an accompanying array of impeccably crafted miniatures, went a long way in enabling them to render the ship's interior and ultimate demise so as to look incredibly authentic (Boles). Whereas the special effects in

Cameron's other films are often used to depict elements of the impossible, in *Titanic* the opposite is true in that they were necessary to show his take on *what actually happened,* which was uncharted territory for Cameron and crew. But the film looks great and audiences, especially teenaged girls, embraced the love story between lead actors Leonardo DiCaprio and Kate Winslet, and the film did phenomenally well, in part because of an unheard of 20 percent viewer return rate, again spurred on in large part by teen girls seeing the movie over and over again (Boles). With box office receipts totaling more than $1.8 billion worldwide, *Titanic* became the highest-grossing film of all time to that point, despite its arduous production and post processes (*Box Office Mojo.com*). It was also nominated for 14 Oscars, winning 11 of them, including the Academy Award for Best Picture and a Best Director Oscar for Cameron.

What does one do after making the most expensive film ever made and turning it into the highest-grossing film in movie history? The question of what's next and how to top it is answered in a lot of different ways, depending on who it is we're talking about. For most folks, it's best to treat each project as a singular thing and judge its success on its own merits, independent of what came before it. Not doing so can result in being haunted by the specter of having created something one can never top, à la Orson Welles and *Citizen Kane* (1941). But Cameron is not a person easily discouraged, and for his next film, he set out to make an epic space opera. In 3D. Even though the 3D process that existed didn't meet Cameron's requirements. Undaunted, Cameron went about helping to invent a new 3D camera that would satisfy his high demands and enhance his legacy as this era's foremost special effects innovator. The result—which took nearly four years to make, not counting the years it took Cameron to invent the technology, the Fusion 3D camera that films in "stereoscopic 3D"—is *Avatar,* about which Cameron said, "This film integrates my life's achievements. . . . It's the most complicated stuff anyone's ever done" (Goodyear). Depending on how one does the accounting—especially whether or not you count the money required to invent the technology as part of the production cost—*Avatar* is the most expensive film ever made, coming in at a mind-boggling $500 million by some accounts, though the official Fox number is a more austere $230 million (Cieply). The question, then, became simple: Can a film with such an enormous production budget, whatever the actual number, turn a profit?

Undeterred, Cameron nicely summed up his filmmaking philosophy, saying, "If you set your goals ridiculously high and it's a failure, you will fail above everyone else's success" (Goodyear). And he was right. *Avatar* is a film about a man who assumes the form—an avatar—of an alien so as to integrate with a colony of aliens and relay information about them back to his corporate masters, who will in turn use the information in their quest to mine the planet for a rare mineral woodenly called "unobtanium." It's easy enough to deride the recycled nature of the film's story, but to do so doesn't account for its appeal, which is in part precisely because it's so familiar. Audiences want to see that which they know, but they want to see it delivered in a new form, and that's exactly what *Avatar* gives them, an elementally mythical tale deftly disguised as a space opera. And the story is in some ways beside the point. If you see *Avatar* in 3D, as it's meant to be seen, it isn't just seen, it's *experienced*. It's a whole new way of going to the movies. The visuals aren't a schlocky gimmick; they give that which you're watching a depth and texture unlike anything ever put on the big screen.

In 2006 James Cameron was the keynote speaker at the National Association of Broadcasters' Digital Cinema Summit. The theme of his speech was the future of cinema, about which he said, "We're in a fight for survival here . . . we just need to fight back harder, come out blazing, not wither away and die. D-cinema [digital cinema] can do it, for a number of reasons, but because d-cinema is an enabling technology for 3-D. Digital 3-D is a revolutionary form of showmanship that is within our grasp. It can get people off their butts and away from their portable devices and get people back in the theaters where they belong." He also took the opportunity to decry the day and date release strategy pioneered by Steven Soderbergh, claiming that, "We're so scared of piracy right now that we're ready to pimp out our mothers. . . . This whole day-and-date DVD release nonsense? Here's an answer: Digital cinema is one of the strongest reasons I've been pushing 3-D for the past few years because it offers a powerful experience which you can only have in the movie theater." Cameron closed by citing his love of movies and his love of making them for the big screen. "I'm not going to make movies for people to watch on their cell phones. . . . I don't want that grand, visionary, transporting movie experience made for the big screen to become a thing of the past" (Crabtree).

In reading Cameron's words at the time, those with an understanding of cinematic history didn't think of the future so much as they did the past. Specifically, folks thought of the 1950s, at which time the popularity of going to the theater to see movies was under assault by the proliferation of new technology, specifically television. In an attempt to differentiate cinema from the small house-bound boxes, the industry tried to reinvent the formats in which movies were shot and screened. They wanted movies to be visually huge and immense in such a way as to make sure that their grandeur could only be experienced in all its glory and enormity on a movie theater big screen. They tried various kinds of wide-screen processes, including CinemaScope and VistaVision, and perhaps most famously and disastrously, they tried various kinds of 3D processes, all of which proved awkward and unwieldy and ultimately failed. Remarkably, Cameron saw that the failure was not the idea but the limits of technology at the time, and in embracing this old idea while armed with new technology, Cameron may well have single-handedly changed cinema forever, finally making the 3D movie experience a financially viable reality. He went back in time to move cinema forward. The rush to film (or convert that which has already been shot) in 3D that has taken place in Hollywood since *Avatar*'s release will surely result in a lot of high-dollar stinkers being made, but that's always the case in the copy-cat phase that invariably happens when someone figures out how to utilize a new technology. Ultimately 3D can be more than just something that puts butts in seats; it can be a new tool to enhance storytelling and filmmakers will surely embrace it.

Whether or not *Avatar* is high art I'll leave to future film scholars, but it's undeniably an immersive visual experience, seamlessly integrating 3D technology with "performance captured" CGI images, and audiences love it, answering the question about whether or not a film with *Avatar*'s production budget can make money. The answer is yes, as evidenced by *Avatar*, with box office in excess of $2.7 billion and counting (Goldsmith). While 3D is likely now here to stay, studios should be loathe to spend hundreds of millions of dollars on a 3D movie just because they can. With that kind of money on the line, they need to be very judicious in their choices and remember that even though *Avatar* seemingly wasn't based on a specific pre-sold property, it did in many ways have one, and that was James Cameron himself, a rare director whose work people want to see specifically because it's his. As for Cameron, he's again faced with the problem of what to do next. He's planning to make a film called *Battle Angel*, another sci-fi film set in the distant future, and then maybe a sequel to *Avatar*. But first, he's doing a little work for NASA, helping San Diego–based Malin Space Science Systems design a 3D camera they can mount on the next Mars Rover, a nuclear-powered machine the size of a car appropriately named "Curiosity" (Hornyak). One only wonders if he'll eventually actually shoot a film in outer space. Don't laugh; he might.

## Notes

1. I'm aware that choosing five directors to feature in a single book chapter can seem arbitrary, as there are certainly many, many other equally deserving directors whose work could be included in this chapter. That said, given the limitations of space, I chose representative influential directors currently working on the large stage of the Hollywood mainstream who I thought were particularly illustrative in proving my points in the hope that it will get readers to reconsider how they think about other directors working within (or outside of) the system as well as those whose work I detail here.

2. The inspiration and some of the text for the Apatow section has its roots in a never-published article on his work that I cowrote with Professor Jana Byars, whose keen insights, as always, have proven invaluable.

## Works Cited

"AFI's 100 Years . . . 100 Movies." *American Film Institute (afi).com.*

Aftab, Kaleem. "Whatever Happened to the Great American Film Director?" *The Independent* [London]. July 3, 2009. *LexisNexis Academic.*

Auletta, Ken. "Beauty and the Beast." *The New Yorker*, Dec. 16, 2002: 64–81. *New Yorker Online Archive.*

Barnes, Henry. "Steven Soderbergh: 'I Can See the End of My Career.'" *Guardian.co.uk* [London]. July 14, 2009.

Bart, Peter, and Michael Fleming. "Sony Scraps Soderbergh's *Moneyball.*" *Variety.com.* July 21, 2009.

Boles, Derek. "James Cameron's *Titanic.*" *Media-Awareness.ca.*

*Box Office Mojo.com.* "The Abyss."

*Box Office Mojo.com.* "Anchorman."

*Box Office Mojo.com.* "The Aviator."

*Box Office Mojo.com.* "Bubble."

*Box Office Mojo.com.* "The Departed."

*Box Office Mojo.com.* "The 40-Year-Old Virgin."

*Box Office Mojo.com.* "Full Frontal."

*Box Office Mojo.com.* "Gangs of New York."

*Box Office Mojo.com.* "The Girlfriend Experience."

*Box Office Mojo.com.* "The Good German."

*Box Office Mojo.com.* "The Informant."

*Box Office Mojo.com.* "The Limey."

*Box Office Mojo.com.* "Out of Sight."

*Box Office Mojo.com.* "Raging Bull."

*Box Office Mojo.com.* "Shutter Island."

*Box Office Mojo.com.* "Solaris."

*Box Office Mojo.com.* "Taxi Driver."

*Box Office Mojo.com.* "The Terminator."

*Box Office Mojo.com.* "Terminator 2."

*Box Office Mojo.com.* "Titanic."

*Box Office Mojo.com.* "True Lies."

Brand, Madeleine. "*Star Wars'* Merchandise." *Morning Edition. npr.org.* May 25, 2007.

Cieply, Michael. "A Movie's Budget Pops from the Screen." *New York Times.com.* Nov. 8, 2009.

Corliss, Richard. "Soderbergh and Tarantino: Warrior Auteurs." *Time.com.* May 22, 2008.

Corliss, Richard. "Guerilla in the Mist: Soderbergh's *Che.*" *Time.com.* Dec. 13, 2008.

Corliss, Richard, and Jeffrey Ressner. "Lies, True Lies, and Ballistics." *Time.com.* July 18, 1994.

Crabtree, Sheigh. "Cameron: D-Cinema Is Exhibition's Salvation." *TheHollywoodReporter. com.* April 24, 2006.

Dwyer, Sean. "*I Love You, Man* Review." *Filmjunk.com.* March 22, 2009.

Dwyer, Sean. "Adventureland Review." *Filmjunk.com.* April 1, 2009.

Goldsmith, Jill. "*Avatar* Gives News Corp. Record Q3." *Variety.com.* May 4, 2010.

Goodyear, Dana. "Man of Extremes: The Return of James Cameron." *The New Yorker. com.* Oct. 26, 2009.

Holson, Laura M. "2 Hollywood Titans Brawl Over a Gang Epic." *The New York Times.* April 7, 2002. *LexisNexis Academic.*

Hornyak, Tim. "James Cameron Building 3-D Cam for Mars Rover." *Cnet.com.* April 29, 2010.

"How George Lucas Got the Rights to the *Star Wars* Sequels." *afi.com.*

*IMDB.com.* "The Aviator."

*IMDB.com.* "Bubble."

*IMDB.com.* "Casino."

*IMDB.com.* "Che."

*IMDB.com.* "The Departed."

*IMDB.com.* "Erin Brockovich."

*IMDB.com.* "Full Frontal."

*IMDB.com.* "The Girlfriend Experience."

*IMDB.com.* "The Good German."

*IMDB.com.* "The Informant."

*IMDB.com.* "The Limey."

*IMDB.com.* "Ocean's Eleven."

*IMDB.com.* "Ocean's Twelve."

*IMDB.com.* "Ocean's Thirteen."

*IMDB.com.* "Out of Sight."

*IMDB.com.* "Raging Bull."

*IMDB.com.* "Schizopolis."

*IMDB.com.* "Shutter Island."

*IMDB.com.* "Solaris."

*IMDB.com.* "Taxi Driver."

*IMDB.com.* "Titanic."

*IMDB.com.* "Traffic."

*IMDB.com.* "True Lies."

Ramos, Steve. "'Adventureland' Interview with Greg Mottola." *Movie Jungle.com.* March 27, 2009.

Truffaut, François. "Une Certaine Tendance du Cinéma Français," *Cahiers du Cinema.* No. 31 January 1954, 15–29.

Wallace, David Foster. "F/X Porn." *Waterstone's* magazine (Winter/Spring 1998). http://www.badgerinternet.com/~bobkat/waterstone.html.

# Chapter 7

# THE RISE AND FALL
# OF THE $100 MILLION PAYCHECK:
# HOLLYWOOD STARDOM SINCE 1990

*By Anne Helen Petersen*

Through the end of the star and studio system, the rise of agents, the inflation of star power, the move to high concept productions, and the all-important summer tent-pole film, the role of the star has fluctuated tremendously. In 1990, the star (and his industrious agent) reigned supreme, able to leverage tremendous salary, participation points, and production credits. Nearly 20 years later, despite sustained reliance on high concept and presold properties, the star remains valuable. Yet his or her ability to open a movie is seriously in question, and the kingly demands of yore are no more. Critics bemoan the fall of the true star and the ubiquity of the reality celebrity, pointing to the death of Michael Jackson as indicative of the decline of a particular type of fame (Segal). While such polemics are not unfounded—stars are certainly not what they used to be—they *are* somewhat premature.

For stars are both industrial *and* sociological phenomena. As such, even as they become less of an industrial imperative, and their services diminish in worth, by no means will they cease to demand our cultural attention. In fact, the reliance on high concept in lieu of stars may revert us to a star system akin to that which accompanied the studio system, when stars were contracted, played both according to and against type, flop films could be leveraged against hit ones, and no single star vehicle could sink a studio. Of course, the parameters of stardom have evolved past the near-indentured servitude that structured the studio system. Yet a return to smaller roles and smaller pictures may indeed be the trajectory of the Hollywood star today.

## A BRIEF HISTORY OF HOLLYWOOD STARDOM

The power of the stars has oscillated significantly through the history of narrative cinema. Richard DeCordova situates the emergence of stars around 1913, when extratextual information concerning those appearing on-screen first became readily available. Early silent stars were larger-than-life figures—Mary Pickford, Charlie Chaplin, Douglas Fairbanks, Gloria Swanson—who quickly realized their value to the studio, demanding and receiving incredible salaries.[1] In response, studio heads moved to reign in the extravagant salaries and demands of the stars, signing talent early—and to long-term contracts—to ensure a long period of service for a bargain-basement price tag. The studios sought out, refined, and exploited talent, practices that defined the star system under the larger studio system of the 1930s through mid-1940s.

If a contracted star refused to do a picture, she would be put on suspension. The time on suspension would then be added on to the existing seven-year contract, effectively forcing the star to cow to the whims of the studio. Star contracts stipulated a certain moral behavior and adherence to a preconstructed public image, including requisite publicity appearances, photo shoots, etc. Star salaries were relatively small and constant, with no bonuses and certainly no share of a particular film's gross.[2] Several stars attempted to fight this particular form of indentured servitude, but none succeeded until Olivia de Havilland sued Warner Bros. in 1945, citing a California statute against contracts longer than seven years. With her victory, the studios' power began to diminish. The enforcement of the Paramount Decree (the 1948 Supreme Court decision that forced the studios to divest themselves of their theaters, thus beginning the end of the classical-era studio system) further handicapped the studios, which soon began to tighten their belts against the onslaught of television, suburbanization, and the resultant loss of audiences, cutting above-and below-the-line talent loose.

When the studios released their stars, the newly vital and vigorous talent agencies were there to scoop them up. While agents had long existed in Hollywood, most studios even forbade their presence on the lot, fearing their intervention with studio policy. With MCA and William Morris's expansion to Hollywood, the talent agency became a formidable industry presence. MCA founder Jules Stein, his protégé Lew Wasserman, and their agent army sought established stars, promised renegotiated contracts, and leveraged their stable of talent against the studios. They pioneered the practice of packaging talent: combining the services of a director, writer, and/or star and selling the talent package to the studio or television network. MCA encouraged its clients to incorporate themselves for tax purposes, thus becoming coproducers (and profit participants) in their own work.

So when Wasserman arranged a deal between Universal and Jimmy Stewart for *Winchester '73* (Mann 1950), promising Stewart a paltry $250,000 paycheck in exchange for a percentage of the profits (which proved substantial), the distribution of power between stars and the studios was forever altered. With the studios in free fall, the promise of a star was one of the few ways to anchor a picture. With the help of a crafty agent, the star could extract promises of profit participation, coproducer credits, and enormous salaries from the desperate studios. By the mid-1960s, almost every major star had self-incorporated and began coproducing his own pictures, listing film profits as capitol gains instead of highly taxable income and regularly exercising veto power over directors, cinematographers, and costars.

In 1963, Elizabeth Taylor was paid a reported $1 million for the big-budget bomb *Cleopatra* (Mankiewicz). In the reckless boom and bust era following World War II, it seemed clear that stars could not function as a reliable predictor of a film's success. Indeed, the largest grosser of the 1960s—*The Sound of Music* (Wise 1965)—boasted no major stars. Yet as the studios reorganized, experimented, and became part of diversified conglomerates, stars nevertheless remained a key means of procuring financing and international distribution deals. While the countercultural films and 1970s art cinema served as a definite turn away from established stars, the most profitable films of the early 1970s—the oft-forgotten disaster films like *The Poseidon Adventure* (Neame 1972), *The Towering Inferno* (Guillermin and Allen 1974), and *Earthquake* (Robson 1974)—boasted tremendous star ensemble casts.

The success of *Jaws* (Spielberg) in 1975 signaled the continued rise of the pre-sold property and the viability of the high-concept film. Many of these 1970s and 1980s blockbusters were purposely bereft of established (and thus expensive) stars. *Star Wars* (Lucas 1977) and *E.T.* (Spielberg 1982) were cast with relative unknowns: the star of these films was the concept. Yet high-concept films are also star machines—an actor enters the narrative an unknown and emerges as a high-priced talent, as evidenced by the careers of Bruce Willis, Sylvester Stallone, Harrison Ford, and Eddie Murphy. With the help of a new generation of agents, the studios paid dearly for such stars.

When MCA moved from agenting to ownership of Universal in 1962, a handful of agencies emerged to form a talent oligopoly: William Morris, Creative Management Associates (composed of former MCA agents), and Famous Talent Agency. The agenting landscape shifted again in 1975, when CMA and Famous Talent merged to form ICM, and a handful of upstart William Morris agents, headed by the young and ambitious Michael Ovitz, left William Morris to start CAA. Through the course of the 1970s and 1980s, CAA continued to rise in prominence and power. Following Ovitz's lead, they dressed in Armani suits, drove matching Jaguars, traveled in packs, and practiced a Zen-influenced philosophy of teamwork and collaboration. While Ovitz is often singled out as a visionary, he was merely reproducing many of the selfsame tactics pioneered by Wasserman: packaging, cultivating anonymity, parlaying CAA's talent monopoly into preferred treatment from producers and studios. Whether or not Ovitz was an original, he was clearly a success, ruling Hollywood through the 1980s and early 1990s while firmly atop the Most Powerful lists of *Premiere* and *Entertainment Weekly* (Slater 223–35).

## STARDOM FROM 1990 TO THE PRESENT: CASE STUDIES

But what, exactly, does it mean to rule Hollywood? Was it Ovitz who had the power, or was it the stars he represented? More to the point, was it the studios, the agents, the stars, or the brains—directors and producers like Spielberg, Lucas, Tony

Scott, Joel Silver—who controlled what films were made, and at what cost? The answer has never been straightforward, but from 1990 on, understanding the dynamics between star and studio has only become more complex. CAA was profoundly shaken by Ovitz's 1995 exit to serve as second-in-command to Michael Eisner at Disney, and by the end of the decade, every major studio and had been sucked up by a massive international conglomerate entity. As the studios continued to morph into glorified distribution arms, the stars turned to armies of personalized assistants to perform the services once supplied for them by the studios. Instead of in-house fixers and massive publicity departments feeding stories to *Photoplay*, stars have publicists strategically offering tidbits to *People* and *Entertainment Tonight*; instead of studio heads slotting talent in pictures, the stars have agents and managers sifting through prospective scripts and managing their brand. Stars employ personal trainers, stylists, and makeup and hair artists; they hire legal teams to negotiate the fine points of contracts and incorporate their interests. During the studio system, all such costs were sheltered under the studio umbrella; in the post-studio, freelance era, these costs are transferred to the star.

The star's salary must rise accordingly. Through the demise of the studio era into the present, as salaries reached phenomenal levels during the 1990s, each superstar must compete for the larger, more lucrative deal. At the turn of the millennium, with DVD sell-throughs posed to generate an ancillary bonanza, stars seemed firmly in control. But a slew of underperforming star vehicles and massively successful starless or mid-star franchises of the 2000s have changed the game, making the $20 million paycheck look thoroughly anachronistic. To illuminate the specific dynamics of stardom over the past 20 years, I turn to the examples of Julia Roberts, Tom Cruise, and George Clooney, as each star's career represents a distinct path to the top, strategy for brand maintenance, and tentative foothold in the Hollywood multiverse today.

## Julia Roberts

Julia Roberts is the most important actress to hit Hollywood since Barbra Streisand. While her most obvious achievement may be her unique ability to garner paychecks on par with her male counterparts, her career trajectory is equally instructive. With the one-two punch of *Steel Magnolias* (Ross 1989) and *Pretty Woman* (Marshall 1990), both of which garnered Oscar nominations, Julia Roberts quickly rose to become the biggest female draw in America. Throughout the course of the 1990s, she rode out her stardom in several lackluster films, skyrocketed into tabloid infamy, retreated from the public eye, and endured a series of incontestable flops. She returned to prominence in 1997 with an impressive string of hits, culminating in an Oscar win for *Erin Brockovich* (Soderbergh 2000) and a $20 million paycheck for *Mona Lisa Smile* (Newell 2003) before she retreated from Hollywood for a second period of relative obscurity. While Roberts's tumultuous career underlines the ability of the celebrity press to sustain interest in a star, her current struggle to return to the game emphasizes the ways in which the industry—and the star's place within it—has shifted during her brief yet significant absence.

Roberts was discovered and shepherded to stardom by Elaine Goldsmith, an agent first with William Morris and soon after with ICM. Goldsmith wrangled for Roberts the role in the long-developing *Pretty Woman*. The film—and Roberts's performance in it—remains iconic, and formed the bedrock of Roberts's stardom. In years to come, films in which she played characters that physically and spiritually resembled Vivian, including those of *My Best Friend's Wedding* (Hogan 1997), *Runaway Bride* (Marshall 1999), and *Erin Brockovich*, would succeed. Roles alien to that creation—including *Something to Talk About* (Hallstrom 1995), *Mary Reilly* (Frears 1996), *Michael Collins* (Jordan 1996), and *Full Frontal* (Soderbergh 2002)—would fail. Following the success of *Pretty Woman,* Roberts appeared in the thriller *Sleeping with the Enemy* (Ruben 1991) (an unexpected success) and weepie *Dying Young* (Schumacher 1991), which performed somewhat poorly. During this period, she also became engaged to Hollywood scion and former costar Keifer Sutherland. When Roberts left Sutherland days before the wedding, she retreated to Ireland to be with Sutherland's good friend Jason Patric. Predictably, the gossip magazines descended with a vengeance upon the wreckage of her love life.

The resultant frenzy was enough to sustain interest in Roberts's star through the next few years, even as she attempted to steer clear of the Hollywood spotlight. A series of minor roles and cameos (including a much-ridiculed turn as Tinkerbell in *Hook* [Spielberg 1991]) were interspersed with a major role in the highly anticipated *The Pelican Brief* (Pakula 1993), along with big-budget Hollywood underperformers *Something to Talk About* and *I Love Trouble* (Schyer 1994) and art film interludes in *Everybody Says I Love You* (Allen 1996), *Mary Reilly,* and *Michael Collins*. To look at Roberts's career in 1997 was to see her tremendous promise unfilled and sustained by tabloid fodder, including a much-ballyhooed barefoot wedding to country-western star Lyle Lovett, ill-advised roles, and nostalgia for her *Pretty Woman* persona.

Cue *My Best Friend's Wedding,* the film David Thomson describes as the moment when Roberts "figured out how people wanted to like her" (745). The string of successes that followed—including *Stepmom* (Columbus 1998), *Notting Hill* (Michell 1999), *Runaway Bride, Erin Brockovich,* and *The Mexican* (Verbinksi 2001)—played up Roberts's natural charisma and *Pretty Woman* personality, reconciling old-fashioned charm and sex appeal. These films likewise paired her with a variety of winning leading men, always in safe yet playful variations on the romantic comedy generic tradition. During this period, Roberts started her own production company, hiring longtime agent Elaine Goldsmith (now Goldsmith-Thomas) to serve as its head and coproducing *Stepmom*. Despite moving into collaborative work with *Ocean's Eleven* (Soderbergh 2001) and *America's Sweethearts* (Roth 2001), Roberts drew a $20 million paycheck for *Mona Lisa Smile*—nearly $1/3$ of the film's $65 million budget. The film grossed only $63 million domestic, with an additional $77 million international. Such numbers underline the appeal of the superstar overseas, but they likewise signal Roberts's descent from the heights of *Runaway Bride* viability.

Following a miraculously quiet romance with then married cameraman Danny Moder, Roberts retreated yet again, this time to her Taos, New Mexico, home. She gave birth to twins, appeared in a few additional ensemble pieces (spoofing herself in *Ocean's Twelve* [Soderbergh 2004], foul-mouthed in *Closer* [Nichols 2004], and voice acting in *Charlotte's Web* [Winick 2006] and *The Ant Bully* [Davis 2006]), and gave birth to a third child. In our celebrity-baby-obsessed culture, her children attracted attention—the first photos of her twins garnered an immense sum from *People* and a cover story—but the remote location of her home continued to shield her from most paparazzi. *People* still loves her, but her life seems altogether too uneventful and scandal-free for the new media gossip forms, whether Perez Hilton or TMZ.

In the meantime, Roberts's production company, now renamed Red Om, has refocused on producing *The American Girl* series for television and the big screen. Roberts herself resurfaced in late 2007 in a notable albeit supporting role in *Charlie Wilson's War* (Nichols 2007). She moved from her longtime agent at ICM to CAA in 2003, presumably in an attempt to reset her career. Roberts was, without a doubt, the biggest female star of the past 20 years. That she holds that clout *despite* two extended periods of inactivity, dabblings in experimental roles, and a slew of unsuccessful films is a testament both to the superlative quality of her blockbusters and the resilience of her star image. While she is no longer young by Hollywood standards, she is still radiant. But is she still a star?

The test seemed to have been in the spring of 2009, when she starred alongside Clive Owen in Tony Gilroy's elaborately plotted caper film *Duplicity* (2009). The film had hit written all over it: Roberts plays a smart, sexy lead alongside a smart, sexy costar. Yet the film seemed homeless, and Universal dropped it in theaters in late March, when movie buzz is at its lowest. Despite positive if not effusive reviews and a strong marketing campaign, the film opened in an embarrassing third place behind high-concept action pic *Knowing* (Proyas 2009), starring the always-reliable Nicolas Cage, and the bromance comedy *I Love You, Man* (Hamburg 2009). *Duplicity* went on to gross only $40.5 million domestic and $36 million international. With a stated budget of $60 million, it clearly underperformed. For *Variety* columnist Anne Thompson, *Duplicity* "boasted the earmarks of a commercial Hollywood vehicle—big budget, exotic locations, thriller genre, two sexy movie stars— but may have been too costly for what was really a smart-house play" ("*Duplicity*"). What's more, Universal paid Roberts a reported $20 million—a full third of the budget—despite the knowledge that no contemporary star, not even Will Smith, has been able to consistently pull in audiences.

Reflecting on Roberts's career, several themes come to the fore. First, her sustained success through the 1990s and 2000s appears to be the exception that proves the rule: no other female star has proven as lucrative. The fickleness of audiences towards female stars has yet to be satisfactorily explained, yet the fact that Roberts consistently figured as the sole female to reside in the upper echelons of star power speaks to this very phenomenon. In 2007 Roberts turned 40, which may account for her inability to draw the massive audiences that bolstered her mid-career come-back. Second, Roberts demonstrates the maxim that a compelling extratextual life can sustain star interest, if not necessarily star power. Yet with an eye to recent flops by tabloid favorite Lindsay Lohan, one becomes keenly aware that a star's name in discourse does not necessarily translate to audience desire to see said star on-screen. Third, a major star will attract greater audiences in roles in accordance with her dominant star image than in roles that deviate from said image. Finally, and perhaps most instructively, even when a star does return to her star image—as Roberts clearly did with *Duplicity*—it will no longer guarantee the type of grosses as before.

At the close of the decade, stars remain larger than life. Nevertheless, their track records simply cannot stack up to those of starless, high-concept films laden with special effects, whether *Transformers: Revenge of the Fallen* (Bay 2009) or *Harry Potter 6* (Yates 2009). For a star like Roberts to remain relevant and employable, she will need to stick with smaller projects with slimmer paychecks. At the same time, as past experimentation made apparent, she must likewise steer clear of films that so clearly subvert her likable, appealing star image. The paradox, then, is she must somehow translate her big-budget persona into small-budget films—or take a significant pay cut to appear in mid-range rom-coms, now the territory of Reese Witherspoon, Kate Hudson, and Sandra Bullock. Can her ego—and career—absorb the hit?

## Tom Cruise

Similar to Julia Roberts, Tom Cruise is readily cited as the biggest star of the past 20, even 30 years. His star power has only grown with time, expanding into coproduction and substantial profit-sharing participation. However, in recent years, with the combination of a high-profile romance, several highly visible em-barrassing gaffes, and a public condemnation from the head of Viacom, Cruise has been forced to work diligently to recover his star prowess. With the quiet international success of *Valkyrie* (Singer 2008), Cruise seems to have rehabili-tated his career—but to what end? What is the place of a star with a pedigree and price tag like Cruise in conglomerate Hollywood?

According to Hollywood lore, Cruise was discovered when Michael Ovitz re-sponded strongly to his performance in *Taps* (Becker 1981) and signed him imme-diately (Slater 106). Through the 1980s, Cruise appeared in a string of massive hits that fine-tuned his cocksure, all-American, playful yet definitively masculine star image: *Risky Business* (Brickman 1983), *All the Right Moves* (Chapman 1983), *Top Gun* (Scott 1986), *The Color of Money* (Scorsese 1986), and *Cocktail* (Donaldson 1988). He branched out, proving his acting range in *Rain Man* (Levinson 1988) and *Born on the Fourth of July* (Stone 1989)—two prestige pictures that still managed to ride Cruise's star power to massive profits and critical adulation.[3] Cruise followed *Born* with a return to traditional Cruise form in *Days of Thunder* (Scott 1990), *Far and Away* (Howard 1992), *A Few Good Men* (Reiner 1992), and *The Firm* (Pollack 1993), meeting and marrying costar Nicole Kidman along the way.

Cruise relied heavily on Ovitz and CAA during this time. They packaged him with Newman in *The Color of Money*; they found the script for *Rain Man*, put Cruise and fellow CAA client Dustin Hoffman in the lead roles, and sustained the project through four changes in director. Even though Cruise ostensibly played variations on a single, albeit immensely appealing, character, the repetition was masked by slight variations in script. Cruise also enjoyed the counsel of Hollywood publicist extraordinaire Pat Kingsley, who ruled press access to the star with an iron hand. As Anne Thompson describes,

> Anyone who has ever dealt with Kingsley knows that going up against her takes guts and the full backing of your organization. That's because she's willing to use her entire arsenal to protect her most powerful clients. With the bat of an eyelash, she'd withdraw the cooperation of her agency's other stars, refuse to cooperate on other stories or ban a publication from getting another star interview. . . . Kingsley controlled the select magazine covers Cruise would do for each picture, the friendly interviewers he was most comfortable with, the photographers who shot him to look his best. Knowing that he didn't have much to say, she controlled his image, preserving his mystique as a movie star. Her PR philosophy has always been, "Less is more." Keep the fans guessing. Hold the star in abeyance. Keep everyone lining up clamoring for more. ("Cruise vs. Pitt")

In other words, Kingsley masterfully protected Cruise from questions and queries concerning Scientology, his sex life, and his divorces, yet still managed to make his brand distinctive, internationally recognizable, and unquestionably valuable.

With the protection of both CAA and Kingsley, Cruise weathered the poor reception of *Interview with the Vampire* (Jordan 1994), going on to major blockbusters with *Mission: Impossible* (De Palma 1996) and *Jerry Maguire* (Crowe 1996)—films that only further reified his established image. He then began juxtaposing risky projects with assured hits: *Eyes Wide Shut* (Kubrick 1999) and *Magnolia* (Anderson 1999) followed by *Mission: Impossible II* (Woo 2000), *Vanilla Sky* (Crowe 2001) followed by *Minority Report* (Spielberg 2002), and *The Last Samurai* (Zwick 2003) and *Collateral* (Mann 2004) followed by *War of the Worlds* (Spielberg 2005). Throughout this period, the vitality of Cruise's image was tantamount to the success of the film, as Edward Jay Epstein makes clear:

> The strategy of Paramount's marketing campaign was to ineluctably link the star to the title so that all the publicity Cruise received in the months leading up to the release would remind people of the film. A back story was then scripted in which Cruise was seen to be indistinguishable from Ethan Hunt, the acrobatic hero he

played, via the claim that he, and not a stunt double, had done the free falls, fire walks, motorcycle leaps, and other perilous stunts that Hunt did in the movie. (*Big Picture* 181)

While publicity has long conflated stars and their roles, this particular move takes such association to the next level. It was understandable, then, that years later, when *Mission: Impossible III* performed below expectations, Cruise was the first and most obvious scapegoat.

Even more important, the biggest hits of the aforementioned bunch—*Mission: Impossible I* and *II*, *Minority Report*, and *War of the Worlds*—were all presold properties in one way or another; that is, they had a built-in audience—whether from a previously established franchise, the best-known director in the world at the helm, or the most famous radio broadcast of all time, which also happened to be based on H. G. Wells's well-known book and had been previously adapted for film and television. While Cruise himself could once open a film on his own—see *Jerry Maguire*—it is crucial to note that the massive hits that sustained his career through the late 1990s and early 2000s were all bolstered by their presold status. What's more, while his films' international earnings portrayed Cruise as a fail-proof star, they masked the steady decline of his films' domestic grosses. *The Last Samurai*, in particular, failed to live up to expectations; Warner Bros. was forced to rely on DVD profits in its "long slog to profitability" (DiOrio 6). In hindsight, Cruise's track record clearly points to the continued ascendancy of the presold, high-concept property.

In 1996, Cruise joined with former CAA agent-turned-producer Paula Wagner to form Cruise/Wagner Production, coproducing Paramount's *Mission: Impossible* series as part of an unprecedented deal. In exchange for a long-term producing partnership with Paramount, Cruise would receive 22 percent of gross revenues on theatrical releases and television licensing; in addition, Cruise would take in 22 percent of *total receipts* from home video sales—a radical departure from the usual percentage off of the studio's 20 percent royalty. Due to the specifics of the deal, Cruise garnered $70 million in final earnings for *Mission: Impossible,* effectively "open[ing] the door for stars to become full partners with the studio in the so-called back-end" (Epstein, "Tom Cruise, Inc.").

Following the rapid proliferation of DVD technology, Cruise renegotiated the deal for *Mission: Impossible II,* this time exacting 30 percent of the theatrical gross and 40 percent of DVD gross revenue, making for a phenomenal $92 million paycheck. But Cruise's relationship with Paramount was not simply about profits: he and Wagner enjoyed offices on the studio lot, between $5 and 10 million a year in operating costs, and Cruise was free to star in side projects with other studios. Apart from Cruise vehicles, however, Cruise/Wagner had little more than a few very modest hits and several expensive clunkers, including *The Others* (Amenábar 2001), *Narc* (Carnahan 2002), *Shattered Glass* (Ray 2003), *Suspect Zero* (Merhige 2004), *Elizabethtown* (Crowe 2005), and *Ask the Dust* (Towne 2006). Nevertheless, the value of Cruise's starring projects was significant enough for Paramount to pay what amounted to a nominal fee to keep Cruise/Wagner on the lot.

Shortly before their tenth wedding anniversary in 2001, Cruise and his then wife Nicole Kidman divorced.[4] Cruise went on to a two-year romance with *Vanilla Sky* costar Penelope Cruz, followed by a series of PR disasters—all completely of Cruise's own making. In the spring of 2004, Cruise fired Kingsley, opting instead to be managed by his sister Lee Anne Mapother De Vette. As *Variety* writer Elizabeth Guider queried, "Does Cruise not know just what ironclad protection Kingsley and her phalanx of PMK minions have been providing for 15 years? And now his *sister* is going to do that?" (6). Cruise had purportedly tired of Kinglsey's dictate to remain mum on the subject of his religion. In contrast, De Vette, a Scientologist herself, would not force her brother to sustain his silence any longer.

Thus the Scientology floodgates broke loose: as Thompson explains, ever since firing Kingsley, "he can't stop talking about Scientology, which is, arguably, his star-sapping kryptonite" ("Cruise vs. Pitt"). He also embarked on a tremendously high-profile courtship of starlet Katie Holmes, punctuated by over-photographed appearances at premieres, murky details on the circumstances of their meeting, and a highly staged proposal atop the Eiffel Tower. The Cruise-Holmes courtship, marriage, and pregnancy extended over the promotional tour for *War of the Worlds* through the buildup to *Mission: Impossible III,* reaching a fever pitch with the in-famous couch jumping incident on *The Oprah Winfrey Show.* Coupled with pub-lic feuds with *Today Show* host Matt Lauer and Brooke Shields over Scientology's stance on depression, Cruise rapidly morphed from favorite superstar into favorite punch line. The footage from the couch-jumping incident was remixed and viewed by millions on YouTube. His Q-score, used to determine celebrity likability/appeal, plummeted.[5] Cruise's image, once so meticulously crafted, had fractured into a mil-lion uncontrollable, unaccountable pieces.

*Mission: Impossible III,* opening on May 5, 2006, grossed $397 million world-wide.[6] Certainly no small figure, but recalling *M:I-iii*'s $150 million budget, Cruise's points off the gross, and the precedent of the first two films of the franchise (*M:I-i* grossed $457 million international; *M:I-ii* grossed $546 million), the in-dustry declared the profits to be "below industry expectations and industry hopes" (Fritz 1). The disappointment over *M:I-iii* was part and parcel of Viacom chairman Sumner Redstone's greater dissatisfaction with Cruise, voiced in an unprecedented statement to *The Wall Street Journal* on August 22, 2006. In Redstone's unclipped words, Cruise's "recent conduct has not been acceptable," prompting the Viacom head to sever Paramount's 14-year relationship with Cruise/Wagner. It was, in one reporter's words, "the potshot heard round the world" (Jensen 13). According to one source, "Talks broke down when Paramount insisted Cruise and Wagner ac-cept $2.5 million annually—a sharp reduction, but on par with what Brad Pitt is getting for producing" (Jensen 15).

Depending on whose account you trust, Paramount and Cruise (and Cruise/Wagner Productions) had called off talks for a renewal of their production deal days before Redstone's announcement. As such, Cruise's representatives claimed that he had not been fired, "but had instead quit and had already lined up $100 million in financing to produce movies on their own" (Halbfinger and Fabrikan C1). Cruise/Wagner had indeed secured financing, and it seems as if talks had also broken down—but Redstone opted to take the proverbial upper hand by issuing his statement first, thus transferring the blame off of Paramount and onto Cruise. Either way, the aftershocks were felt across the industry: if a former behemoth like Cruise could be publicly filleted and cut loose, what was the future of stardom? Writing for the *New York Times,* Neal Gabler extrapolated that the split signaled a return to studio control. Contextualizing the Sumner-Cruise feud with similar studio-star skirmishes, including the high-profile cancellation of a Jim Carrey film and the "public rebuke" of Lindsay Lohan by the head of Morgan Creek for her hedonistic lifestyle, Gabler concluded that "this isn't only a Tom Cruise problem. In disengaging from Mr. Cruise, Mr. Redstone issued a warning to other puffed-up stars with inflated salaries and demands. After decades of studios threatening to draw the line, Paramount actually had the chutzpah to do it. Everyone is now on notice: The moguls want their power back." For Gabler, the era of enormous star salaries and bargaining power was effectively over. Cruise—and stars in general—seemed on the decline.

Fast-forward to November 2006. With rumors of hedge-fund backing, Cruise and Wagner finagled a deal with MGM to restart the long-dormant United Artists, thereby "rebranding" themselves in the vaunted tradition of quasi-independent, star-headed production (LaPorte 1). By the summer of 2007, UA had secured $500 million in financing from Merrill Lynch to finance eighteen films over five years—a lucrative rebound indeed. Cruise had rehired a professional publicist, and the memory of couch-jumping missteps began to slowly fade. He appeared markedly younger in photos and enjoyed a well-publicized, much-praised cameo as Les Grossman, a Harvey Weinstein–esque exec in the summer blockbuster *Tropic Thunder* (Stiller 2008). After Cruise appeared as the Grossman character at the 2010 MTV Movie Awards, it was reported that a spin-off movie for the Grossman character was in the works. It was, in one media observer's words, "Tom Cruise 2.0" (Sperling 10).

Despite MGM's vote of confidence in Cruise/Wagner, the relationship quickly turned sour. UA's first release, the star-studded, self-serious *Lions for Lambs* (Redford 2007), fell flat at the box office, grossing a regrettable $15 million domestic. The problem, according to one industry expert, was Cruise-size expectations: UA needed to "educate the public and consumer press that box office grosses aren't what United Artists are about; rather, Cruise and Wagner want to continue the company's legacy of nurturing talent and creativity" (McClintock and McNary 1). In other words, *Lions for Lambs* was never intended to be the next *Mission: Impossible.* But with Cruise attached, such associations were all but impossible to shake.

Still reeling from *Lions for Lambs,* Cruise/Wagner was faced with overwhelmingly negative buzz surrounding Cruise's forthcoming star vehicle *Valkyrie.* Germans had already objected to a Scientologist playing a German personage; there were unfortunate paparazzi shots of Cruise with an eye patch; and the film's release date had been repeatedly postponed (Barnes and Cieply). *Valkyrie* was set to bomb. Even worse, in light of UA's underperformance, Wagner exited UA in August, leaving Cruise to repatch the deal. Wagner had released just *one* film since taking over UA—despite promising four to five a year (Thompson, "Tom on the Spot" 1). MGM head Harry Sloan quickly endorsed the studio's continued relationship with Cruise, but the split augured poorly—as Michael Cieply points out, if UA continues to fail, "Mr. Cruise will certainly bear much of the blame."

But UA fought back, embarking on a massive rebranding of *Valkyrie,* including a new trailer, ad campaign, and press materials. Crucially, the rebranding deemphasized Cruise, choosing instead to frame the film as an ensemble action/thriller (Graser 5). To put it bluntly, "Saving the movie meant soft-pedaling the star" (Barnes and Cieply). The stakes were high: the film would "test the mettle of the 46-year-old Cruise: if it fails, his status as a superstar, damaged by a rough parting with Paramount . . . slips another notch" (Barnes and Cieply). *Valkyrie* proved a moderate success, pulling in $83 million domestic, $117 million foreign, for $200 million worldwide (McClintock and Thomas 10). But with a production budget of $75 million (rumored to be $90 million) and the costly rebranding, the film barely cleared a profit theatrically, if it did at all.

At the time of this writing, Cruise's future in the industry is unclear, although the heavy box office thud that met the high-profile film *Knight and Day* (Mangold 2010), which costars Cameron Diaz, doesn't bode well for his continued place on the A-list. He boasts of nearly half-a-dozen projects in development, including several old-school Cruise thrillers. But is there a market for a Cruise thriller that is neither presold nor part of a larger franchise? In other words, is Cruise's star brand still a strong enough presell to warrant the massive budgets that accompany his films? He might not have many other options: as *Lions for Lambs* demonstrated, audiences do not know how to respond to Cruise in non-blockbuster mode. He has effectively backed himself into a corner, forced to replay the sorts of roles that sustained his star through the 1980s and 1990s.

The Cruise model of stardom—distinguished by massive participation points, star-headed coproduction, and reliance on star-as-selling-point—appears, by all accounts, to be on the decline. What's more, the dramatic fall of Cruise's star, taken in context with its gradual, albeit partial, recovery, speaks to the continued necessity of excellent management, agenting, and publicity. But Cruise's career is by no means dead. He is still an international draw and will remain so for the foreseeable future. Small, artsy films featuring mid-level stars and serious actors may turn strong profits on small budgets domestically, but they will never supply the tremendous international and ancillary draw associated with Cruise and his middle-aged big-movie brethren: Tom Hanks, John Travolta, and Nicolas Cage. Unlike Roberts, who is faced with the difficulty of reprising her traditional rom-com roles, Cruise still has the market cornered in his particular brand of cocky action hero. It remains a

matter of finding the right films, the right studio arrangement, and the right publicity management to pull it off again. Tom Cruise, as David Thomson has noted, is
indeed very professional (193). Time will tell if he will be able to shift that consum-
mate professionalism to the new parameters of conglomerate Hollywood.

## George Clooney

George Clooney has twice been named *People Magazine*'s Sexiest Man Alive. He
signifies strongly as a sexy, debonair, next-best-thing to Cary Grant. He plays the
social role of avid philanthropist and United Nations ambassador of peace; he is
good friends with Brad Pitt, Angelina Jolie, Julia Roberts, and Matt Damon and
hosts lavish summer getaways at his Lake Como home. He remains a consum-
mate bachelor and pledges never to marry again, attracting fanatical attention to
his various casual romantic exploits. His *ER*-era hairstyle was emulated by hundreds of thousands; he has garnered millions in ad deals; and he has a Q-score
through the roof.[7] Clooney has directed, produced, and worked extensively with
friend and indie auteur Steven Soderbergh. But is he a movie star? Can he open
a film? Does his presence in a film warrant a massive paycheck or points off the
gross? Absolutely not.

Clooney is certainly a star: he comports himself like a star, he lives like a star,
and his presence in a film certainly lends it credit and a modicum of box office
promise. But he is a minor star at best: his ensemble films do well; his small productions do proportionally good business. But the few times he has been entrusted to
open a film—*Batman & Robin* (Schumacher 1997), *The Peacemaker* (Leder 1997),
*Out of Sight* (Soderbergh 1998), *Three Kings* (Russell 1999), *Solaris* (Soderbergh
2002), *Intolerable Cruelty* (Coen Brothers 2003), *The Good German* (Soderbergh
2006), and *Leatherheads* (Clooney 2008)—resulted in disappointments of one order or another. He has performed relatively well with smallish pictures, including
*O Brother Where Art Thou?* (Coen Brothers 2000) and *Good Night, and Good Luck*
(Clooney 2005), along with the ensemble *Ocean's* trilogy and surprise hit *Burn After
Reading* (Coen Brothers 2008). But Brad Pitt was there to anchor several of those
pictures, not to mention Matt Damon, Julia Roberts, and a handful of other mid-
level stars.

Why, then, is Clooney as well known and respected as he is? He has a solid
pedigree—his aunt was singer Rosemary Clooney; his father had a long history
in television news. But George Clooney scrapped his way through his early Hollywood career, working through supporting bits on *Sisters* and *Roseanne* before ultimately landing the role of heartthrob pediatrician Doug Ross on *ER*. As a TV
star, however popular, Clooney struggled to break into film. He appeared in horror flicks (*From Dusk 'Til Dawn* [Rodriguez 1996]), romantic comedy (*One Fine
Day* [Hoffman 1996]), and an exhausted franchise (*Batman & Robin*) in an embar-
rassingly nippled Batsuit. He feuded publicly with *Three Kings* director David O.
Russell and weathered failures in *Out of Sight* and *The Peacemaker*. After nearly six

years of attempting to find his niche, he restarted his star brand with a kooky performance in the much-beloved *O Brother Where Art Thou?* and a solid gross from
the otherwise unremarkable *The Perfect Storm* (Peterson 2000).

Again, a few solid roles did not a movie star make. Yet in 2000, Clooney began to
bolster his artistic credentials, joining Soderbergh, fresh off the double-triumph of
*Traffic* (1999) and *Erin Brockovich* (1999), to form Section Eight Pictures. Section
Eight would produce projects helmed by Soderbergh or Clooney, several Clooney
star vehicles, and other miscellaneous small indie fare. The two aimed to "recreate
the heady days of Hollywood in the late 1960s and early 1970s, when innovative
filmmakers like Francis Ford Coppola and Stanley Kubrick worked free of corporate constraints" (Holson). In other words, they wanted to work without pressure
to deliver a certain type of movie, with a certain type of conclusion, or a certain
type of star role, high concept, or presold property. They wanted to make *art.*

Clooney and Soderbergh pitched the idea to Warner Brothers, where Clooney
had a long-standing relationship dating to his start with *ER.* The pair stated upfront
that "neither of us are looking to get rich as a company, so we can bring you the
lowest overhead of any company you'll ever have" (Holson). Warner Bros. jumped
at the proposition, offering Section Eight Jack Warner's storied office, around
$1 million a year, and a small staff (Holson). Unlike other star-headed produc-
tion companies (such as Cruise/Wagner), Section Eight aimed to function as a safe
haven for risk-taking directors. With Section Eight's assistance, Todd Haynes could
make *Far from Heaven* (2002), Christopher Nolan brought in *Insomnia* (2002),
and Richard Linklater directed the roto-scoping noir *A Scanner Darkly* (2006).
Using the *Ocean's* franchise as their financial engine, the two were able to take risks
of their own: Clooney directed *Confessions of a Dangerous Mind* (2002); Soderbergh
experimented with micro-budget faux-vérité in *Full Frontal* (2002) and nonactors
and simultaneous theater/DVD release with *Bubble* (2006). All three films, as well
as Section Eight's two dabblings in quasi-reality television drama (*K Street* and *Un-
scripted*), garnered a modicum of critical praise, but failed to attract a broad audience. Yet as Soderbergh averred, "My motivation is not to make money which, on
occasion, makes us a sorry proposition" (Holson).

With Section Eight, Clooney and Soderbergh were able to function as a different type of producer—the type who "find commercial stuff that doesn't make you
feel bad in the morning" (Holson). They did so by engaging the "one for them, one
for us" paradigm, first popularized by the 1970s movie brats, in which talent (an
actor, director, producer, writers) alternates between major commercial products
and smaller, more personal and experimental films. With the *Ocean's* movies as
its anchor, Section Eight was able to eke out small, profitless projects by keeping
budgets low and diverting producing fees back into other projects. In 2005,
Clooney's artistic experimentation finally paid off: he directed and costarred in
*Good Night, and Good Luck* and costarred in *Syriana* (Gaghan 2005), both coproduced by Section Eight. Clooney received lauds on all sides, complementing his
existing profile as suave leading man with that of a socially and politically conscious

artist as he garnered an Oscar nomination for Best Director and an Oscar win for Best Supporting Actor. Both films turned modest profits: *Good Night, and Good Luck* grossed $54 internationally on a $7 million budget; *Syriana* grossed $94 million on $50 million. Clooney's cachet—as star, actor, director, artist—had never been greater.

Following this success, Clooney continued to take artistic and professional risks. This time around, however, such chancy endeavors have failed to fulfill their promise. Soderbergh and Clooney split amicably to pursue other projects in 2006. Clooney immediately created a new production home, Smoke House, headed by longtime Section Eight collaborator Grant Heslov, which continued to partner with Warner Bros. Both Clooney and Soderbergh claimed that Section Eight was always intended to be a temporary arrangement, looking back on it as a "worthwhile experiment" (McLean). But the aftermath of the breakup bespeaks greater obstacles for the future of Clooney's attempted reconciliation of art and commerce. Apart from the surefire *Ocean's Thirteen* (Soderbergh 2007), Clooney's fortunes have, at least financially, soured. The last of the Section Eight productions, *The Good German* (Soderbergh 2006), was an unmitigated failure, while *Michael Clayton* (Gilroy 2007) performed below expectations despite widespread critical praise and an additional Oscar nomination for Best Actor. Finally, *Leatherheads* (Clooney 2008), Clooney's third turn behind the camera and his first film to open wide, was deemed a "theatrical non-starter," grossing a meager $31 million domestic and $9 million international on its $58 million budget (McCarthy 34).

Nevertheless, Clooney is still considered a star. The celebrity magazines and gossip blogs continue to feature him prominently. And he's in demand. On June 30, 2009, Clooney announced that he would move Smoke House, heretofore a shingle at Warner Bros., to Sony. At Sony, Smoke House would enjoy a two-year first-look pact—remarkable "at a time when studios are cutting back on production deals, no matter how big the producer may be" (McLean). Since its inception in 2006, Smoke House had been most successful in nabbing deals for films outside of Warner Bros.; Warner Bros. was also likely disappointed with the performance of *Leatherheads,* one of the few Smoke House films it did option and distribute. Or, as interpreted by cutthroat industry observer Nikki Finke, "As a writer and director and producer, he's not a moneymaker. (Looking at his films in development, I predict there's not a $20 million opening weekend among them at a time when the average marketing cost of studio fare is $30M–$50M.) Believe me, if he were generating decent grosses, Warner Bros would have wanted to hang onto him. So Warner's gain is Sony's loss."

Indeed, in the summer of 2009 Clooney had a staggering thirteen films in various stages of completion and development, three of which—*Up in the Air* (Reitman), *The Men Who Stare at Goats* (Heslov), and *The Fantastic Mr. Fox* (Anderson)—were released in the subsequent fall. *Up in the Air* resulted in another Oscar nomination for Clooney; still, unless paired with other big names, his films will never be blockbusters. Nevertheless, as evidenced by the Sony deal, Clooney remains eminently employable—he is a sparkly, respectable jewel in any studio's crown. Regardless of Finke's derision, Clooney occupies an enviable position, especially when compared with Roberts and Cruise. His production company recently made a lucrative deal; he is neither planning nor expected to shoulder large, risk-laden films. He is no tent-poler. Instead, he's free, as it were, to choose and develop his own projects in which to either star and/or direct. He may not be receiving the massive paychecks and points that Roberts and Cruise enjoyed over the past two decades, but his position in the revamped Hollywood is certainly more secure.

In this way, Clooney keenly resembles his star antecedent Cary Grant. Like Clooney, Grant had to toil through several films and genres before finding his niche. Grant persisted in avoiding long-term contracts, instead opting to shop his services to various studios at will. Similar to Clooney, Grant was rather inscrutable to the press, operating with discretion in all facets of his life. Both are internationally recognizable names, but neither garnered runaway salaries. Each partnered with a specific director—Grant with Hitchcock and Clooney with Soderbergh—to produce films that either deliberately played on or exploited their star images, often with tongue firmly in cheek. Both moved between more audience-pleasing genre work and more challenging, intricate pieces. Finally, both radiate a rare sense of *charisma*—which, as Roberts and Cruise demonstrate as well, will forever sustain them as celebrities, even if not super-salaried stars. Grant is remembered today as a tremendous leading man, and his star presence in a film absolutely upped its gross. Yet Grant also weathered his share of failures—but due to the structure of the studio system, none cost the studio too much, and could thus be readily absorbed as he proceeded to his next project.

While differences certainly exist between Grant and Clooney, the comparison is useful in illuminating not only the position of Clooney but the potential future of Hollywood stardom in general. What seems to be taking shape, as the stars become less of an assurance and more of a liability, is a revamped version of the tried-and-true star system. Only under this new model, stars do not necessarily pledge their services to one company—at least not for seven years. With that said, many do place themselves in a long-term working relationship with a single studio/conglomerate, oftentimes with their production company in tow. The star is no longer afforded the extravagant demands of the era before *Mission: Impossible III*; instead, he is held on a tight leash, accountable for extracurricular activities that may degrade or devalue his star brand and, in turn, the products in which he appears. While this is a far cry from the morality clauses of yore, the messages sent to Cruise and Lohan in 2005 bear a striking resemblance to the moral censorship of classic Hollywood.

What occurred in the late 1990s was a rise in salary incommensurate with the rise of services—and likewise disproportional to the true box office draw of the star. After the relative failure of *Mission: Impossible III*, retrenchment seemed the most reasonable option. Thus when Redstone and Paramount appeared to fire Cruise and came up with their own set of new rules as to the price they were willing to pay for talent, the rest of the industry more or less began to follow suit. Realizing their tent-pole films stood on comic books, children's fantasy, cartoons, and Disney rides, it has only become easier to relegate stars to smaller films, prestige pictures, and supporting roles (often single–story line villains and sidekicks) in tent-pole films, thereby circumnavigating any contracts for future films.

Perhaps we should approach this from a different perspective. As Tom Schatz points out, "The indie surge has relied heavily on the mobility of top stars who are willing to work on indie projects for far less than their studio rates" (34). Perhaps, as Cruise, Roberts, and others who can no longer draw the paychecks of yore look to smaller films, they will bolster the vital but flagging independent film sector of the industry—whether through small indie arms of larger conglomerates or in true indies made completely outside the system. Or maybe they won't. Maybe the studios, still desperate for success and franchise, will continue to rely on stars to anchor large properties, even when, as is the case with Eddie Murphy, they fail again and again. Maybe the reliance on big stars is too entrenched and the alternate Clooney model of art wedded with small commerce too unique.

Regardless, the role and power of Hollywood stars is at a turning point, a familiar position for stars through the ages. The recent merger of Endeavor and William Morris has incited yet another sea change in the agenting landscape, and Ari Emanuel seems primed to become the Ovitz of the new millennium. And it's not just the studios that are under conglomerate control: all celebrity access is now under the control of two monster publicity firms.[8] The future of most stars is now consolidated into the hands of the few. Ten years from now, we will know how this epic battle between stars, conglomerates, and the impulse towards profit ended. For now, we can only watch, watch movies—whether featuring real stars, cheap young talent, skyscraping robots, CGI Statue of Liberties, man-eating waves—and see.

## NOTES

1. Swanson earned $7,000 dollars a week on contract with Paramount.

2. As Edward Jay Epstein points out, "The average earnings per film of the top ten stars in 2003 was roughly thirty times what the equivalent stars had earned in 1948 under the studio system" (even *after* correction for inflation) (*Big Picture* 261).

3. *Rain Main* grossed $354 international on a $25 million budget; *Born* grossed $161 million international against its $14 million budget.

4. The date was not without significance: by beginning divorce proceedings before their tenth year of marriage, Cruise prevented Kidman from claims to crucial assets—a move undoubtedly orchestrated with the help of his personal retinue.

5. Ratings in 2006 from The Q Scores Co., a firm that measures celebrities' likability and appeal, show that Cruise's popularity continued to drop, particularly with women. The actor's Q-score was at its lowest since 2000, with a 40 percent drop in positive perception among men, who reported a 170 percent increase in negative perception. The outlook is worse among women: Cruise's appeal dropped 45 percent; negative perception is up 300 percent (Thomas).

6. *Mission: Impossible III* grossed $134 million domestic and $263 million international.

7. Official Q-scores are notoriously difficult to come by without significant financial backing. According to a Q Scores Company's press release, Clooney's Q-score hovers in the top five of all male stars, accompanied by Tom Hanks, Johnny Depp, Denzel Washington, and Will Smith.

8. The two firms that control access to most Hollywood stars are Baker/Winoker/Ryder and Interpublic, which owns PMK/HBH, Rogers & Cowan and Bragman Nyman Cafarelli.

## WORKS CITED

Barnes, Brooks, and Michael Cieply. "A Studio, a Star, a Fateful Bet." *The New York Times.com.* Nov. 7, 2008.

Cieply, Michael. "Memo Re Tom Cruise: The Star Is Staying Here." *The New York Times. com.* Aug. 15, 2008.

DeCordova, Michael. *Picture Personalities: The Emergence of the Star System in America.* Urbana: University of Illinois Press, 1990.

DiOrio, Carl. "B.O. Doesn't Tell 'Samurai' Tale." *Variety,* Jan. 19, 2004: 6.

Epstein, Edward Jay. *The Big Picture: The New Logic of Money and Power in Hollywood.* New York: Random House, 2005.

Epstein, Edward Jay. "Tom Cruise, Inc." *Slate.com.* June 27, 2005.

Finke, Nikki. "George Clooney Exits Warner Bros. for Sony." *Deadline Hollywood Daily. com.* June 30, 2009.

Fritz, Ben. "Par's 'Mission': Impossible?" *Variety,* May 8, 2006: 1.

Gabler, Neal. "Risky Business." *The New York Times.com.* Aug. 25, 2006.

Graser, Marc. "UA Patches Things Up." *Variety,* Oct. 6, 2008: 5.

Guider, Elizabeth. "PR Maven Loses Cruise Control." *Variety,* April 12, 2004: 6.

Halbfinger, David, and Geraldine Fabrikan. "Fired or Quit, Tom Cruise Parts Ways with Studio." *The New York Times,* Aug. 23, 2006: C1.

Holson, Laura M. "Confessions of a Perplexed Mind." *The New York Times.com.* Jan. 17, 2005.

Holson, Laura M. "Trying to Combine Art and Box Office in Hollywood." *The New York Times.com.* Jan. 17, 2005.

Jensen, Jeff. "A Star Is Shorn." *Entertainment Weekly,* Sept. 8, 2006: 13–16.

LaPorte, Nichole. "UA Lighting the Cruise Fuse." *Variety,* Nov. 8, 2006: 1.

McCarthy, Todd. "Review of *Leatherheads*." *Variety,* Apr. 7, 2008: 34.

McClintock, Pamela, and Archie Thomas. "*Valkyrie* Cruises to the Top of the World." *Variety,* Feb. 9, 2009: 10.

McClintock, Pamela, and Dave McNary. "UA's Screen Test." *Variety,* Nov. 9, 2007: 1.

McLean, Thomas. "Section Eight Goes Up in Smoke." *Variety.com.* Oct. 6, 2006.

Schatz, Tom. "The Studio System and Conglomerate Hollywood." In *The Contemporary Hollywood Film Industry,* ed. Janet Wasko and Paul McDonald, 11–42. Malden, MA: Blackwell, 2008.

Segal, David. "After Jackson, Fame May Never Be the Same." *The New York Times.com.* June 27, 2009.

Slater, Robert. *Ovitz: The Inside Story of Hollywood's Most Controversial Power Broker.* New
        York: McGraw-Hill, 1997.

Sperling, Nicole. "A Star Is Reborn?" *Entertainment Weekly,* May 6, 2008: 10–11.

Thomas, Karen. "Tom Cruise Gets His Game On." *USA Today.com.* Sept. 4, 2006.

Thompson, Anne. "Cruise vs. Pitt: Tale of 2 Publicists." *The Hollywood Reporter.com.*
        June 10, 2005.

Thompson, Anne. "Tom on the Spot." *Variety.com.* Aug. 15, 2008: 1.

Thompson, Anne. "*Duplicity*: What Happened?" *Variety*.com. Apr. 2, 2009.

Thomson, David. *The New Biographical Dictionary of Film.* New York: Knopf, 2002.

# Chapter 8

# TV: The Last Best Hope?

U pon hearing that his death had been reported in the *New York Journal,*
Mark Twain was quoted as saying, "Reports of my death have been greatly
exaggerated." Similarly, time and again contemporary audiences read
about the demise of the movies, actual, impending, or otherwise. Truth be told,
reportage on the expiration of the movies, like Twain's death, has been greatly exaggerated. After all, from 2000 to 2009, the annual cumulative yearly gross of Hollywood films reached a new record high 8 out of 10 years. Additionally, in 2000
the cumulative total was just over $7.5 billion, whereas in 2010 it was just over
$10.6 billion, which means that in 10 years the total box office rose by around
40 percent, which is remarkable growth in any business and indicative of a pretty
healthy industry (*Box Office Mojo.com,* "All-Time"). Or is it?

For comparison, consider the U.S. housing market, which grew by leaps and
bounds in the early and mid-2000s as well. But, as the growth was fueled by wild
speculation and sub-prime lending, the numbers belied the reality, which was an
industry in disarray and long overdue for a correction, which came with a vengeance
in 2008. While claiming the film industry is due for a reality check as harsh as that
faced by the real estate sector is perhaps going too far, I would still argue not all is
as rosy as it seems. Not even close. In particular, there are two things that merit further consideration. One is that fewer films are accounting for more of the money,
as Hollywood, not immune to the international credit crunch caused by the global
financial crisis, scales back production from 600 or so films a year to a more modest 450 or less (Pilkington). So in 2000, only 3 films made at least $200 million,
with the Jim Carrey vehicle *How the Grinch Stole Christmas* (Howard) on top with
a $260 million gross (*Box Office Mojo.com,* "2000"); conversely, in 2009, 10 films
made over $200 million, the top 6 of which, led by *Avatar's* (Cameron) jaw-
dropping $750 million—which, as it was released in December, was accrued in less
than a month—made more than *The Grinch's* $260 million. The other issue to
consider, as Edward Jay Epstein observes, is that attendance has remained fairly
stagnant over the years: "Today, less than 10 percent of the public on the average
go to the movies in a week. Now, even with movies like *Avatar,* they score enormous
numbers but the percentage still doesn't go above 10 percent. They take their
numbers from other movies that are playing at other theaters. You still have less
than 10 percent of the population and it's been this way for the last 10 years." The

numbers back up his assertion. According to the National Association of Theater Owners (NATO), in 2000, 1.38 billion tickets were sold, whereas in 2009, there were 1.41 billion sales, an increase of less than two percent, which hardly matches up to the 40 percent in box office growth during the same time ("Total Number"). What gives?

The obvious conclusion is that ticket prices have gone up, and this is true as average ticket prices have risen from $5.39 in 2000 to $7.50 in 2009, a growth rate of around 39 percent, which nicely accounts for the concurrent growth in box office even as attendance stagnated (NATO, "Average"). As we move into an era in which 3D productions are increasingly the norm, this will certainly continue as the privilege of seeing 3D movies comes with a surcharge of three or more extra dollars on top of what it costs to see a film in standard format. In fact, in the first quarter of 2010 alone, the cost of a movie ticket rose 8 percent, mostly fueled by the three highest-grossing films of the quarter—*Avatar, Alice in Wonderland* (Burton), and *How to Train Your Dragon* (DeBlois and Sanders)—not coincidentally all of which had wide releases in 3D. Theater owners counter gouging charges by noting that when adjusted for inflation, tickets are actually cheaper now than they were in the late 1960s (Fritz). Of course, that doesn't account for the fact that when adjusted for inflation, the real median income of American households has dropped around 3.5 percent as well, rendering the theater owners' claims a bit toothless (Rampell). Still, while the move to more 3D productions will continue to artificially disguise the fact that viewership remains flat even while grosses seemingly rise—in the aforementioned first quarter, receipts were up 8.6 percent whereas attendance rose by only .05 percent (Fritz)—it won't solve the fundamental issue of the increasing difficulty of getting audiences into theater seats. No industry can succeed indefinitely while experiencing zero growth.

But the truth of the matter is that the industry itself played a big part in keeping audiences away from movie theaters, first with the advent of VHS tapes and later with DVDs. Home video became the holy grail of ancillary income, to the point that by some estimates 70 percent or more of the profits for movies comes from DVD sales, which was by design (Grover). In some ways theatrical releases often served the equivalent of being an advertisement for the eventually forthcoming DVDs. And when DVD sales boomed, this was a great thing for the industry. The problem is that Hollywood apparently believed that DVD sales would go on unfettered forever. While they couldn't possibly have actually believed this, they might as well have when they remained complacent as the digital revolution brought consumers cheaper pay-per-play alternatives to owning DVDs, including video on demand (VOD) and digital delivery. Furthermore, new super-easy renting methods such as Redbox and Netflix made getting films efficiently and inexpensively a snap for consumers.

And still Hollywood plodded along, making high-dollar movies and assuming that the post–theatrical release sales of DVDs would continue to remain an open window. In an attempt to slow the death knell of DVDs, Hollywood attacked the competition, striking an agreement with Netflix for a month delay between when a DVD title goes on sale and when it's available for rental, thus allowing the studios to put the product with the highest profit margin first in line—the studios take a larger percentage on sales than they do from various kinds of rentals (Fritz and Chmielewski). But the numbers tell the tale, as evidenced by DVD/Blu-ray sales falling by 7 percent in 2008 before falling off a cliff in 2009, during which they fell another 13 percent (Schiffman). DreamWorks Animation CEO Jeffrey Katzenberg neatly sums up the situation, saying that the studios' "greed killed the goose": "Two, three years ago people had no problem purchasing a DVD for $18. . . . Suddenly, $20 is something you think about . . . in a world where there's Netflix, Blockbuster, Redbox, many VOD services, digital delivery, Amazon—we can go through the list of options on a per play basis where you can watch for $5 or $3 or $2.50. . . . The overall movie world is having to deal with the change in consumer habits" (Smith, "DreamWorks").

Deals with Netflix and the like are only going to delay the inevitable, as in the digital age the idea of following a movie's theatrical release with a series of subsequent windows in which you can over time repeatedly sell consumers the same product is a nonstarter. Audiences don't want to wait, and they certainly won't when the only reason for their having to do so is an artificial time structure concocted by the studios to ensure that they're able to maintain the same percentage of profits. And new formats like Blu-ray might not solve the issue either, as people have to date been slow to buy new players and TVs, and no one wants to replace their perfectly good DVD collections with Blu-ray versions, even if they do look a little better. As former 20th Century Fox studio head Bill Mechanic says, "If I can buy *Titanic* for under $5 in some stores, why am I so eager then to rush out to pay $30 or so when it's released on Blu-ray? Is the quality that great? How many formats are yet to come? They [the studios] simply accepted the idea that they could resell their libraries at higher prices" (Smith, "DVD Sales.").

Regardless, it still won't solve the issue of declining sales anyway. So where should Hollywood look for a new model that might enable them to reinvent their business plan? I would suggest that they look to one of their supposed primary competitors: Television, which may well be the movies' last best hope, at least as concerns the industry's ability to make diversified product that extends beyond their tent-pole and other high dollar releases.

It might seem a bit of a stretch to think that contemporary TV has anything to offer the movies. After all, the long-lasting network affiliate model for the industry has been in a slow decline for the past 30 or more years. The problem is the same as it is for the movies: increased competition and a fractured audience. Because of these two things, the validity of carrying on with big-tent, scripted televisual entertainments is being severely tested. TV has tried its own kinds of experimentation to counteract its issues, from cheaper-to-produce reality programming, which comes with its own difficulties as it has no real viable financial afterlife either in the form of syndication or DVD sales, to NBC's ill-fated and short-lived attempt to get rid of the 10 P.M. prime-time hour altogether by giving talk-show host Jay Leno the spot five nights a week, which was a fiscal and ratings disaster. TV has become much harder to program, and the fact is that the death of the network/affiliate model means we have lost something culturally in that we're not likely to have the kind of shared moments that we had for series finales such as *M\*A\*S\*H, Cheers,* and *Seinfeld.* Now, we'll share only Super Bowls and national tragedies. That said, with only four (or five or six, depending on your point of view) major networks, creators had no choice but to try for big-tent entertainments, shows that offered something for as wide a swath of people as possible, something that's really hard to do in the contemporary milieu given all the channels vying for eyeballs. Indeed, when perusing a list of the Nielson ratings' Top 100 shows of all time in terms of the highest percentage of U.S. households that watched them, what stands out is that there's nothing from the 2000s other than Super Bowls on the list, which is not a comment on the quality of any recent shows (the best of which, I'd argue, are as good or better than any other era's) as much as it is a fact that neatly illustrates the reality of diminished audiences for singular shows, which is a natural by-product of there being more shows on air and way more hours to program than at any other point in human history (Gorman). The major TV networks, like the movie industry's major studios, are also experiencing a lot of problems caused by new technologies. As the blogger known as the Masked Scheduler, who also happens to be an exec at CBS, writes, "Although most people still watch television the 'old fashioned' way, the simple fact that there are so many alternatives now (iTunes, HULU etc.), coupled with the lack of urgency due to re-cording and time shifting, threatens the communal experience of watching a tele-vision show. We just better figure out how to monetize all these platforms or we're screwed" ("Another One").

Indeed, in the current milieu, the networks are struggling, especially when compared to their own historical standards. There are a lot of reasons for this, but as acerbically noted by Kurt Sutter, creator and showrunner of the critically ac-claimed F/X series *Sons of Anarchy,* on his blog *Sutter Ink,* a major part of the bigger issue is the process through which shows must now go to get on air:

> The reason most network scripted dramas suck is because of the process. For the most part, you have a collection of young, half-bright development executives who wouldn't know a good story idea if it set itself on fire and f\*\*\*ed their moth-ers while singing "Cheyenne Anthem" from *Leftoverture.* So they do what most chimpanzees do—they ape and throw s\*\*t. Developing shows based on what they think people want to see. Churning out clones of semi-successful shows. Look-ing for a "hook" to market. It's never about the story or characters. That would demand talent, patience and an open mind. Commodities that have long up and deserted ABC, NBC, CBS, FOX and the CW.
>
> I have a director friend, let's call him . . . CJ, who says the job of a network ex-ecutive is to turn everything to s\*\*t. They hire you to stop them from doing that.

Unfortunately, the s\*\*t-turners are winning. Nowadays it's all about formula. You get rights, attach a hot writer, develop it into the f\*\*\*ing ground until it's so middle-of-the-road it has no point-of-view, then attach a waning movie star, throw tens of millions in promotion at it and hope that no one notices that it's the same old crap repackaged. But folks always do. In recovery, the "definition of insanity" is doing the same thing over and over and expecting a different result. Primetime is an active asylum.

Interestingly, Sutter's complaints about the networks apply to the processes in play at the major film studios as well, which are ever increasingly turning out products with little variance. That said, I'm less concerned about the quality argument than I am the lack of variety that comes about from current studio practices. You can't knock the studios; they're in a business and they're making money. But I would argue that they could be making even more money if they increased the variance in their products so as to attract a greater audience to theaters and more customers to the subsequent ancillary exhibition markets, and they could do so by following the model of the cable television stations that have stolen so much of the networks' thunder. The truth is that while the networks were floundering, cable channels were flourishing, and other than an unwillingness to think creatively and go against established industry practice, there's no reason the movie industry can't mimic their results.

So what is it that cable channels were able to do that attracted audiences away from the networks? Well, first and foremost the more famously successful of them presented themselves oppositionally to the networks by selling the idea that they were presenting "quality" fare that the networks, subject to the rules by which free over-the-air channels must operate, weren't able to match. In other words, quality TV can be defined by what it isn't, which is network TV. By taking advantage of looser restrictions as concerns content, especially in terms of language, nudity, and violence, cable channels such as F/X, AMC, Showtime, and HBO have been able to create their own brand, which is often characterized by what Jason Mittell convincingly posits is a "narrative complexity as an alternative to the conventional episodic and serial forms" that the networks, which are advertising dependent to a much greater extent than smaller cable channels and subscription channels, can't afford to incorporate for fear of alienating viewers. Indeed, Mittell believes that the best of "American television of the past twenty years will be remembered as an era of narrative experimentation and innovation, challenging the norms of what the medium can do" (29).

The most renowned and arguably successful of the cable channels working in this vein is HBO, which has had a number of highly acclaimed original scripted shows that have helped to boost and maintain its subscriber base. While HBO had other original shows before 1999 (most notably *Oz,* a drama set in a prison that vividly detailed aspects of that specific subculture), it wasn't until *The Sopranos* came out in that year that things really took off for the network as concerns its originally scripted shows. The show has achieved an iconic place in popular culture, perhaps in part because it's squarely situated in the gangster genre, a form with which audiences are quite familiar and comfortable. Interestingly, the networks had a chance at it but ultimately passed, despite the strength of the story and the vision of its creator, David Chase, who "originally pitched it to the four major networks, and came close to a deal with Fox, writing a pilot script without swearing, nudity and violence. What put the networks off, he says, were, 'the details and the complexity and the different pacing. They are afraid to trust the audience'" (Bradberry). Chase isn't wrong per se, but I don't think it's "trust" in their audience that they're lacking so much as it is the luxury of time that HBO, as a subscription-based network not dependent on advertising, has to wait and see if its shows catch on. As Grace Bradberry notes, "On the networks, shows are cancelled after as little as two weeks, because audiences don't instantly get them. On HBO a series will be given at least one complete season to find its viewers." HBO carefully picks and chooses its programs. Additionally, "Latitude to tell stories differently, creative personnel given the autonomy to work with minimal interference and without having to compromise, has become the HBO trademark—how they endlessly speak about and sell themselves, how the media talks about them, and how their customers have come to understand what they are paying for" (McCabe and Akass 87).

In addition to *The Sopranos,* HBO has enjoyed enormous critical success, Emmy Award nominations and wins, and continued financial gains in the form of its enlarging subscription base as a result of shows such as *The Wire, Sex and the City,* and *Entourage* and original movies and series such as *Band of Brothers* and *The Pacific.* Other channels quickly followed suit, taking advantage of their not having to garner the same kind of audiences as their network brethren in order to be financially successful. And so F/X aired *The Shield, Rescue Me,* and *Damages*; TNT *The Closer*; AMC *Mad Men* and *Breaking Bad,* and so on. While shows like these get all the rapturous press and credibility, it's important to note, as Mittell points out, that "complexity and value are not mutually guaranteed" (30). Even HBO has had its fair share of missteps, including *John From Cincinnati, Carnivale,* and *Rome,* the latter two of which were fairly well received critically but didn't result in enough new subscriptions to warrant their continuation. More to the point, cable channels don't have to field exclusively quality shows to be a successful network. They just have to make shows that people want to watch. So while we can look to HBO and understand that the "cachet of HBO—and in particular its original programming—[is] as a haven for creative integrity, initiating diversity and bucking convention that breaks the rules in terms of language, content, and representation," it's important to remember that very little of its programming is scripted (McCabe and Akass 89). They run a lot of the same kind of critically derided but popular stuff that other channels run and they do it because people watch it. It's easy to think poorly of comparatively lowbrow MTV shows like *Jersey Shore* and VH1's *Flavor of Love, Rock of Love,* and *A Shot of Love with Tila Tequila,* but they are essentially doing the same thing as HBO and are successful with their niches. It's just that their niches aren't as elite, but that doesn't necessarily make them any less profitable. Conversely, by "advertising itself with the audacious marketing claim, 'It's not TV. It's HBO,' the channel brands itself as something worth paying for. In fact, HBO has made much capital from cultural snobbery around televisions as it sets out to appeal to the college-educated audience who supposedly do not watch TV" (McCabe and Akass 85).

But just like every other channel, they have to program all the hours in the day, which means they can have the best of both worlds, running cheaply produced dreck that still pulls in viewers, but putting the weight of its marketing machine behind its more high-profile fare. As Bradberry notes,

> Executives and producers at the "free" TV channels are insanely jealous and rather scared of HBO, which fills the bulk of its schedules with films (the same ones over and over), relatively cheap documentaries, including the notorious *G-String Divas* [and *Real Sex* and *Cathouse*] and boxing matches. The channel then saves its subscriptions to produce mini-series such as *The Gathering Storm* and *Band of Brothers,* and a handful of expensive series that run for no more than 13 episodes. HBO can also spend more on its programmes—an episode of *Six Feet Under,* for example, costs more than $2 million, almost twice as much as a typical network drama [at the time].
>
> The networks, meanwhile, have to fill primetime with dozens of series a week, all of which have to attract a mass audience and hence advertising dollars. "Network TV is chosen and written to alienate as few people as possible," says James Poniewozik, TV critic for *Time* magazine. "You're doing well if you can get 20 million people watching your show, even if they wouldn't be willing to pay out of their pocket if they had to. On HBO a better goal is to put on a show only four million people want to watch, but they want to watch it so badly they will pay to do so."

And that's it in a nutshell; in competing with the networks, the cable channels in some ways have a huge advantage in that they've realized that it's not meeting the need for quality that matters in success (although it doesn't hurt); it's meeting the needs of various niches. Cable shows don't have to attract the huge audiences necessary to justify the prices they charge for the advertising or subscription fees that support their networks; the model is the same, but the scale is not. They just need to make enough money to keep doing what they're doing, and that's enough to keep them succeeding.

So for a point in comparison, one can look at the number of viewers and see that the difference in audience that makes a show a hit on network TV is dramatically different from a cable corollary. For example, during the week of May 3, 2010, the most-viewed network show was a tie between *American Idol* (Fox) and *Dancing with the Stars* (ABC), which had 19.6 million viewers each. *CSI: NY* (CBS) and

*The Big Bang Theory* (CBS), with 10.3 million viewers each, tied to round out the top 20. Conversely, the highest-rated cable show was an NBA playoff game on TNT between the Boston Celtics and the Cleveland Cavaliers, which attracted 5.5 million viewers, a number sure to lead to cancellation were it to recur for a network show. Interestingly, NBA playoff games, wrestling, and *NCIS* reruns dominate the cable ratings for this given week. In fact, only 4 original shows, *iCarly* (#5), *Victorious* (tied for #7 with a Phoenix Suns vs. San Antonio Spurs NBA playoff game and *WWE Raw* on USA), and *Big Time Rush* (tied at #10 with another Suns/Spurs playoff game) on Nickelodeon, and *Good Luck, Charlie* (#12) on Disney, all of which are targeted at the burgeoning tween market, make the top 15 (*USA Today*). During the fall and winter, when more scripted shows are in the midst of their run the numbers for hit cable series can be higher, with shows such as USA's *Royal Pains* and TNT's *Rizzoli & Isles* getting upwards of 7 million viewers, a lot by cable standards but still nowhere near the kind of ratings a network show needs to sustain to stay on the air (McPherson).

And what of highly revered series such as AMC's *Mad Men* or F/X's *Rescue Me* and the like? Well, for comparison sake the most viewers an episode of *Mad Men* has ever had is 2.92 million for the premier episode of Season Four, which debuted during the summer of 2010 (McPherson). This seems like nothing, especially given the fact that in the spring of 2010 NBC, citing high costs and low ratings, unceremoniously cancelled *Heroes* in the middle of a story line. For the 2009/2010 season, *Heroes* averaged 6.5 million viewers, a number that would put it in the mix for the highest-rated scripted cable show by a long shot, but that gets it nothing more than walking papers from NBC (Rice). But as for *Mad Men* and its seemingly paltry numbers, as Ryan DeVault observed after *Mad Men*'s Season Three premier, which attracted 2.8 million viewers, its largest audience to that point, "while that may not seem like a lot of viewers when compared to a show like *American Idol*, it is definitely a great ratings share for a cable show. Before the estimated 2.8 million viewers tuned in . . . , the highest ratings numbers for *Mad Men* was the Season Two season premiere, where an estimated 2.1 million viewers tuned in to watch the show. That is an increase of about 34 percent in total viewers as estimated by the Nielsen ratings scale, and spells a lot of success for the producers and creators of *Mad Men*." And while that success has continued right on into Season Four, the much smaller audience increase may signal that the show is nearing its maximum viewership, which is decidedly lower than the 15 to 20 million or more viewers a high profile network show can expect to attract. So long as cable channels produce shows that fill their desired niches and meet the needs required of them by the business reality of their particular situation, ratings are relative, as is quality, perceived or otherwise. After all, "as the number of channels has grown and the size of the audience for any single program has shrunk, networks and channels have grown to recognize that a consistent cult following of a small but dedicated audience can suffice to make a show economically viable" (Mittell 31). This is especially true of the cable channels that are supposedly giving network programmers fits.

The television and film industries have lot in common as concerns their respective structures, and that commonality goes beyond the fact that in many instances they're owned by the same companies. Both are huge endeavors at the top end that require enormous financial investments in the hopes of getting the viewership necessary to make a buck (or a billion, as the case may be). So just as the major networks need to produce big-tent entertainments to attract as wide an audience as possible, so too has the film industry turned to tent-pole productions to do likewise. It's no accident that the metaphors are similar as the charge is essentially the same for both mediums. The challenges to their dominance aren't from direct competitors as much as they are from niche programmers that are sucking from their viewership one precise viewership at a time. Why, then, are the networks allowing the cable channels to clean their clocks and steal their thunder without countering their moves? The truth is that they aren't, and the movie industry could learn a lot about where to go from here by copying the model laid out in plain sight by the TV industry.

So the truth of the matter is that the networks aren't really in competition with the cable companies at all; rather, they are in collusion with them in creating the illusion of competition that allows viewers of all tiers to believe that the results of said competition allow for them to have choices they wouldn't otherwise have. As William M. Kunz writes, "The fragmentation of the television audience, and the media marketplace as a whole, fuels the claim that the prominence of television has diminished, and, in turn, rendered questions related to ownership unimportant. This argument has justified the deregulation of media industries over the last two decades" (8). Accordingly, there was a time in the past during which cable TV was a legitimate competitor to the networks, but, as a result of the deregulation of media companies that began in earnest with the onset of the Reagan administration in 1980, the structural barriers that limited media companies from owning too much of any one thing have long since fallen, and the subsequent consolidation has rendered the cable channels and the networks partners rather than competitors. Take, for example, HBO, which, as Deborah Jaramillo convincingly lays out, isn't so much an independent entity "looming over broadcast networks" as it is a cog "in a larger conglomerate's entertainment holdings," which in the case of HBO is as a subsidiary of Time Warner. But Time Warner doesn't simply own HBO; it is the world's largest media company, and, as such, also owns all the Turner Networks (TCM, TNT, and TBS, etc.), CNN and all of its stations, part of Comedy Central and the CW, and so forth, all of which would seem to be HBO's competitors, as would many of the network shows that are actually produced by Warner Bros. Television, including such longtime network stalwarts as *Friends* (NBC, 1994 to 2004) and *ER* (NBC, 1994 to 2009) and contemporary CW shows such as *Gossip Girl* and *Smallville* (588–89). Time Warner is able to play both sides against the middle as they create shows for consumption by the masses on network television while at the same time propagating the idea that HBO is somehow better than regular TV, which results in the desired demographic, up-scale viewers between 18 and 49, wanting to subscribe to the premium channel.

As Jaramillo writes, this strategy for HBO has been incredibly successful, as its perceived prestige is the result of viewers being sold on the idea that they're getting programming they can't get elsewhere:

> The critics then blame the mass exodus to cable on "quality." As popular dis-course moves from numbers of households to lofty intangibles such as "quality," the generative mechanisms are left behind. An instrument for determining mon-etary worth has become what many presume is an interactive game complete with democratic votes. An AOL Time Warner Publication such as *Entertainment Weekly*, with its rating reports and annual issue on ratings winners and losers, has solidified this presumption and naturalized the mere existence of ratings, just as Nielsen has worked to naturalize its methodology in its own publications (591).

In the end, I would argue that the secret to HBO's success isn't so much that it's of a higher quality than a lot of network fare as it is that it attracts the desired de-mographic for its parent company, Time Warner. HBO is just a small part of the whole. It's when we see how it works it in combination with other properties owned by Time Warner that we can see its value to the company. The parent com-pany is surely delighted to have the audience HBO attracts, but it's important to remember that HBO is but one piece of the pie, and that what Time Warner has done is approach the market in terms of niches so as to capture a nice portion of each market entirety rather than trying to totally dominate any one share at the ex-pense of another. More to the point, Time Warner isn't alone in this endeavor. All of the big media companies are structured the same way—in addition to having movie studios that both produce and acquire films, they also own and/or create con-tent for network and cable channels, they have vast holdings in print and digital media, they own multiple music companies and book-publishing houses, and so on—which is in part what makes them multinational conglomerates that control the production, distribution, and exhibition of the entertainment industry.

TV is effectively wholly owned by the big media companies and they control most of the content that gets made and shown on TV, from the costliest network dramas, like *Lost* and *Desperate Housewives,* to the cheapest cable reality shows and everything in between. Why haven't these companies done the same thing with their movie industry holdings? Sure, for a while they did when they got into in-dependent styled production, but as they began competing with each other, costs of said productions skyrocketed and began to outweigh the potential returns and the studios dumped their independent arms like so much chattel. Their move to the high-dollar top end of tent-pole productions has created a vacuum at the bottom end, which I would argue makes the time right for them to jump back in and begin truly low-cost niche production, which would allow them to dominate both ends of the industry, just as they already do in TV. Let's not forget, we can and often do talk about the TV industry and the movie industry as separate entities, but just as HBO and Time Warner TV aren't really independent competitors, neither are the TV and film industries. The same companies that own most of the market's cable and network TV stations also own the major film studios. When considering the TV and film industries, what is often overlooked but is essential in understanding their nature is the "concentration of ownership in the motion picture and television industries, and the degree to which a small cadre of corporations dominate both of them, utilizing their market position to extend their influence into more and more endeavors. When one traces the ownership of motion picture studios, broadcast networks, and cable programming services, the same corporations appear time and again" (Kunz 9).

Accordingly, just as they do with TV, the big media companies are in a position to dominate the movie industry at all ends of the spectrum. And I'm hoping they do. I'm not condoning the efficacies of monopolies as concerns their providing the public with more choices. Indeed, as many have pointed out, because of the consolidation and the subsequent concentration of the ownership of media outlets, the fact that we have more choices than ever before doesn't translate to more diversity, especially in light of the lack of a diverse cross section of ownership in the film sector. What Kunz writes about the TV industry—"There is no question that the penetration of cable and satellite systems increased the number of available services, but far less convincing is the contention that this resulted in more owners, more variety, more diversity" (10)—equally applies to the film industry. But we have to acknowledge the reality of the current landscape in media, which is that it is what it is and it's not going to go backwards; there is no indication that the FCC or Congress will ever do anything to roll back the deregulation that got us where we are today. It's just not going to happen. That said, the marketplace still can be the ultimate arbiter of content, but the marketplace in the digital age is becoming so fractured into tiny niches that in order to meet consumer demand, film studios will have to make a wider variety of movies to fill the desires of all the audience niches, just in the same way TV has. You can argue that the heyday of the networks is long since past and you'd be right, but that doesn't mean TV is on the way out. Hardly. And the same with the movies; the film industry is splintering but not dying, and if studios reassert their primacy over lower-cost productions then viewers looking for more choices at the multiplexes just might benefit.

In a lot of ways, the studios already make niche movies to meet the demands of specific audiences; we call them genre films instead of niche films, but the effect is the same. The catch is that genre films like romantic comedies, crime movies, or even horror movies still cost millions to produce and millions more to advertise and exhibit. As famed zombie movie writer/director George Romero says, "Genre stuff is difficult and if it's expensive, then it has to have stars and then somebody says, 'no', and then you have to rewrite it, you know? 'Well, let's rewrite it for Sharon

Stone,' or 'let's rewrite it for Alec Baldwin,' or whoever [is] happening at the time" (Masters, "George"). Still, niche and genre certainly overlap, as they do in the case of filmmaker Tyler Perry, who has made a career of writing, directing, and acting in films and TV shows that feature African American actors and are heavily marketed towards African American audiences. That his films aren't critics' darlings and that he's been accused of making simple-minded films based on stereotypes that exploit "the preconceptions that Hollywood has about blackness" in order to make a buck is besides the point (Als). Collectively Perry's films have made upwards of $450 million at the box office and earned him a dedicated audience, and whether you like them or not, his films are successful because they meet the needs of an audience whose desires aren't otherwise fed by mainline Hollywood's filmic output. As Michael Z. Newman puts it, "If one function of art is to please its audience, a commercial incentive for spreading and intensifying pleasure dovetails with the goals of the artist. . . . Mass art strives for accessibility and ease of comprehension" (17). Perry's films inarguably achieve both.

But Perry's films still cost millions of dollars to make—typically ranging from the mid-seven to the low-eight figures—which requires the swath of folks to which his films appeal to be fairly large, lest they wouldn't make money. But what if they didn't, or at least if the studios chose to make movies that didn't require the same amount of money to achieve success? What if a low-budget film was defined by six-figure budgets instead of seven or eight? Hollywood could still content itself with the high dollar returns of its tent-pole productions, but could also make similar returns on the dollar, or even greater for the matter, with a lot less expenditure on the opposite end of the playing field. Yeah, the Brad Pitts and Steven Spielbergs of the world might not participate at this end of the spectrum—nor would the Tyler Perrys for that matter—but so what? It's an admittedly much smaller niche—or array of niches—but that doesn't mean it couldn't be well filled and smashingly successful. For comparison's sake, think of Wall Street's so-called penny traders, the high-frequency traders who buy and sell stocks so quickly that they normally only make a few pennies per trade. When they first started out they were laughed at. According Julie Cresswell of the *New York Times,* they're now responsible for 40 percent to 70 percent of all daily NYSE trades and a key part of the business of Wall Street titans such as Goldman Sachs. Sometimes David wins and keeps winning.

By definition these films would almost have to be "quality," although I use the term with some reservation, as cost neither automatically dictates quality nor predicts success, as evidenced by the runaway success of films like *Napoleon Dynamite* and *Paranormal Activity.* Those kinds of films will continue to break big once in a while, but they will remain the exception to the rule and they are filling another niche regardless of their budgets. But the fact is that if you're making films with $1 or $2 million or less, you can't do things that feature high-dollar actors or that require extensive special effects or location shooting in exotic locales as the budget prohibits it. But why can't you make character-driven narrative fare for adults in the same way that cable channels do? And if you're spending less to make them, you don't need to get as much back to make them profitable, hence worth doing. The average cost of an episode of *Mad Men* is some $2 million, as opposed to $3 million for a comparative network drama, which for a company like AMC is still a veritable fortune (or at least would be if it wasn't actually Lionsgate that provides most of the funding), given that it has to repeat the cost for 13 episodes per season (as opposed to the 22 or more episodes a network show typically has), year in and year out (Witchel). But because it's not a network show, that relative lack of money also comes with the added benefit of creative freedom and, as such, a lot of people want to work on the show. It's not that they don't want to get paid, it's that they understand that by taking what is in comparison a lower salary in return they get artistic freedom they wouldn't otherwise have. So, for example, according to *TV Guide, Mad Men*'s lead actor Jon Hamm makes $75,000 per episode as opposed to Charlie Sheen's $875,000 on *Two and a Half Men* or Keifer Sutherland's $550,000 for *24* (*omg!*). And it's important to remember that we're talking about salaries for scripted network shows here; folks like Fox TV's *American Idol*'s Simon Cowell ($75 million per year) and NBC's *The Apprentice*'s Donald Trump ($50 million), who double dip by serving as producers for the shows upon which they star, make a lot more money. As Gary Susman notes, when looking at any list noting TV's top earners, what is clear is that "nobody who makes a living on basic cable (such as *Rescue Me* actor/writer/producer Denis Leary)" is to be found, which is illustrative of the fact that "network TV, despite its shrinking audience, is still the place to go to earn big bucks." Still, despite the clear disparity between network and cable salaries, most actors recognize that $75,000 per episode for a 13-episode season is a ton of money compared to what the average person on the street makes, and that if the show hits big the rewards far outweigh the risks.

Admittedly, the structure of TV is very different from that of the movies, and I'm not suggesting that the movie industry should start making serials again so as to replicate what's done on TV. It just wouldn't work, as Mittell notes, for the kinds of complexity that can sometimes result in quality that he sees as having emerged on American TV over the past 20 or so years are "predicated on specific facets of storytelling that seem uniquely suited to the series structure that sets television apart from film" (29). Perhaps more to the point, "While innovative film narration has emerged as a 'boutique' form over the past years . . . the norms of Hollywood still favor spectacle and formulas suitable for a peak opening weekend; comparatively, many narratively complex programs are among the medium's biggest hits, suggesting that the market for complexity may be more valued on television than film" (31). He's right assuming he means it's more valued on TV than film if we're comparing smaller TV shows to high-dollar film productions, the kind that have to open big to have any hopes of turning a profit. But maybe he wouldn't be right if the Hollywood studios also turned out smaller-scale, more-adult fare with the same alacrity as they do their more stereotypical products.

And I don't think attracting talent would be an issue. There's a ton of people out there who would give their eyeteeth for a shot at making, writing, or acting in features, and many never get a shot given the limitations of current Hollywood production practices. What if writers and directors and the like were hired for two or three small-scale picture deals? It would allow them the flexibility to make things they wanted to make, and given the relatively low financial stakes, they'd have a lot more latitude with which to work. After all, it's that desire for creative control that resulted in so many people who had their roots in the film business to go into television anyway. As the monetary stakes in filmmaking go higher and higher and the kinds of films which you can make that hit the broad four quadrants (young, old, male, and female) are shrinking exponentially, the opportunity for narrative innovation and developing unique and quirky characters lessens commensurately. With that in mind, it's no surprise that, as Mittell observes,

> The rise of narrative complexity on contemporary television is the changing perception of the medium's legitimacy and its appeal to creators. Many of the innovative television programs of the past twenty years have come from creators who launched their careers in film, a medium with more traditional cultural cachet: David Lynch (*Twin Peaks*) and Barry Levinson (*Homicide: Life on the Street* and *Oz*) as directors, Aaron Sorkin (*Sports Night* and *West Wing*), Joss Whedon (*Buffy, Angel,* and *Firefly*), Alan Ball (*Six Feet Under*), and J. J. Abrams (*Alias* and *Lost*) as screenwriters. Part of the appeal is television's reputation as a producer's medium, where writers and creators retain control of their work more than in film's director-centered model. (31–32)

Many of the well-known producers in TV are better known as showrunners, who typically, though not always, are also the show's creator and have primary responsibility for not just the storytelling but just about everything else as well. As Fox Broadcasting president Kevin Reilly describes it to *The Business*'s Kim Masters, it's a seemingly impossible job:

> One of the things that kills a lot of shows is that what makes up a showrunner in television is two diametrically opposed things. Number one, you've got to be an artist, a writer. Most people who become writers did not really want to go study management courses, business courses, marketing courses; they liked creativity, they wanted to be alone, they had no problems sitting in a room looking at a blank page . . . now, you've got a television show, you have hundreds of people that are reporting to you, they're all looking at you saying, "what do we do?" You have got to keep a machine, a multi-million dollar machine that comes with budgets and responsibilities, you've got to deal with the politics of the network and the studio and the different agendas, you've got to deal with marketing, you have to keep your own writers on track and keep a story afloat in the pipeline. That is a tremen-

dous management responsibility which quite often is not the skill set the great writer has. It's very rare to get them both in the same person. ("Got an Idea")

Still, despite the enormous difficulties that come with the job, for those who succeed, the payoff is huge. They become permanently associated with the show in the minds of both the public and the programming execs at the networks, so that when we think of *The Sopranos* we think of David Chase, *Deadwood* brings to mind David Milch, *Lost* J. J. Abrams, *The L Word* Ilene Chaiken, and so on. Just like their movie director counterparts, they are thought of as auteurs in accordance to the way François Truffaut defined them. So when we think of the great TV shows over the past several years, we also think of their creators, with whom we've come to identify the show. And for good reason. Like film, TV is a collaborative endeavor as well, but when a show fails, the showrunner takes the hit, which, given the amount of influence their vision has in shaping a show's content and arc, seems fair, just as it seems fair when they get the accolades for a show's success. Take, for example, the case of *Mad Men*'s creator and showrunner Matthew Weiner, who got his big break as a writer on *The Sopranos,* a job he famously landed when he sent *Sopranos*' creator David Chase his pilot for *Mad Men* as a writing sample, which he had written in his off-hours when he was a staff writer on CBS's *Becker.* Now that *Mad Men* has become a popular culture phenomenon, Weiner is a king in the world of cable television. But it's a tough gig:

> He wrote the pilot; he writes every episode of every show (along with four other people); he's the executive producer who haggles for money . . . ; and he approves every actor, costume, hairstyle and prop. Though he has directed episodes, most of the time he holds a "tone meeting" with the director at which he essentially performs the entire show himself so it's perfectly clear how he wants it done. He is both ultimate authority and divine messenger, some peculiar hybrid of God and Edith Head. "I do not feel any guilt about saying that the show comes from my mind and that I'm a control freak," he told me. "I love to be surrounded by perfectionists, and part of the problem with perfectionism is that by nature, you're always failing." (Witchel)

Weiner sets the bar high for himself, but it's paid off handsomely for him, just as it has for other successful showrunners. And even though TV doesn't have quite the same prestige as working in the high end of the motion picture industry (although that's presently changing pretty rapidly given that folks such as Martin Scorsese, who is an executive producer and also directed the pilot for HBO's *Boardwalk Empire,* are trying their hands at TV), what showrunners lose in perceived prestige and salary, they more than gain in the artistic freedom they get on cable TV, and even on network TV in some instances. Aaron Sorkin, for example, is a very successful Hollywood screenwriter, with scripts such as *A Few Good Men, The American President,* and *Charlie Wilson's War* to his credit. That said, he gravitated to TV, first with *Sports Night* and later with *The West Wing,* in large part because of the control doing so allowed him over his material. As actor Oliver Platt, who played Oliver Babish on *The West Wing,* put it in an interview with Terry Gross on *Fresh Air,*

> You have to say all of [his] words exactly the way they're written . . . there's this nice little lady who sits behind the camera . . . and she would come out and tell you afterwards if you literally got an "A" or a "Z" or a "but" wrong, and you'd have to do it all again. . . . So I had a little hazing that went on as I figured out that you had to say it exactly as it was written and sweat it out.
>
> Television is much more of a writer's medium, and I hadn't done a lot of television at that time. And I'd done a lot of movies and . . . I came up doing movies . . . when . . . movies were very concept heavy and . . . the script wasn't always the most important thing. . . . He's [Sorkin] very fastidious, and he has every right to be. And there's an absolute music and a rhythm to the way he writes. And it was a wonderful exercise for me as an actor, you know, because God knows, that's what we're supposed to do.

The movies are stagnant right now, despite the money they're making. The industry has backed itself into a corner in which it is hugely dependent on high-end tent-pole productions for survival, while comparatively less expensive productions still run into the many millions of dollars and don't warrant the risks associated with their cost. Interestingly, the showrunners who came to TV did so to enjoy the same kind of creative control that many of the legendary Hollywood filmmakers of earlier eras enjoyed over their work. As the monetary stakes are so high in contemporary Hollywood, studios are loathe to give creators freedom that may result in product that runs contrary to their business model. They don't need to completely change their business model as concerns film production— distribution and exhibition are another story—but they certainly need to adapt and diversify it. As Newman writes, over the past quarter century, "American television has undergone enormous changes with the introduction of more than one hundred new channels, pervasive new structures of media ownership and synergy, and transformations in the technologies of media production and distribution" (16). The TV industry is massive and has been slow to adapt, but it's way ahead of the film industry and has adapted in that it realizes that to be successful, it needs to still make programming that appeals to a mass audience while also making shows that appeal to niche audiences of different demographics so as to capture the largest possible share of all audiences. Despite the Chicken Little lamentations of network executives, the diversification of programs has been healthy for the business. In particular, the cable channels, and to a lesser extent the networks, have been quite successful in their wooing of upwardly mobile audiences who might not otherwise have been compelled to watch. As Jaramillo notes, "If a series appeals to (and captures) decent numbers of an upscale demographic, larger numbers of lower income viewers are secondary—quality of quantity" (585).

Thus the film industry would be well served to engage in producing its own brand of niche programming. In particular, I'd like to see them embark on their own move towards lower-budget, high-quality films (the two things absolutely don't have to be mutually exclusive) so as to fill the vacuum left for fans of truly independent filmmaking that occurred when the movement collapsed under the weight of its own excesses in the late 1990s and early 2000s. Studios would do well to heed the lessons of their own failures with their various independent arms and control costs, as doing so is essential to this new niche's success. But by hiring new talent and paying them well enough so that they don't have to worry about how they're going to live and giving them anywhere from $100,000 to $1,000,000 to make a movie without interference, they'd surely get some winners, and the costs would be such that bombs wouldn't much matter to the bottom line. There's not enough cinemas to support an influx of more films than are already being made, but where Hollywood can cut production is in the middle ground of films priced in the $20 to $60 million range, as that's where they're having the hardest time making money anyway. Those films cost too much to hope for word of mouth to lead them to catching fire at the box office, but too often they aren't based on the kinds the presold properties that would justify the enormous outlay of money required to produce, distribute, promote, and exhibit them. Filmmakers can't make the kinds of complex serial narratives that we see on TV, as the medium just won't allow it. But that doesn't mean that given the opportunity and the freedom to do so, they couldn't follow the model of quality TV and make more sophisticated adult-themed fare than Hollywood normally makes. And if they did, I'm convinced the audience that now stays in to watch TV (or DVR recordings thereof ) for such entertainment would gladly come to the movie theater more often (or pay to watch simultaneously released new movies at home), which would be great for not only the audience that desires these kinds of movies, but also for the studios who would have a new niche on their belt, as it were.

Many of the more successful of the showrunners in recent years moved to television so that they could replicate what they saw on the big screen in an earlier era, as illustrated in Alex Witchel's on-set observation of *Mad Men*:

> Matthew Weiner stood on the set of his hit show, *Mad Men,* ready for his close-up in extreme anxiety. He was watching the rehearsal of a scene that seemed fine to me, better than fine, but his staccato commentary was a scene in itself.
>
> "He should be standing," he said of an actor who was seated.
>
> "That should be on the table," he said of an accordion folder that an actress had placed on the floor.
>
> "They're overreacting, paying too much attention to each other." He heard himself and looked slightly sheepish. "You'll see it turn from theater to movie in the next take," he told me. "I want them not to pay too much attention to each other, so it feels real, more perfunctory. Not that TV thing." His smile was wry. "I'm very impatient. . . . I just don't want it to look like a TV show."

Conversely, Hollywood would be well served if it made more movies that looked like TV shows and it's high time they do so.

## WORKS CITED

Als, Hilton. (Interviewed by Allison Keyes). "Tyler Perry Simplifies, Commodifies Black Life." *NPR: Tell Me More.* May 12, 2010.

"Another One Bites the Dust." *Masked Scheduler Blog.* May 28, 2010.

*Box Office Mojo.com.* "All-Time Domestic Gross."

*Box Office Mojo.com.* "2000 Domestic Grosses."

Bradberry, Grace. "Swearing, Sex, and Brilliance." *The Observer* [London]. Oct. 20, 2002. *LexisNexis Academic.*

Cresswell, Julie. "Speedy New Traders Make Waves Far from Wall Street." *The New York Times.com.* May 16, 2010.

DeVault, Ryan Christopher. "*Mad Men* Season Premier Sets Ratings Record for Show." *associatedcontent.com.* Aug. 17, 2009.

Epstein, Edward Jay. (Interviewed by Dave Davies). "Crunching Numbers in the Hollywood Economy." *NPR Fresh Air Podcast.* April 1, 2010.

Fritz, Ben. "Movie Tickets Rise 8% in First Quarter." *Los Angeles Times.com.* May 4, 2010.

Fritz, Ben, and Dawn M. Chmielewski. "Netflix Agrees to Delay in Renting Out Warner Movies." *Los Angeles Times.com.* Jan. 7, 2010.

Gorman, Bill. "The Top 100 Rated TV Shows of All Time." *tvbythenumbers.com.* March 21, 2009.

Gross, Terry. "Oliver Platt Gives His All on Film, TV, and Stage." *NPR Fresh Air Podcast.* April 27, 2010.

Grover, Ronald. "Hollywood Is Worried as DVD Sales Slow." *Bloomberg Business Week.com.* Feb. 19, 2009.

Jaramillo, Deborah. "The Family Racket: AOL Time Warner, HBO, *The Sopranos,* and the Construction of a Quality Brand." In *Considering Television. Television: The Critical View,* 7th ed., ed. Horace Newcomb, 579–94. New York: Oxford University Press, 2007.

Kunz, William M. *Consolidation in the Motion Picture and Television Industries.* Oxford: Rowman & Littlefield, 2007.

Masters, Kim. "Got an Idea for a Great TV Show?" *The Business Podcast.* April 27, 2010.

Masters, Kim. "George Romero: Grandfather of the Zombie Film." *The Business Podcast.* May 17, 2010.

McCabe, Janet and Kim Akass. "It's not TV, it's HBO's original programming; Producing quality TV." In *It's Not TV: Watching HBO in the Post-Television Era,* ed. Marc Leverette, Brian L. Ott and Cara Louise Buckley, 83–93. New York: Routledge, 2008.

McPherson, Sam. "Record Ratings for 'Mad Men' Season 4 Premiere." *TVovermind.com.* July 31, 2010.

Mittell, Jason. "Narrative Complexity in Contemporary American Television." *The Velvet Light Trap* 58 (Fall 2006): 29–40.

*natoonline.org.* The National Association of Theater Owners. "Average U.S. Ticket Prices.".

*natoonline.org.* "Total Number of U.S. Admissions."

Newman, Michael Z. "From Beats to Arcs: Toward a Poetics of Television Narrative." *The Velvet Light Trap* 58 (Fall 2006): 16–28.

*omg! News from Yahoo.com.* "Charlie Sheen, Mariska Hargitay Among TV's Highest Paid Stars." Sept. 20, 2009.

Pilkington, Ed. "Hollywood Film Output to Fall by a Third." *Guardian.co.uk* [London]. Oct. 18, 2009.

Rampell, Catherine. "Poverty Rate Rises: Uninsured Rate Stays Flat." *The New York Times. com.* Sept. 10, 2009.

Rice, Lynette. "*Heroes* Cancelled by NBC." *Entertainmentweekly.com.* May 14, 2010.

Schiffman, Betsy. "*Avatar* DVD Sales Are Out of This World: Is It the Last Hurrah for Discs?" *dailyfinance.com.* April 26, 2010.

Smith, Shane. "DVD Sales Decline; Blame the Studios?" *insideredbox.com.* Sept. 30, 2009.

Smith, Shane. "DreamWorks Exec on DVD Sales Decline: 'Greed killed the Goose.'" *insideredbox.com.* May 12, 2010.

Susman, Gary. "Simon Cowell Tops TV's Male Earners (So Kids, Being Mean Does Pay)." *TV Squad.com.* Nov. 11, 2009.

Sutter, Kurt. "Why Most Network Scripted Dramas Suck." *Sutter Ink Blog.* Oct. 22, 2009.

*USA Today.com.* "Nielsen Ratings for Week of May 3." May 10, 2010.

Witchel, Alex. "*Mad Men* Has Its Moment." *The New York Times.com.* June 22, 2008.

# Chapter 9

# "THE FUTURE, MR. GITTES. THE FUTURE": NEXT WAVE FILMMAKING AND BEYOND

As the movie industry moves into the digital age, it's undergoing cataclysmic industrial changes. But when the dust finally settles for a while, neither its more than a century-old basic premise, providing for-profit entertainment to consumers, nor the underlying structure required to control the market—production, distribution, and exhibition—will have changed. What likely will have changed is how things are produced, distributed, and exhibited. This doesn't mean that the major media companies won't still control them, but that the methods used to maintain that control will by necessity have morphed, and some very interesting things will come about as a result of it.

Production, the making of movies, remains the core of the business, as you have to have product that customers want. As has been discussed at length, the industry is for the most part moving away from producing smaller-scale films, opting instead to anchor its production slate with a few (hopefully) well-chosen tent-pole franchise films around which it can fill out the rest of its slate with acquisitions and more modest endeavors. The idea is that spectacle is something that's required to get people coming to the theaters. Why leave the house for intimate drama, which can be just as satisfying to watch at home? To get fannies in seats, the movies need to differentiate themselves from that which can be watched elsewhere, hence the current onslaught of 3D tent-pole pictures. It's only a matter of time before all tent-pole movies are in 3D and it makes sense. It's been a long time coming, as making going to the movies in a theater a unique experience that can't be replicated at home was the goal of many of the goofier cinematic innovations of the 1950s—Cinerama, CinemaScope, VistaVision, 3D, etc. The processes required to produce and exhibit films utilizing those early innovations proved too unwieldy and costly and so they faded away, but the idea behind them didn't, and 3D technology has recently become cost effective and finally caught up with the dream and appears to be here to stay this time; it's easy to wear the glasses, which no longer give most viewers a headache, when done right the technology works well, and it now really is more than just a gimmick. In fact, it can make watching movies better, although it can't make a bad movie good. But it can make a good movie even better to watch, adding a texture, a depth, a visual resonance that isn't quite there in 2D. It's just a more full visual experience. And no home theater can replicate seeing *Avatar* in 3D at a great movie house. The fact that Martin Scorsese followed up *Shutter Island* by choosing to film a 3D adaptation of Brian Selznick's children's book *The Invention of Hugo Cabret* pretty much tells you all you need to know about 3D's place in the movies' digital future (Siegel).

Still, there's a gold rush mentality with 3D technology right now, which has resulted in slapdash postproduction conversions of films that were never meant to be seen in 3D (e.g., *Clash of the Titans* [Leterrier 2010]); additionally, studios are green-lighting new 3D productions at a breakneck pace. So far, audiences have flocked to see 3D movies, choosing 3D versions of a movie that's playing in both 2D and 3D at a more than 2 to 1 margin, which is saying something given that there's still a lot more 2D than 3D screens in America. (Although that's changing rapidly, as according to the MPAA's 2009 Theatrical Market Statistics Report, in 2005 there were only 84 digital 3D screens in the world, all of which were in the United States. By 2009, there were 3,548 in the United States and 8,989 total worldwide, a remarkable growth rate [MPAA.org].) And Hollywood is taking advantage, trying to make up for the revenue lost from the hemorrhaging DVD market by raising 3D ticket prices at what will certainly be an unsustainable rate. From *Clash of the Titans* in March 2010 to the release of *Shrek Forever After* (Mitchell) in June 2010, in some places around the country prices rose more than $3.50 per ticket, which is nothing short of "inflation on an Argentinian scale" (Masters, "Cannes"). While the technology has yet to fail at the box office, it's only a matter of time before a high-budget bomb gets Hollywood to rethink when and how it will use 3D, but that's probably a good thing. And what about those movies that aren't tent-pole films? Do we need to see *Little Miss Sunshine* or *Napoleon Dynamite* in 3D? Probably not, but that doesn't mean that future indie-style films won't be made in 3D, especially as the equipment gets cheaper and more accessible to lower-budget filmmakers. And it will. It's a paradigm shift, and some filmmakers will definitely use 3D to enhance the spectacle of their work, but it's also a new tool in the way stories can be told on film—or, more accurately, digitally via 1s and 0s—and it's hard to imagine filmmakers not flocking to utilize it.

Not everyone likes 3D or thinks that it's more than a passing fad. Of its critics, it's perhaps Roger Ebert who has been the most loudly excoriating. He's written a fair amount about 3D, but it was in a twitter tweet that he boiled his pointed views down to their essence when he wrote, "3-D is a distracting, annoying, anti-realistic, juvenile abomination to use as an excuse for higher prices." Still, a lot of powerful folks in the industry are betting on the long-term viability of 3D, including Jeffrey Katzenberg, who has reportedly had *12 Angry Men* (Lumet 1957) converted into 3D as a tool to convince skeptical industry execs that 3D has the capacity to make any kind of movie more interesting (Masters, "Clash"). He screens it to naysayers and they come out singing a different tune. Apparently, it puts you right in the room with the jury and makes the tensions even more palpable. This sort of intimacy may prove to be irresistible for future filmmakers of all stripes.

But that future, though fast approaching, is still a ways off, and there remains a ton of young filmmakers who want to make films but don't have the financial wherewithal to make anything close to the kinds of high-dollar films Hollywood currently favors, 3D or otherwise. Rather than trying to make low-budget versions of high-end Hollywood films, a number of filmmakers have instead made the films they want to make on their own terms, with no consideration of what might make a film commercially marketable. At the forefront of these filmmakers are folks like Andrew Bujalski, Joe Swanberg, Aaron Katz, and Mark and Jay Duplass, who are considered founders of and key players in the so-called "mumblecore" movement. There is far from critical consensus as to the value of their work, but much of the extant criticism is misplaced and focuses too much on what they're doing in comparison to Hollywood and not enough on how they're doing it, as it's the how that may ultimately prove to be much more influential over the long haul.

Legend has it that the name "mumblecore" was coined in Austin during the 2005 South by Southwest Film Festival (SXSW), which featured the Duplass Brothers' *The Puffy Chair,* Bujalski's *Mutual Appreciation,* and Swanberg's *Kissing on the Mouth.* While out at a bar one night, Eric Masunaga, Bujalski's sound mixer, jokingly used the term and it has stuck, much to the chagrin of those associated with the movement (Lim, "Generation"). It's a terrible name for a variety of reasons, not the least of which is the way it's been pounced on by its detractors, who use the term derisively to emphasize what they see as its shortcomings as compared to higher-dollar Hollywood movies. Take, for example, Amy Taubin (who, having selected Bujalski's *Funny Ha Ha* as one of the best films of 2010, clearly isn't wholly opposed to all films of this kind), who asserts that "on a technical level, these are micro-budget movies where sound is almost always a neglected element," which just isn't the case. Is it the artificially crisp Hollywood sound where every syllable is clearly enunciated? Most definitely not, but while the technical acumen isn't in the same league as a Hollywood production, the sound is fine. And regardless, I'd argue that the term is less about the sound quality than it is the way the characters talk, which is in halting, hesitant, elliptically clipped phrases, full of "ums," "you knows," "likes," and other thought gaps that rarely make it into Hollywood films but are the lingua franca of the 20-somethings these films typically feature. It's inarticulate to be sure, but that inarticulateness is representative of what is typically an inability and/or unwillingness on the part of the characters to connect with one another on an emotional level that goes beyond their normal superficial but safe mode of communication.

While there are a lot of differences in the work of these directors, there are some unifying elements as well. Visually, most of them shoot on digital video. There are a lot of really long handheld shots. Part of this is surely intentional and a part of their aesthetic, but part of it is also functionally and financially imperative. With small, often nonprofessional casts and crews that are donating their time, it's just a lot easier to do longer, uncomplicated shots. While the shots themselves may be simple, the editing often isn't, at least in the sense of its rhythms, in that they frequently cut where you wouldn't expect them to, resulting in a kind of unsettling effect on the viewer. They tend to favor nonprofessional actors and are much more open to improvisation than most filmmakers. The reasons for this are also as much financial as they are aesthetic. With budgets that can be as little as a couple of thousand dollars, it's not like they're hiring SAG actors or professional crew. They get the friends they think might have the ability to act (or crew or create the music, etc.) to do it for free or not much. Likewise, because they typically shoot on digital video it means that the only extra cost that comes about as a result of improvisation is time, which, as they aren't paying union rates for cast and crew, doesn't translate to monetary cost in the same way that shooting extra footage does on a Hollywood production. As Taubin writes, "In relation to meaning, these nonactors are perfect choices for these films because their insecurity and embarrassment about voicing their characters' ideas, desires, and feelings is not merely symptomatic of their lack of technique, it dovetails with a defining characteristic of the particular cohort (white, middle-class, twenty-something) to which the filmmakers and their quasi-fictional characters belong. The mumblecore films literally speak in the voice of that cohort, and the best of them do so with remarkable and revealing precision."

As Taubin rightfully notes, the subject of these films almost always centers around the characters' "quarterlife crises," which come part and parcel with the difficulty many postgrads have in transitioning from college to the working world. Dennis Lim evocatively describes this period as "the blurry limbo of post-collegiate existence, a period at once ephemeral and cruelly decisive" (Lim, "Graduates"). This is far from a new subject, having long been treated in film—such as *The Graduate* (Nichols 1967)—and literature—such as in Jack Kerouac's *On the Road* or Douglas Coupland's landmark 1991 book *Generation X,* in which he coined a linguistic precursor to "quarterlife crisis," the term "mid-twenties breakdown," which he defines as "a period of mental collapse occurring in one's twenties, often caused by an inability to function outside of school or structured environments coupled with a realization of one's aloneness in the world. Often marks the induction into the ritual of pharmaceutical usage" (27). As several critics have noted, not always complimentarily, this crippling fear of growing up and putting yourself out in the world professionally, romantically, and emotionally is also the theme of pretty much every film Judd Apatow has directed, written, and/or produced; the difference is that things turn out much more realistically in these films than they do in their larger-budgeted, more mainstream Hollywood counterparts. Whereas in an Apatow film we're asked to believe in the veracity of a world in which not only does Seth Rogen actually sleep with Katherine Heigl, but ends up winning her heart as well, these films "thrum with ambivalent dread—underlying the characters' inert indecision is a reluctance to let the rest of their lives begin, not least for fear that it might prove an undifferentiated haze" (Lim, "Graduates").

This has resulted in these filmmakers being dubbed the "voices of their generation," a sobriquet with which they are justifiably uncomfortable, even while they acknowledge the possibility. As Bujalski posits, "I don't think that was ever my intention per se. Nor was it any kind of grand attempt to make a generational statement—it was always a little more specific. Though another maxim that I'm given to quoting a lot is that the more specific something is, the more universal it is. Certainly that was some kind of guiding principle." Still, in the same interview he does go on to concede that "fear of adulthood is a theme that pervades [my] films . . . and . . . maybe that is something that is specific, if not to 'my generation,' then at least my subset of it. I feel like a lot of people I know, myself included, are still figuring out what we're doing, are single and so forth, even though we're now at a point where we're older than our parents were when they married and had us" (Foundas).

While the constancy of 20-somethings in crisis is part of the reason folks have tried to lump these films together as part of a movement, it's also resulted in no small amount of backlash. As Lim writes,

> For potential haters, mumblecore offers plenty of ammunition. The films are modest in scope, but their concentration on daily banalities can register as narcissism. Despite the movement's communitarian ethos, from the outside it can seem incestuous and insular. Hardly models of diversity, the films are set in mostly white, straight, middle-class worlds, and while female characters are often well drawn, the directors are overwhelmingly male. ("Generation")

Taubin goes even further in her criticism of their perceived homogeneity when she writes,

> The directors are all male middle-class Caucasians, and they make movies exclusively about young adults who are involved in heterosexual relationships and who have jobs (when they have them) in workplaces populated almost exclusively by SWMs and SWFs. As a few bloggers who had their fill of the hype have noted, So Yong Kim's lovely *In Between Days* (06) would seem to fit the mumblecore parameters (DIY production, a protagonist whose problems with language and communication frustrate her desire for a romantic relationship), but because the filmmaker is a Korean-American woman and her heroine is a Korean immigrant, no one thought to invite the movie to the party. Instead, the mumblecore guys selected Ry Russo-Young, who plays a supporting role in Swanberg's *Hannah Takes the Stairs* (07), as their token female director even though her first feature, *Orphans* (07), with its heavy-handed visual metaphors and anguished examination of the symbiotic bond between two sisters, seems closer to Bergman than Bujalski.

Taubin's implying that the directors associated with mumblecore rejected So Yong Kim because she's female and Korean is no less absurd than the idea that they hand-picked Russo-Young for inclusion in the party. More likely is that critics trying to define the movement or genre overlooked Kim, even though, as Taubin accurately notes, she certainly fits the bill. Conversely, the inclusion of Russo-Young in the pantheon is no doubt because she had a connection with the gang, as it were. But it's not like they have any money and are deciding what films to green-light and back or what films get into film festivals. They don't like being called mumblecore directors themselves, so it's not like they're working to deny others the privilege on the basis of race or gender or anything else for that matter. It's an odd kind of criticism. There's certainly truth to the claim that many of those identified as mumblecore filmmakers are white guys making films about predominantly well-educated 20-somethings, but there isn't anything wrong with that. That's where they are in their lives, it's where the people they know and hang out with are as well, and they are simply making movies about that which they know, the scope of which also happens to be particularly conducive to the budgets and technology that are allowing them to make movies in the first place. No one told the young Spike Lee that his films should have had more white people in them, nor, for that matter, is anyone saying that Kim should consider making films that aren't about Korean Americans, nor should they. There's no problem in not liking a filmmaker's work, but as David Denby gracefully notes, a critic "should grant a filmmaker his subject."

But even if one views the term "mumblecore" as being more about the emotional stuntedness of its characters than a snide reference to its perceived technological deficiencies, it's still a rotten term that doesn't do the importance of the work justice. In describing the current state of independent cinema, John Patterson claims that the "last independent generation has been co-opted by the studios, and the next one still labours in digicam/web-based/mumblecore obscurity, with its auteurs and iconoclasts yet to establish themselves." Again, the idea that these filmmakers are working in mumblecore is derogatory in that they're simply marking time until they get to the big league of Hollywood cinema. But what's important to take from this is that many of them *are* going to eventually make their way to Hollywood; they are the next wave of filmmakers, and that's exactly what they should be called: Next Wave filmmakers. There's a lot of contention over whether or not the work of these filmmakers to date comprises a genre. David Denby refers without comment to "a recent genre of micro-budget independent movies," as though it's a given that their work collectively forms a genre. Amy Taubin goes the other way, arguing that mumblecore was "never more than a flurry of festival hype and blogoshpere branding" and definitely not a movement in "the grand sense of the French New Wave or the postwar American avant-garde. At most, one might think of mumblecore as an update of the 'New Talkie,' the strand (not quite a genre) of no-budget indies that emerged in the early nineties with such landmark films as Richard Linklater's *Slacker,* Kevin Smith's *Clerks* and Rose Troche and Guinevere Turner's *Go Fish.*" I certainly wouldn't call the output of the Next Wave a genre in that there just aren't the kind of unifying characteristics necessary to comprise a genre along the lines of say, westerns or romantic comedies. Conversely, I do think there's no doubt that a movement is afoot, and history may well prove it to be every bit as grand as those cited by Taubin. In fact, the French New Wave is a particularly apt analogy, in that it was composed of a bunch of different filmmakers making all kinds of different films, genre and otherwise. The variance of their output prevented their being generically categorized (although there has been some contention about this as well), but the fact that they were making movies at the same time and that their work, often funded by the French government, was an anarchical alternative to mainstream European cinema—the "tradition of quality"—is what made it a movement.

Kim Masters describes the output of Next Wave filmmakers as simply being "made with tiny budgets, shot on hand-held digital cameras, with unknown actors who talk a lot about their lives" ("Brothers Duplass"). While this is accurate, there is more to their work than broad similarities that could just as accurately describe most home movies. In fact, there is a lot more unity among the output of Next Wave filmmakers than there ever was among New Wave filmmakers. Again, part of this is economic in that it's much more financially feasible to make a movie about the minutiae of everyday life than it is to make anything that includes heavy special effects or action sequences. As Lim notes,

> Mumblecore concerns itself with the mundane vacillations of postcollegiate existence. It can seem like these movies, which star nonprofessional actors and feature quasi-improvised dialogue, seldom deal with matters more pressing than whether to return a phone call. . . . But what these films understand all too well is that the tentative drift of the in-between years masks quietly seismic shifts that are apparent only in hindsight. Mumblecore narratives hinge less on plot points than on the tipping points in interpersonal relationships. . . . Artists who mine life's minutiae are by no means new, but mumblecore bespeaks a true 21st-century sensibility, reflective of MySpace-like social networks and the voyeurism and intimacy of YouTube. ("Generation")

Certainly, the press has done a lot to pigeonhole and limit Next Wave filmmakers, in no small part because the articles typically focus on Bujalski, Swanberg, Katz, and the Duplass Brothers, which makes it seem more like an exclusive fraternity than a broad-scale movement. Taubin is absolutely right when she taps So Yong Kim as deserving inclusion in what I would argue is the Next Wave movement. In fact, there are a ton of young Next Wave filmmakers of all colors, genders, sexual orientations, and nationalities out there who are embracing the freedom and opportunity that comes with low-budget filmmaking, digital or otherwise, and some of them will definitely break through and make their marks as filmmakers. The club as touted by the media is small, but that's not reflective of the groundswell that's taking place in the world of filmmaking right now. To whit, in the winter of 2010, the Sundance Film Festival, which the media has for a long time now made seem as being more about a Hollywood marketplace where deals are made than a festival that supports independent filmmaking (which isn't true—it's just that the glossies aren't going to cover true indies with no chance for distribution, which far and away make up the bulk of the festival's programming), featured for the first time a new section that featured low- and no-budget films, tellingly titled "Next." Eight films were selected for Next, all of them shot on digital video by a multiethnic array of directors who range in age from 24 to 32 (Wood). While not identified as part of the mumblecore gang, there's no doubt they are all working in the same ballpark. In "A Generation Finds Its Mumble," Lim argues that Next Wave filmmakers are a part of "more a loose collective or even a state of mind than an actual aesthetic movement," but I would argue that they are at the forefront of a technological movement that will undoubtedly have long-term effects on some of the directions the industry ultimately takes in the future.

Next Wave filmmakers are truly, refreshingly independent. Rather than make what they think Hollywood might want to buy, they make what they want, marketplace be damned, which results in their having a limited appeal, which is not necessarily a bad thing. As Joe Swanberg says, while it's disconcerting when people don't care for your work, "when you weigh that frustration against having to make other kinds of movies, making the kinds of movies you want to wins out in the end. It's always hard to put so much love and energy and work into a film and then say, 'Oh, but only 1/100 of the people are going to see it.' But I'm stubborn, and I'd rather have the audience change to like my films than to change my films so the audience likes them" (O'Hehir). This is a rather refreshing attitude for a filmmaker to have, although there's a trade-off, one of which is that you're exchanging the freedom that comes with micro-budget digital filmmaking with the reality that you're not likely to make a living as a filmmaker if you keep working in this mode forever. Indeed, upon the festival release of his second film, *Mutual Appreciation* in 2005, Bujalski (who iconoclastically shoots in 16mm) wistfully said, "Of course I'd love to do another film. If I could find a way to keep pulling these off, I'd be delighted," indicating he was already keenly aware that making films "on the cheap, with nonprofessional actors and a skeleton crew . . . may be unsustainable" (Land). Indeed, in a later interview Bujalski was even more blunt, referring to his mode of moviemaking as "completely unsustainable. . . . As I get older and my friends get older, it's hard to say to people, 'Take a month off from your life and work for me for free.'" (Lim, "[Mumbled]"). But that hasn't stopped Next Wave filmmakers from trying, and in addition to making the films they want to make, a lack of industry affiliation allows them to market and distribute their movies as they want to as well, which is part of a larger undercurrent of paradigmatic change in movie distribution.

When they realized they weren't going to be able to walk through the front doors of a studio and get a job making movies, the previous generation of indie filmmakers made their assault on Hollywood via the festival circuit backdoor. It wasn't self-distribution in that they were playing festivals so as to attract the interest of larger entities that had the financial wherewithal to distribute their films and get them to the masses. Before the studios got into making independent movies themselves, it was a win-win for all concerned, as film companies picked up product without having to pay for production and filmmakers, at least those who were lucky enough to score deals, were able to get their films seen and earn the cachet necessary to get a foothold in the industry. For the current generation, the death of studio specialty arms and the subsequent drying up of money in the wake of the global financial meltdown in the late 2000s means that these opportunities, always rare in the greater scheme of things despite the media aggrandizement of movies like *Clerks* and *The Blair Witch Project,* are now virtually nonexistent. But unlike their predecessors, Next Wavers have plenty of alternate distribution opportunities not previously available that has resulted in a deluge of new models for distribution.

Forever, the cinema has been seen as the end all, be all for filmmakers. "Video" was derogatory, something used to describe inferior products, an attitude that was reinforced by the unwillingness of established filmmakers to even consider working on video. But Next Wave filmmakers have grown up in an era in which the lines have blurred considerably. They watch streaming videos online via laptops and smart phones, and understand that there's plenty of YouTube videos that have been seen by millions of more folks than would ever have been possible had they been released theatrically, which isn't really feasible for these filmmakers anyway in an era in which the MPAA estimates that the average cost of marketing a studio specialty film is upwards of $25 million, which is in many cases thousands of times more than what these filmmakers are spending to make their films (Barnes). And Next Wavers are much more comfortable with the technology than their predecessors and don't see it as inferior at all; they see it as a god-send that allows them to take their films directly to the people in a way they never could have in earlier eras. And it starts with production and the willingness to see shooting on DV as an advantage rather than a hindrance. In the summer of 2009, I had a conversation with filmmaker Mark Duplass at the CineVegas Film Festival after a screening of Lynn Shelton's *Humpday* (2009), in which he stars, about what he likes about shooting digitally (he had been making *Cyrus* [2010] with his brother and they'd specifically contracted to shoot it digitally). He cited digital video—the Red Cam in particular—as nothing less than "a gift" that allowed he and his peers to do that which they'd never be able to do otherwise. Things have changed accordingly:

> "Real" has come to mean not color-saturated, 35mm film stock shot by a camerman named Andrzej, but a "low-fi" digital look, which is a boon to self-made filmmakers everywhere. [Mark] Duplass and Aselton [Katie, his wife and sometime collaborator] say that what began as a budgetary limitation has become their visual style. Improv or scripted, digital shooting allows for instant feedback and endless takes. "Now we're addicted to it," Aselton says.
>
> "Before this there was [this belief that] the aesthetic of film is better than video," says [Ted] Barron [curator of the Harvard Film Archives' New American Independent Cinema series, which featured the Duplass Brothers' *The Puffy*

*Chair*]. "[Now] all kinds of viewing experiences are changing." He cites gadgets such as laptops and iPods as the new platforms for indie cinema. (Gilsdorf)

And then, as Michael Cieply notes, once the films are made, it's a whole new world in which final cut is not the end of the process but just the start of the next phase in which filmmakers are doing it themselves, "paying for their own distribution, marketing films through social networking sites and Twitter blasts, putting their work up free on the Web to build a reputation, [and] cozying up to concierges at luxury hotels in film festival cities to get them to whisper into the right ears." And in many ways, it's by necessity that Next Wave filmmakers have taken to the streets to promote their own work. Films that 10 or 15 years ago would have likely been snapped up for distribution by a studio specialty arm now languish on the festival circuit, where they become audience favorites that generate good buzz but still aren't able to make it into movie theaters, as was the case with Bob Byington's well-liked *Harmony and Me* (2009), which played to adoring audiences at top festivals such as Edinburgh, the Los Angeles Film Festival, and CineVegas (where I saw it). But it was just never quite able to score a distribution deal that satisfied Byington. Rather than wallowing in self-pity about how the dying off of so many indie distributors has made his row a much tougher one to hoe, Byington instead tried to distribute it himself by booking it into theaters directly without the backing of a distributor:

> "How can you lament the passing of a [distributor]?" Byington asks. "A lot of those companies went down because they had nothing to offer. Like in *Heathers,* when Christian Slater says it wasn't so bad that the jock guys die, because what did they have to offer? Date rape? I think people who make movies will soon expect to disseminate the movies themselves, rather looking around for someone to do it for them." (Longworth)

Things are certainly changing and quickly. While Swanberg is far from alone in his methods, he's received a lot of attention for them, in no small part due to his being unbelievably prolific. He's posted his movies online, he's sold them on DVD via his Web site, he's tirelessly traveled the festival circuit with his movies, he uses social networking sites to keep folks up to date on his projects, and he's also created a Web series called *Young American Bodies* that now runs on the Independent Film Channel's Web site. He has made a name for himself, and he's done it completely outside of the system and for very little money; for nothing, really, if you consider his expenses in the context of Hollywood:

> Working cheaply, with off-the-shelf video cameras and a nonprofessional crew, Swanberg says, is the price of artistic freedom. "It takes tremendous weight off your shoulders in terms of what you're going to tackle. If I'd had to do *Kissing on the Mouth* on a cheap film budget of, like, $50,000, I don't think I would have even

set out to make the film, because it would be so unrealistic to think that it would make that money back. But knowing that it was only going to cost a few thousand dollars, and knowing that it was *my* few thousand dollars, allowed me to say, 'Cool, this is the movie I want to make. So I'll make it.'" (O'Hehir)

At the 2009 SXSW Film Festival, Swanberg debuted his film *Alexander the Last*. But the night before it played SXSW, it had already debuted on the Independent Film Channel's IFC in Theaters, a movies-on-demand channel that's available in 55 million American homes through which viewers can purchase and stream movies that are currently playing festivals and/or are in limited theatrical release. Additionally, they have Festival Direct, which plays six films a month that IFC Films has picked up from festivals. It's available in upwards of 37 million American households (Snyder, "Film Festival"). Whereas Soderbergh's much-ballyhooed 2006 day and date release of *Bubble* caused much hand-wringing about the future of films in Hollywood, IFC's ventures are barely creating a ripple of protest, perhaps in part because more often than not the films they're featuring never really had a chance for wide theatrical distribution anyway. Neither did *Bubble* for that matter, but I would argue it was that it was made by Steven Soderbergh that caused all the concern. Had the movie been made by Joe Blow (or Swanberg, as the case may be), no one would have batted an eye, as it wouldn't have been seen as a threat to the status quo, even if the status quo is in need of a good shot in the arm. It's also no surprise that it's Next Wave filmmakers who are so keen to explore new opportunities such as this to get their work seen. Frustrated by how difficult the mainstream cinema is to break into, they're creating a system of their own. As for *Alexander the Last*'s simultaneous multi-platform release, Swanberg himself summed it up nicely when he said, "I feel like this is a watershed moment. The promise of the digital revolution, this democratization of movies, is now really happening" (Snyder, "The Film Festival"). And in a neat case of reverse osmosis, some of what they're doing is trickling back upstream; when Soderbergh's *Che* (2008) failed to get a mainstream distribution deal in the States, he opted to show it on demand through IFC Films' networks. And in a testament to how far we've come in such a short period of time, Hollywood didn't raise one eyebrow.

Nor, for that matter, did Wayne Wang's *The Princess of Nebraska* being released online via streaming video in the YouTube Screening Room. Wang adapted two films, *A Thousand Years of Good Prayers* (2008) and *The Princess of Nebraska* (2008), from a collection of Yiyun Li stories about three generations of Chinese natives resettled in America. While Wang has made fairly mainstream films in the past, most notably the Jennifer Lopez vehicle *Maid in Manhattan* (2002), these two fall squarely in the realm of the art house and making them together created a problem. Releasing tent-pole franchise films months or more apart happens all the time (*Twilight, Harry Potter,* etc.), but there wasn't much precedent in which to place stock as concerns the releasing of thematically related art house films. Tarantino's *Kill Bill* was split into two parts and they performed somewhat poorly, and they were ostensibly a lot more commercial than Wang's films. A double feature wasn't much of an option either, as the only film in the recent past that was released that way, Robert Rodriguez and Tarantino's *Grindhouse* (2007), also underwhelmed at the box office. So, in a novel approach, Magnolia Pictures, the film's distributor, released *A Thousand Years of Good Prayers* theatrically in art houses and *The Princess of Nebraska* via YouTube. The theory was about eyes and future DVD sales, the idea being that you can attract a lot more viewers on YouTube for a lot less money, which results in greater interest in the DVD once it comes out (Snyder, "YouTube"). The films weren't financially successful, but that doesn't mean it was a failed experiment. By not spending the million or more likely required to release and market *The Princess,* Magnolia was able to limit its losses substantially. And *The Princess* did get almost a quarter-million-page views on YouTube, which is around the same size as the theatrical audience garnered by *A Thousand Years,* which had a worldwide box office gross of $1.65 million. While this isn't yet a viable option for a multimillion-dollar film, for smaller films with less margin for error, Web releases are certainly worth exploring.

It's not just Next Wave films or art house films by more established filmmakers that are going alternative routes; other kinds of films, like documentaries, are doing so as well, and for good reason. As the traditional avenues for indie distribution dry up, docs are tanking at the box office. And this is after a brief period in which films like *March of the Penguins, Fahrenheit 9/11, Super Size Me,* and *An Inconvenient Truth* became box office smashes, which many thought might be signaling a strong era for docs. Part of that has come to pass; with the advent of cheap digital technology, we really have entered a golden age of documentary filmmaking, with a plethora of fantastic films being made annually the world over. The problem is saturation, and documentary filmmakers have good reason to be scrambling for new ways to get their films seen. Docs were never going to dominate at the box office anyway, and now there are way too many films for too few slots, so that the ones that do get theatrical distribution tend to cancel each other out, while the best of the rest play to rapt festival audiences only to then fade into obscurity, never to be seen or heard from again. To whit, Alex Gibney's 2007 Best Documentary Oscar winner *Taxi to the Dark Side* made only $275,000 domestically; *Standard Operating Procedure* (2008), Errol Morris's acclaimed Abu Ghraib film, $209,000; and festival fave *Crazy Love* (Klores and Stevens 2007) barely broke the $300,000 mark (Ansen). Alternatively, Michael Moore took his film *Slacker Uprising* (2007), which chronicles his college tour during the 2004 election cycle on which he tried to inspire 18- to 24-year-olds to turn out and vote, and released it online as a free download. This is a great approach if you're Michael Moore, the most commercially successful documentarian in the history of the planet. Not so much if you're a young filmmaker trying to make a name for herself.

What's happening is a shift away from the cinema, where it just costs too much money for a documentary, which has a limited likelihood of being a breakout hit, to make it worth the investment a theatrical release requires. So, like Next Wavers, doc filmmakers are turning towards the Web, television, and home video

DVD sales, rental, and video on demand companies like Netflix and are having some success. As Magnolia Pictures' Eamonn Bowles notes, "Docs perform disproportionately well on Netflix, relative to the theatrical marketplace. . . . I do think that's where a lot of the doc business is going" (Kaufman). Similarly, docs are now TV staples on channels such as HBO, PBS, Discovery, The History Channel, and so forth. In fact, HBO documentary head Shiela Nevins once famously sent Michael Moore a TV in an attempt to get him to make a movie for HBO, which he has so far declined to do ("Doc Ethics"). Moore isn't buying, in part because he believes that "going to the movies is an active experience . . . TV is passive" (Ansen). But Moore might be the only documentarian in the world able to hold that view and still believe he can get his work seen. As Nevins says, documentaries make for great TV and there's a market for them there that doesn't exist theatrically. "Several million people, she claims, see even the lowest-rated documentaries shown on HBO. 'You're paying for it, and you want to get your money's worth'" (Ansen). With the price of bringing a film to the movie theaters running the equivalent of dozens or more DIY docs or Next Wave films, it's no wonder young filmmakers are so intensely pursuing alternative forms of distribution; it's not like they have a lot of other choices.

Alternative distribution methods are good for filmmakers in that they can use them to create a calling card of sorts, but the problems for the small fry are the same as they are for the big boys: there's no money in them. As Johanna Schneller puts it, "The thing that really chafes Hollywood is this: they haven't figured out a way to make money off the Internet. At best, they use it for marketing; at worst, they spend a lot of time and dough trying to keep their unauthorized stuff off of it. But what to make now—they have no idea. So far they're making the same old stuff, only louder, faster, and stupider." For those who use it to try to get seen, there's something freeing about it; they can make whatever they want with nary a nod to commercial viability, and that's allowed them to take chances their Hollywood counterparts never would. But that cuts both ways. They make want they want, but they also keep their day jobs as there's no money to be made in working outside of the mainstream. In a telling example, in order to interview Andrew Bujalski about his second film, *Mutual Appreciation,* Scott Foundas had to accompany him to his part-time job in a Boston bookstore; working on the margins is fun, but it doesn't pay the bills. As Mark Duplass wryly put it when asked by Kim Masters about making the jump to studio filmmaking with his brother Jay, "Contrary to popular belief, there's not a hefty living to be made in micro-budget filmmaking. And while our movies were showing up on blogs everywhere and on Netflix' instant viewing, there wasn't a hefty revenue stream coming in so at a certain point Jay and I knew we wanted to make a living as filmmakers, so keeping some sort of eye on the studio system in the future was always happening for us" ("Brothers Duplass").

The Duplass Brothers are the most widely known of the Next Wave filmmakers to make the jump from mumblecore to the bright kliegs of a studio. But that doesn't mean that their doing so is selling out, even though it definitely does mean certain compromises have to be made. And there's nothing wrong with making

Hollywood-style films if you have the chance to do so and that's what you want to do. But the Duplass Brothers have a working method and narrative style that's very counterintuitive to what Hollywood does, and they are very interested in continuing to work in the same vein, albeit with larger budgets and a better chance of actually getting their work seen. After turning down several offers to make films in the $40 to $50 million range, the brothers finally struck a deal with Fox Searchlight, the specialty arm of 20th Century Fox, to write and direct *Cyrus,* a film about a man (John C. Reilly) who starts dating a woman (Marisa Tomei) whose needy and obstreperous 20-something son, Cyrus (Jonah Hill), still lives at home. The brothers discovered the realities of Hollywood right away. They wanted to keep their small crews of no more than 15 and shoot in the same heavily improvisational, loose documentary style sans actors' sightlines and blocking that they always had (Masters, "Brothers Duplass"). The studio did let them shoot sequentially in HD with a Red Camera, a high-end digital camera, so they were able to shoot endless footage, as much as five hours a day, much of which was composed of long takes of 15 minutes or more (Levy).

This kind of filmmaking is beyond unorthodox in the world of Hollywood studios, but the fact that digital is so much cheaper to use than film resulted in Fox Searchlight taking a chance and allowing the brothers the opportunity to test their method in a mainstream environment. But there are some things in Hollywood you just can't get around. Like union contracts. As they told Masters, the brothers really wanted to keep using tiny crews, but because of the realities of the various labor unions' contracts, more often than not there were 75 or even 100 people on-set, all of whom were on the clock and getting paid ("Brothers Duplass"). The brothers found workarounds, but were they making this film sans studio affiliation, they would have been able to make it for thousands instead of the $7 million or so it cost to do so under the auspices of Fox Searchlight. The film was well received, but it only barely made its production budget back and it's not the kind of film likely to do well overseas. On the one hand, at $7 million, it needed to perform worlds better than anything any Next Wave filmmaker has ever done to break even, let alone turn a profit. On the other hand, at least if money does get lost in the end its not their own or that of their friends and family. Ultimately, as Emanuel Levy writes, "The result is a very personal film that reflects the Duplass brothers' singular worldview. 'This movie feels very homemade and I think that's their intention,' says Jonah Hill. 'And when I say "homemade," I mean it's not like something you get at The Gap—it's the sweater your grandma made you. It's not like any other film I've ever made.'"

Still, in trying to bring the Next Wave to the mainstream, the Duplass Brothers are bearing a burden in that their success or failure will likely play a role in if and when other Next Wavers get their shot. Their next film, *Jeff Who Lives at Home,* which was made for a major studio, Paramount, and stars Jason Segal, Susan Sarandon, and Ed Helms and was produced by Jason Reitman of *Juno* and *Up in the Air* fame, is already in the can and slated for a 2011 release. The Duplass Brothers have made it into the Hollywood firmament. But so far, the only other Next Waver that seems to be transitioning to Hollywood is Greta Gerwig, the darling of mumblecore cinema faves such as *Hannah Takes the Stairs* (which J. Hoberman says "is something like the Mumblecore equivalent to *Gone with the Wind*"), *Baghead,* and *Nights and Weekends.* She stars opposite Ben Stiller in Noah Baumbach's 2010 film *Greenberg* (Baumbach is clearly a fan of Next Wavers, having produced Swanberg's *Alexander the Last*), an awfully talkie film that owes a lot to the deeply personal and reflexive narrative style of Next Wave filmmakers. Gerwig is the poster child of the Next Wave's nonchalant acting style, about which Steve Rose writes, "You wouldn't exactly call it method acting, but mumblecore nailed something about the social habits of educated but aimless young, white Americans, and it presented its findings unapologetically; a shaky mirror held up to a demographic that would rather be looking at a flattering Facebook profile of itself. As such, it ended up being just the shot of fresh indie realism the mainstream needed."

Writing in *The New York Times,* A. O. Scott went even further, asserting that Gerwig "may well be the definitive screen actress of her generation." She's firmly on the road to Hollywood rewards, and it's only a matter of time before others make the jump as well. As derided as the so-called mumblecore filmmakers ("aka Generation DIY, aka Cine Slackavetes, aka MySpace Neorealists" [Hoberman]) have been, the fact remains that some of them are incredibly talented. And to be able to make the waves in cinema they have sans any money whatsoever is nothing short of phenomenal. Add to that the fact that they are much more open to change and new methods than their elders, and it seems inevitable that they will play a role in the future of Hollywood. It's not if, it's when.

While the Next Wave definitely doesn't comprise a genre, it most certainly is a movement, and for better or worse, Hollywood has noticed. And as Andrew O'Hehir cynically notes, "Under capitalism, of course, there is no such thing as a revolution too strident (or too warm and fuzzy) to be turned into a commodity." While that's certainly true, and with the Duplass Brothers and Gerwig and surely others entering the realm of multimillion-dollar filmmaking, there are ostensibly reasons for believers in indie cinema to wring their hands about the accompanying loss of purity Hollywood affiliation can bring. But there's also reason to believe that Hollywood is looking to the Next Wave not just for new talent but for production inspiration as well. When Paramount folded its specialty arm, Paramount Vantage, into the parent company, indie filmmakers lamented the loss of yet another distribution avenue; they retained the brand, but Paramount had taken Paramount Vantage mainstream. And then something potentially magical happened. In the spring of 2010, Paramount jumped back into indie filmmaking, only this time, their proposed business plan owed a lot more to Next Wave filmmaking than it did to the traditional way that studio specialty arms operated. Rather than scouring the festival circuit for acquisitions, Paramount's new company, Insurge Pictures, will instead fund 10 movies a year at approximately $100,000 each. As

John Horn notes, other companies have tried to create lower-budget film divisions, such as 20th Century Fox's Fox Atomic and Universal Studios' Rogue Pictures, now owned by Relativity Media (Horn, "Paramount to Launch"). But Insurge is the first time a major has tried its hand at truly micro-budget filmmaking. As Adam Goldman, president of Paramount's film group, says about Insurge, "I feel very strongly we need to be contrary in our thinking . . . everybody has the ability to create content now" (Horn, "New Paramount Division"). Not surprisingly, the new studio is to be helmed by Amy Powell, who played a big part in shepherding Paramount's $15,000 *Paranormal Activity* to the biggest return on the dollar in the history of Hollywood (Hernandez). As Patrick Goldstein blogs in the *LA Times,*

> It's a fascinating, potentially game-changing concept, since it's a wonderful way for studios to replenish the pipeline with new ideas, but ideas that can be executed on a cheap budget. Even if most of the films never see the light of day, it could serve as a valuable way for Paramount to gain access to new talent, since presumably the studio would retain the right to make a movie with anyone participating in the program. . . .
>
> But, of course, there are drawbacks. Studios are notoriously control-freak-style institutions. So will Paramount executives really be able to keep their mitts off these projects and refrain from trying to buff away all the rough edges? Can the studio execs refrain from giving the kind of soul-killing notes ("Can you make this character a little bit less unlikeable? Shouldn't we have a little more jeopardy in the second act?") that have been endlessly parodied by every writer who's ever spent more than a weekend doing a studio rewrite?

Despite the obvious risks, whatever happens with Insurge it's still a sign of what's to come next. Hollywood, always the last to realize that change is already here, is finally realizing that their output doesn't all have to be the *Sturm und Drang* of tent-pole franchise films. There's a whole generation of folks for whom shaky cams and lo-fi production values are perfectly acceptable. As the industry bifurcates towards a high and low end, mid-level art films are what's likely going to get caught in the crunch, too expensive to make back the returns that would justify their costs. Fortunately, in addition to an emerging audience that doesn't mind watching films that don't look like Hollywood's high-end products, there are also Next Wave filmmakers that don't want to make them either and would instead rather focus on much smaller, more resonantly personal narratives. Here's hoping that in the digital future, there's room for them alongside their more bombastic Hollywood siblings.

## WORKS CITED

Ansen, David. "Multiple Choice: How Much Did *Taxi to the Dark Side* Earn at the American Box Office?" *Newsweek.com.* July 14, 2008.

Barnes, Brooks. "Indie Films, Coming to a Small Screen Near You." *The New York Times. com.* May 25, 2008.

Cieply, Michael. "For Independent Filmmakers, Final Cut Is Now Just Step One." *The New York Times.com.* Aug. 13, 2009.

Coupland, Douglas. *Generation X: Tales for an Accelerated Culture.* New York: St. Martin's Press, 1991.

Denby, David. "Youthquake: Mumblecore Movies." *The New Yorker.com.* March 16, 2009.

"Doc Ethics." *WNYC's on the Media Podcast.* Sept. 25, 2009.

Ebert, Roger. "3-D Is a Distracting . . ." *twitter.com.* March 24, 2010.

Foundas, Scott. "Mutual Appreciation Society: The World of Andrew Bujalski." *LA Weekly. com.* Sept. 7, 2006.

Gilsdorf, Ethan. "New Wave of Indie Cinema Fights Power of Hollywood." *The Boston Globe.com.* May 28, 2006.

Goldstein, Patrick. "Hollywood Films on the Cheap: Paramount's Low-Budget Movie Gamble." *The Los Angeles Times.com.* Dec. 11, 2010.

Hernandez, Eugene. "Hollywood Studio to Back Micro-Budget Movies." *Indiewire.com.* March 11, 2010.

Hoberman, J. "It's Mumblecore! Films By, For, and About Twentysomethings Are Having a Moment. IM Someone About It." *The Village Voice.com.* Aug. 14, 2007.

Horn, John. "Paramount to Launch Micro-Budget Movie Division." *The Los Angeles Times. com.* Dec. 10, 2010.

Horn, John. "New Paramount Division Will Think Small." *The Los Angeles Times.com.* Dec. 11, 2010.

Kaufman, Anthony. "*Sicko* Success Can't Cure Ailing Reception to Docs." *Variety.com.* Oct. 1, 2007.

Land, Joshua. "Funny Because It's True." *The Village Voice.com.* April 19, 2005.

Levy, Emanuel. "*Cyrus:* The Duplassian Method." *Cinema 24/7. Emanuellevy.com.*

Lim, Dennis. "The Graduates: Indie Captures Twentysomething Indecision, Like, Perfectly." *The Village Voice.com.* April 19, 2005.

Lim, Dennis. "The (Mumbled) . . . Halting . . . Voice—of a Generation." *The New York Times.com.* Jan. 8, 2006.

Lim, Dennis. "A Generation Finds Its Mumble." *The New York Times.com.* Aug. 19, 2007.

Longworth, Karina. "*Harmony and Me* and Frustration." *LA Weekly.com.* March 25, 2010.

Masters, Kim. "Clash of the 3D Titans." *KCRW's The Business Podcast.* April 12, 2010.

Masters, Kim. "Cannes Market Report." *KCRW's The Business Podcast.* May 24, 2010.

Masters, Kim. "The Brothers Duplass Go Studio." *KCRW's The Business Podcast.* June 21, 2010.

Motion Picture Association of America (MPAA). "2009 Theatrical Market Statistics." *MPAA.org.*

O'Hehir, Andrew. "The DIY Generation Gets Its Big Moment with John Swanberg's Bittersweet *Hannah Takes the Stairs*." *Salon.com.* Aug. 23, 2007.

Patterson, John. "The Last Indie Film Generation Has Been Co-opted by the Studios, While the Next Still Labours in Digicam, Mumblecore Obscurity." *The Guardian* [London].*com.* July 18, 2008.

Rose, Steve. "*Greenberg* Star Greta Gerwig Steps from the Shadows of Mumblecore." *The Guardian* [London].*com.* June 5, 2010.

Schneller, Johanna. "I Have Seen the Future of Cinema, and It Looks Homemade." *The Globe and Mail* [Canada].*com.* May 17, 2008.

Scott, A. O. "No Method to Her Method." *The New York Times.com.* March 24, 2010.

Siegel, Tatiana. "Scorsese to Shoot *Hugo Cabret* in 3D." *Variety.com.* April 13, 2010.

Snyder, S. James. "A YouTube Opening for Wayne Wang's New Film." *Time Magazine.com.* Oct. 17, 2008.

Snyder, S. James. "The Film Festival Comes to Your Living Room." *Time Magazine.com.* March 18, 2009.

Taubin, Amy. "All Talk? Supposedly the Voice of Its Generation, the Indie Film Movement Known as Mumblecore Has Had Its 15 Minutes." *Film Society of Lincoln Center.com.* Nov./Dec. 2007.

Wood, Jennifer M. "Sundance's 'Next' Wave of Indie Moviemakers." *Moviemaker.com.* Jan. 19, 2010.

# INDEX

# ABOUT THE AUTHOR AND CONTRIBUTORS

**ROBERT C. SICKELS** is Professor of American Film and Popular Culture in the Department of Rhetoric & Film Studies at Whitman College in Walla Walla, WA. In addition to publishing numerous journal articles, he is also the author of *American Popular Culture through History: The 1940s* (Greenwood Press 2004), the editor of the three-volume collection *The Business of Entertainment* (Praeger Publishers 2008), and an independent filmmaker whose work has appeared in festivals around the world.

**YANNIS TZIOUMAKIS** is Lecturer in Communication and Media at the University of Liverpool. His research specializes in American cinema and the business of media entertainment. His books include: *American Independent Cinema: An Introduction* (2006), *The Spanish Prisoner* (2009), *Hollywood's Indies: Classics Divisions, Specialty Labels and the Independent Film Market* (2011) (all for Edinburgh University Press) and, as a coeditor, *Greek Cinema: Texts, Forms, Identities* (2011) for Intellect. He is also coediting the "American Indies" series for Edinburgh University Press.

**ANNE HELEN PETERSEN** is a PhD Candidate in the Department of Radio-Television-Film at the University of Texas-Austin, where she studies the industrial history of stardom and celebrity gossip. The former editor of *FlowTV.org*, her work has been published in *Feminist Media Studies, Celebrity Studies, Television & New Media,* and *Jump Cut.* She blogs on "Celebrity Gossip, Academic Style" at http://www.annehelenpetersen.com.